Essential ASP.NET

with Examples in C#

Microsoft .NET Development Series

John Montgomery, *Series Advisor*
Don Box, *Series Advisor*
Martin Heller, *Series Editor*

"This Microsoft .NET series is a great resource for .NET developers. Coupling the .NET architects at Microsoft with the training skills of DevelopMentor means that all the technical bases, from reference to 'how-to,' will be covered."
    —JOHN MONTGOMERY, Group Product Manager
    for the .NET platform, Microsoft Corporation

"The Microsoft .NET series has the unique advantage of an author pool that combines some of the most insightful authors in the industry with the actual architects and developers of the .NET platform."
    —DON BOX, Architect, Microsoft Corporation

Titles in the Series

Keith Ballinger, *.NET Web Services: Architecture and Implementation with .NET,* 0-321-11359-4

Don Box with Chris Sells, *Essential .NET Volume 1: The Common Language Runtime,* 0-201-73411-7

Microsoft Common Language Runtime Team, *The Common Language Runtime Annotated Reference and Specification,* 0-321-15493-2

Microsoft .NET Framework Class Libraries Team, *The .NET Framework CLI Standard Class Library Annotated Reference,* 0-321-15489-4

Microsoft Visual C# Development Team, *The C# Annotated Reference and Specification,* 0-321-15491-6

Fritz Onion, *Essential ASP.NET with Examples in C#,* 0-201-76040-1

Fritz Onion, *Essential ASP.NET with Examples in Visual Basic .NET,* 0-201-76039-8

Damien Watkins, Mark Hammond, Brad Abrams, *Programming in the .NET Environment,* 0-201-77018-0

Shawn Wildermuth, *Pragmatic ADO.NET: Data Access for the Internet World,* 0-201-74568-2

http://www.awprofessional.com/msdotnetseries/

Essential ASP.NET

with Examples in C#

■ **Fritz Onion**

♦ Addison-Wesley

Boston • San Francisco • New York • Toronto • Montreal
London • Munich • Paris • Madrid
Capetown • Sydney • Tokyo • Singapore • Mexico City

The publisher offers discounts on this book when ordered in quantity for special sales. For more information, please contact:

U.S. Corporate and Government Sales
(800) 382-3419
corpsales@pearsontechgroup.com

For sales outside of the U.S., please contact:
International Sales
(317 581-3793
international@pearsontechgroup.com

Visit Addison-Wesley on the Web:
www.awprofessional.com

Library of Congress Cataloging-in-Publication Data

Onion, Fritz.
  Essential ASP.NET with examples in C# / Fritz Onion.
    p. cm.
  Includes index.
  ISBN 0-201-76040-1 (alk. paper)
  1. Web site development. 2. Active server pages.
3. C (Computer program language) I. Title.

TK5105.8885.A26 O53 2003
005.2'762--dc21

2002038295

ISBN 0-201-76040-1
Text printed on recycled paper
1 2 3 4 5 6 7 8 9 10—MA—0706050403
First printing, February, 2003

Contents

Figures

Tables

Foreword

I WAS DRAWN to Microsoft explicitly for the opportunity to work on ASP.NET. It had a different name at that point, but the promise was to build a language-neutral, compiled Web platform that was friendly enough for the novice, and powerful and performant enough for the world's largest Web sites. I was intrigued by that promise, and working on it has indeed been a fascinating and rewarding journey.

The Web platform is built on the new Microsoft developer platform: the .NET Framework and the Common Language Runtime. This platform offers a rich set of services and capabilities upon which the Web application model was built. This platform let us change many of the rules of the game. For example, it became possible to have performance approaching the realm of compiled native code without losing the benefits of the rapid development experience associated with scripting environments.

ASP.NET was designed with a grand goal: to be a comprehensive platform for developing and delivering dynamic content to the Web. Among the challenges that entails is building a system with appeal to many different backgrounds and competencies: the Web developer scripting applications with Active Server Pages or other systems, the Visual Basic forms developer, and the ISAPI developer. What evolved was a rich platform that can be approached gradually, leveraging one's existing skills to become productive quickly, and then acquiring new skills to take advantage of new features of the platform.

The team started by building on the considerable merits of Active Server Pages and then expanding from there, constantly asking how tasks could be made easier and expressed in fewer lines of code. Support for declarative design, aided by good tools, was a key design goal. While this was being done, there was a constant awareness that the system must be extensible and support the sorts of advanced usage that many real-world, highly scalable Web sites demand.

An oft-repeated mantra during the development of ASP.NET was "No black boxes!" This is a goal that the development team intends to continue working on for quite some time, and it involves a commitment to a factored architecture that can be extended or customized to suit the problem at hand, whatever that might be. As a result, the core ASP.NET primitives are modularized and have a rich extensibility model.

In the following pages, you'll learn about where the points of extensibility are and how to use them. Fritz has carefully chosen the key concepts and explained how to weave them into an application. The critical building blocks of real Web applications are all well represented: request processing, pages and controls, configuration, error handling, security, caching, data presentation, and state management.

To develop ASP.NET applications, one does not need to understand the whole of what is a vast and complex system. However, as one begins to build more complex applications with challenging requirements, a thorough grounding in the basics and a reliable guide to what lies beyond become truly indispensable.

And with that, I commend the following work to you. It succeeds admirably as a guide to ASP.NET. It leads the reader through a solid understanding of the ASP.NET architecture and the core tenets of building Web applications. It then moves into more advanced applications of the technology that are indispensable for solving many of the real-world problems that face Web applications today. I think that the reader will agree that this work is indeed an essential guide to getting the most from ASP.NET.

Erik Olson
Program Manager
Microsoft Corporation
Redmond, Washington

Preface

IT WAS LATE at night in Torrance, California, in August 2000. I had spent 12 hours of the day teaching DevelopMentor's Guerrilla COM course with Mike Woodring and Jason Whittington. Don Box had come over after class, and, as usual, we were staying up late into the night after the students had long since gone to bed, discussing technology and hacking. Microsoft had just released its preview version of .NET at the PDC in July, and we had been spending much of the year up to that point digging into "the next COM" and were excited that it had finally been released so we could talk about it. It was that evening that Don, in his typical succinct way, showed me my first glimpse of ASP.NET (then called ASP+). He first typed into emacs an .aspx file that looked like this:

```
<%@ Page Language="C#" src="TestPage.cs"
    Inherits="TestPage" %>

<html>
<h1 runat=server id=ctl/>
</html>
```

He then wrote another file that looked like this:

```
using System;
using System.Web;
using System.Web.UI;
using System.Web.UI.HtmlControls;

public class TestPage : Page
```

```
  {
    protected HtmlGenericControl ctl;
    void Page_Load(object src, EventArgs e)
    {
      ctl.InnerText = "Hello!";
    }
  }
```

He then placed the two files in `c:\inetpub\wwwroot` on his machine and showed me the rendering of the .aspx page through the browser, exclaiming, "Get it?" Perhaps it was the late hour or the fact that I had been teaching all day, but I have to admit that although I "got" the technical details of what Don was showing me, I was somewhat underwhelmed by being able to change the `innerText` of an `h1` element from a class.

The following week, after a couple of good nights of sleep, I revisited the .aspx example and began to explore ASP.NET in more detail. After a day of reading and experimenting, I finally "got it" and I was hooked. This technology was poised to fundamentally change the way people built Web applications on Windows, and it took full advantage of the new .NET runtime. I spent the next six months researching, building ASP.NET applications, and writing DevelopMentor's Essential ASP.NET course, and I spent the subsequent year and a half teaching, speaking, and writing about ASP.NET. This book is the culmination of those activities, and I hope it helps you in your path to understanding ASP.NET.

C# versus VB.NET

Before .NET, Visual Basic was not just another language—it was a platform unto itself. Building applications in Visual Basic 6.0, for example, was completely different from using C++ and MFC. With .NET, this distinction is gone, and Visual Basic is indeed just another .NET language that uses the same libraries, the same development tools, and the same runtime as all others. As a consequence, we can now talk about technologies like ASP.NET from a language-neutral standpoint. The code samples, however, must be shown in a particular language, so this book is published in two versions: one with examples in C# and one with examples in VB.NET. All content outside the examples is nearly identical between the two books.

Sample Code, Web Site, Feedback

All the code samples in this book are drawn from working samples available for display and download from the book's Web site at http://www.develop.com/books/essentialasp.net/. This site also contains any errata found after publication and a supplemental set of more extended examples of the concepts presented in this book for your reference. The author welcomes your comments, errata, and feedback via the forms available on the Web site.

Prerequisites

This book focuses exclusively on ASP.NET and does not spend time reviewing .NET programming, object-oriented programming techniques, database access, or general Web application development techniques. You will be able to get the most out of this book if you have spent some time gaining experience in each of these areas.

Organization of This Book

This book approaches ASP.NET from the ground up, beginning with a look at the core elements of the architecture in Chapter 1 and continuing with the server-side control model in Chapter 2. It is recommended that the reader be familiar with the contents of Chapters 1 and 2 before reading any of the subsequent chapters. However, all chapters after 2 can be read independently and in any desired sequence.

Chapter 1, Architecture, covers the fundamentals of the ASP.NET architecture, beginning with a look at the parsing of .aspx files and their subsequent compilation into assemblies. This chapter explains the details of the Page class, demonstrates the new code-behind model, and discusses the shadow copy mechanism used to prevent file locking. The chapter concludes with a look at the new classes in ASP.NET that replace the intrinsic objects of traditional ASP.

Chapter 2, Web Forms, looks at the control-based programming model supported in ASP.NET called Web Forms. This chapter looks at the details of state retention across post-backs using both POST body data and View-State, and describes how to effectively use server-side controls to create dynamic Web pages. The chapter concludes with a look at the various server-side controls available in ASP.NET.

Chapter 3, Configuration, describes the configuration model used by ASP.NET, starting with the XML format used by all configuration files and the hierarchical application of configuration settings. This chapter inspects several configuration elements in detail, including the processModel and appSettings elements. The chapter concludes by demonstrating two techniques for adding custom configuration sections to your configuration files.

Chapter 4, HTTP Pipeline, explores the details of the classes involved with servicing HTTP requests in ASP.NET. This chapter first walks through all the elements in the HTTP pipeline used to process a request, and then discusses the three points of extensibility in the pipeline: custom application classes, custom handlers, and custom modules. The chapter concludes with a discussion of threading and object pooling in the pipeline.

Chapter 5, Diagnostics and Error Handling, covers the new diagnostic features of ASP.NET, including page and application tracing as well as the new performance monitor counters. This chapter also discusses techniques for debugging ASP.NET applications and exception handling. The chapter concludes with a look at how to define custom error pages for your applications.

Chapter 6, Validation, describes the new validation architecture built into ASP.NET. This chapter begins by looking at how validation is performed in Web applications in general and proceeds to show how ASP.NET's validation architecture provides a general solution to the problem of validating user input. The chapter includes a detailed look at how both client-side and server-side validation work, as well as a look at all the available validation controls.

Chapter 7, Data Binding, explores the process of binding server-side data to controls in an ASP.NET page. This chapter starts by explaining how data binding works with several different data sources, including collection classes, DataReaders, and DataSets, and then looks at how to bind data to several controls, including the DataGrid class. The chapter concludes with a look at templates and how to use them effectively with the Repeater, DataList, and DataGrid classes.

Chapter 8, Custom Controls, covers the fundamentals of building your own custom controls for use in ASP.NET applications. This chapter explains how custom controls are built, how to use the `HtmlTextWriter` class to achieve some browser independence, how to further support browser-independent rendering, how to define properties and subproperties, how to extract the inner content of a control's tag, how to generate client-side script, and how to manage control state. The chapter also covers the details of building composite controls, user controls, controls that support validation, and controls that support data binding. The chapter concludes with a look at how to integrate your controls with the Visual Studio .NET designer.

Chapter 9, Caching, looks at both output caching and data caching in ASP.NET. This chapter discusses the mechanism of output caching and how to precisely control which versions of a page are placed in the cache, as well as how to cache portions of a page using page fragment caching with user controls. The chapter explains how to use the new application-wide data cache and includes a discussion of considerations and guidelines to observe when caching data.

Chapter 10, State Management, discusses the various types of state in an ASP.NET Web application and how and when to use each type. This chapter begins with a look at application state and explains why it should typically be avoided in ASP.NET. It then looks at the improvements in session state, including out-of-process storage and cookieless key management, as well as techniques for optimizing your use of session state. The chapter concludes with a look at using cookies and view state as alternatives, or in addition, to session state.

Chapter 11, Security, describes the security features of ASP.NET and how to control client authentication and authorization in your applications. This chapter starts by reviewing the concepts of security for Web applications and then shows how to build and manage applications that need to authenticate clients using the forms authentication architecture provided by ASP.NET. The chapter also covers the management of authentication cookies in Web farms, safe password storage, building role-based authentication systems, and how to control the process identity used by ASP.NET.

Acknowledgments

I would first like to thank my wife, Susan, and my children, Zoë and Sam, who supported me without hesitation during the writing of this book. Thanks also to my parents, Pat and Dan Onion, for their support and direction.

Thanks to all my colleagues at DevelopMentor for the many discussions and constant feedback both for the course and for this book. In particular, thanks to Bob Beauchemin for his always timely and useful feedback; Keith Brown, for showing me how to salt my hashes and otherwise reinforcing my security chapter; Simon Horrell, for his detailed feedback; Dan Sullivan, for leaving no stone unturned; Ted Pattison, for commiserating on writing and for his always positive comments; Stu Halloway, for making my writing more concise; and Mike Woodring, for thinking through the threading implications of asynchronous handlers with me.

Thanks to my official reviewers, Justin Burtch, Amit Kalani, Daryl Richter, Martin Heller, and Matt Milner, all of whom provided invaluable feedback. Thanks to the members of the ASP.NET team at Microsoft for building such an interesting product and for fielding many questions. In particular, thanks to Rob Howard for his input on caching and to Erik Olson for explaining thread allocation and pooling in the pipeline. Thanks to Don Box for introducing me to ASP.NET and for getting my writing career started at *C++ Report* back in 1995.

Thanks to my editor, Stephane Thomas, for all her hard work, and to my copy editor, Debby English, who more than lives up to her last name. Much gratitude also to the more than 1,000 students who have taken the Essential ASP.NET course—your input has shaped the stories in this book more than anything else. Thanks in particular to the students at the Essential ASP.NET course offered in Washington, D.C., in October 2002 for helping choose the color of the book covers.

Fritz Onion
Wells, Maine
October 2002
http://staff.develop.com/onion/

▪ 1 ▪
Architecture

ASP.NET INTRODUCES A slew of new features for the Web application developer, including compiled server-side code, a technique called code-behind to separate server-side logic from client-side layout, an extensible server-side control model, a well-designed and easy-to-use data binding model, xcopy deployment, and support for form validation on both clients and servers. More than all that, however, ASP.NET gives us unification: a unification of languages, tools, libraries, deployment models, system design, and diagnostics. Web application developers no longer need to differentiate between components used by their pages and components used elsewhere in their architecture. They no longer have to deal with a script debugger to diagnose problems in their pages. They are no longer subject to the often mysterious subtleties of untyped scripting languages and can now use whatever .NET language they prefer in building their pages. Building Web applications is now like any other software development on the .NET platform.

In this chapter, we introduce the architectural foundations of building Web applications with ASP.NET. We look at the new compilation model used to process requests, how to build code-behind classes, how the shadow copy mechanism enables xcopy deployment, and the new directives and intrinsics available.

1.1 Fundamentals

At its core, ASP.NET is a collection of .NET classes that work together to service HTTP requests. Some of these classes are defined in system assemblies as part of the base class libraries that are installed with the .NET runtime, some of these classes may be housed in assemblies deployed in the global assembly cache (GAC), and some of these classes are loaded from local assemblies that live in the virtual directory associated with this application. All these classes are loaded into an application domain within the ASP.NET worker process and interact to generate a response for a given request. Figure 1-1 shows this architecture.

The fundamental shift that most developers face when moving to ASP.NET is the fact that everything is a class loaded from an assembly. As in other class-based architectures, you build applications in ASP.NET by constructing classes that interact with other classes in the base framework. Some of your classes will derive from base classes in the framework, others may implement interfaces defined by the framework, and still others may simply interact with base classes in the framework by calling methods on them. Although ASP-style syntax is still supported, ASP.NET files with server-side code are turned into class definitions housed in assemblies when first accessed. The end result, therefore, is a collection of classes interacting within a process to service a request.

Another significant shift is the process model. The ASP.NET worker process is a distinct worker process, aspnet_wp.exe,[1] separate from inetinfo.exe (the Internet Information Server, or IIS, process), and the process model in ASP.NET is unrelated to process isolation settings in IIS. Although IIS is still typically used as the entry point to an ASP.NET application,[2] physically listening on the appropriate ports and dispatching the requests,

---

1. In IIS 6.0, which ships with Windows Server 2003, the worker process model is somewhat different and is discussed in Chapter 3. At this point, it is worth noting that unless you are running IIS 6.0 in IIS 5.0 isolation mode, ASP.NET is housed in a worker process named w3wp.exe.

2. There are already several examples of using ASP.NET without IIS as the front-end Web server. Cassini is a sample Web server produced by Microsoft and is available with full source code at http://www.asp.net, which, among other projects, has been used to host ASP.NET with Apache.

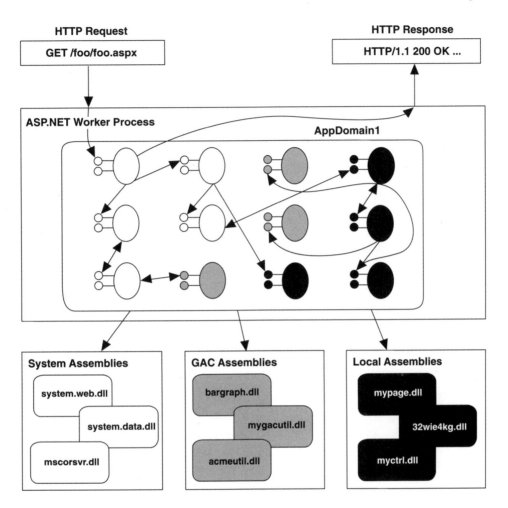

HTTP Request

GET /foo/foo.aspx

HTTP Response

HTTP/1.1 200 OK ...

ASP.NET Worker Process

AppDomain1

System Assemblies

system.web.dll

system.data.dll

mscorsvr.dll

GAC Assemblies

bargraph.dll

mygacutil.dll

acmeutil.dll

Local Assemblies

mypage.dll

32wie4kg.dll

myctrl.dll

FIGURE 1-1: High-Level Architecture of ASP.NET

its role has been lessened, and many of the tasks it used to handle are now handled by ASP.NET in its own worker process.

1.2 **ASP 4.0**

Although ASP.NET is not technically labeled ASP 4.0, in many ways it is just that—the next version of ASP. Because most people starting to work with ASP.NET come from an ASP background, we start our exploration by describing the similarities shared by the two technologies. Listing 1-1 shows a simple ASP page that intermingles server-side JavaScript with static HTML. Note that several server-side coding techniques are demonstrated in this file. There is a script block marked with the `runat=server` attribute containing a function called `Add`. The server-side evaluation syntax "`<%=`" is used to invoke the `Add` method and output the results of the expression to an h2 tag. The server-side script syntax "`<%`" is used to programmatically generate ten rows in a table, and finally, the intrinsic `Response` object is used to programmatically add a final h2 tag to the bottom of the page.

LISTING 1-1: Sample ASP Page

```
<!- File: test.asp ->
<%@ language=javascript %>

<script language='JScript' runat=server>
function Add(x, y)
{
  return x+y;
}
</script>

<html> <body>
<h1>Test ASP Page</h1>

<h2>2+2=<%=Add(2,2)%></h2>
<table border=2>
<%
  for (var i=0; i<10; i++) {
%>
  <tr><td>Row<%=i%> Col0</td><td>Row<%=i%> Col1</td></tr>
<%
  }
%>
</table>

<%
  Response.Write("<h2>Written directly to Response</h2>");
%>

</body> </html>
```

All these server-side programming techniques are supported in ASP.NET as well. In fact, if you take this file and simply change the extension from .asp to .aspx, you will find that it behaves exactly as the .asp version did. What is really happening under the covers when these two pages are accessed is dramatically different, as we will see, but on the surface, many traditional ASP pages can be brought forward as ASP.NET pages with no modifications.

In ASP.NET, we are no longer constrained to the two scripting languages available in traditional ASP: VBScript and JScript.[3] Any fully compliant .NET language can now be used with ASP.NET, including C# and VB.NET. To see an example, we can rewrite the ASP page presented in Listing 1-1 as an ASP.NET page using C# as the server-side language. Although it is not strictly required, we include the language preference within a `Page` directive, which is where most of the page-level attributes are controlled for ASP.NET pages. Listing 1-2 shows the page rewritten using C#, complete with an ASP.NET `Page` directive.

LISTING 1-2: Sample .aspx Page

```
<!— File: test.aspx —>
<%@ Page Language='C#' %>

<script runat=server>
int Add(int x, int y)
{
  return x+y;
}
</script>

<html> <body>
<h1>Test ASP.NET Page</h1>

<h2>2+2=<%=Add(2,2)%></h2>
<table border=2>
<%
  for (int i=0; i<10; i++) {
```

continues

---

3. Although, as we have seen already, JScript is a fully supported .NET language and can be used in ASP.NET pages. VBScript, in contrast, is not directly supported in ASP.NET, although full-fledged Visual Basic .NET can be used.

```
%>
  <tr><td>Row<%=i%> Col0</td><td>Row<%=i%> Col1</td></tr>
<%
  }
%>
</table>

<%
  Response.Write("<h2>Written directly to Response</h2>");
%>

</body> </html>
```

1.2.1 Compilation versus Interpretation

The first time you access the ASP.NET page shown in Listing 1-2, the most remarkable thing you will see differentiating it from the traditional ASP version is the amount of time it takes for the page to load. It is slower. Quite a bit slower, in fact. Any subsequent access to that page, however, will be markedly faster. The overhead you will see on the first access is the launching of the ASP.NET worker process plus the parsing and compilation of the .aspx files into an assembly. This is in contrast to how the ASP engine executes server-side code, which is always through an interpreter (JScript or VBScript).

When a traditional ASP page is requested, the text of that page is parsed linearly. All content that is not server-side script is rendered as is back to the response. All server-side script in the page is first run through the appropriate interpreter (JScript or VBScript), the output of which is then rendered back to the response. This architecture affects the efficiency of page rendering in several ways. First, interpreting the server-side script on the fly is less efficient than executing precompiled code on the server. As a side effect, one common optimization for ASP applications is to move a lot of server-side script into precompiled COM components to improve response times. A second efficiency concern is that intermingling server-side evaluation blocks with static HTML is less efficient than evaluating a single server-side script block, because the interpreter has to be invoked over and over again. Thus, to improve efficiency of rendering, many ASP developers resort to large blocks of server-side script, replacing static HTML elements with `Response.Write()` invocations instead. Finally, this ASP model actually allows different blocks of script within a page to be written in different script languages. While this may be appealing in some ways, it also degrades performance by requiring that a particular page load both scripting engines to process a request, which takes more time and memory than using just one language.

In contrast, ASP.NET pages are always compiled into .NET classes housed within assemblies. This class includes all of the server-side code and the static HTML, so once a page is accessed for the first time (or any page within a particular directory is accessed), subsequent rendering of that page is serviced by executing compiled code. This eliminates all the inefficiencies of the scripting model of traditional ASP. There is no longer any performance difference between compiled components and server-side code embedded within a page—they are now both compiled components. There is also no performance difference between interspersing server-side code blocks among static HTML elements, and writing large blocks of server-side code and using `Response.Write()` for static HTML content. Also, because the .aspx file is parsed into a single code file and compiled, it is not possible to use multiple server-side languages within a single .aspx file.

There are several other immediate benefits to working with a compilation model instead of an interpreted one. In addition to improved performance over the interpreted model, pages that are compiled into classes can be debugged using the same debugging tools available to desktop applications or component developers. Errors with pages are generated as compiler errors, and there is a good chance that most errors will be found at compilation time instead of runtime, because VB.NET and C# are both strongly typed languages. Plus, all the tools available to the .NET developer are applicable to the .aspx developer. In fact, this distinction between Web application script developers and component developers, which has traditionally been very clear, is gone completely. Web developers using ASP.NET are constructing classes and building hierarchies using the same technologies and languages as their component developer peers, even when they are simply writing .aspx files with embedded server-side code. This is a fundamental shift in design from traditional ASP and bears repeating. *Whenever you author an ASP.NET page, you are authoring a new class.*

1.3 System.Web.UI.Page

Now that you understand that every page is compiled into a class definition, the next step is to understand exactly how that class is created and
what control you have over its creation. As a first experiment, because we
know that our page is turned into a class, we can display the type of our
page and the class from which it inherits. Figure 1-2 shows a sample .aspx

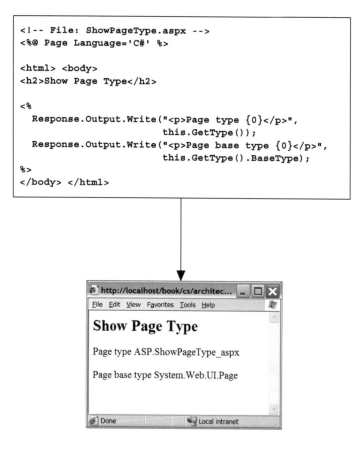

```
<!-- File: ShowPageType.aspx -->
<%@ Page Language='C#' %>

<html> <body>
<h2>Show Page Type</h2>

<%
  Response.Output.Write("<p>Page type {0}</p>",
                        this.GetType());
  Response.Output.Write("<p>Page base type {0}</p>",
                        this.GetType().BaseType);
%>
</body> </html>
```

http://localhost/book/cs/architec...

File Edit View Favorites Tools Help

Show Page Type

Page type ASP.ShowPageType_aspx

Page base type System.Web.UI.Page

Done   Local intranet

FIGURE 1-2: ASP.NET Page Type

file, along with its output, that prints out the type of the page and its base class, using the GetType() method and the BaseType property.[4]

Notice that the type of the page is ASP.ShowPageType_aspx, which is simply the name of the file with the "." replaced by an "_" character. More interestingly, the base class is System.Web.UI.Page, which defines most of the functionality for processing requests in ASP.NET. By default, every .aspx page you author derives from the Page base class. As with any other class hierarchy, it is important to understand the features and functionality of the class from which you inherit. Listing 1-3 shows some of the most interesting members of the Page class.

LISTING 1-3: Important Members of System.Web.UI.Page

```
public class Page : TemplateControl, IHttpHandler
{
        // State management
    public HttpApplicationState Application {get;}
    public virtual HttpSessionState Session { get;}
    public Cache Cache {get;}

        // Intrinsics
    public HttpRequest Request {get;}
    public HttpResponse Response {get;}
    public HttpServerUtility Server {get;}
    public string MapPath(string virtualPath);

        // Client information
    public ClientTarget ClientTarget {get; set;}
    public IPrincipal User {get;}

    // Core
    public UserControl LoadControl(string virtualPath);
    public virtual ControlCollection Controls {get;}
    public override string ID { get; set;}

    public bool IsPostBack {get;}
    protected void
            RenderControl(HtmlTextWriter writer);

    //...
}
```

---

4. In this example, note the use of the Output property of the Response object. This is an instance of the TextWriter class, which writes to the response buffer. This class is convenient to use when you need to construct strings, because it supports the formatting of strings, which is more efficient than string concatenation.

The `Page` class provides facilities for state management, including the familiar `Application` and `Session` state objects plus a new `Cache` object, the details of which are discussed in Chapter 9. All the familiar intrinsics ASP programmers are used to can be found exposed as properties in the `Page` class, including the `Response`, `Request`, and `Server` objects. This means that the familiar ASP-style syntax of accessing something like the `Response` object will compile because it maps onto a property of the class from which your page inherits. The details of the new classes that replace the ASP intrinsics are discussed later in this chapter.

Once you are aware that your pages are turned into classes, you can start taking advantage of this fact by adding features to your page as you might add features to a class. For example, consider the page shown in Listing 1-4.

LISTING 1-4: Sample ASP.NET Page with Data Members

```
<!- SamplePage.aspx ->
<%@ Page Language="C#" %>
<html><body>
<script language="C#" runat=server>
  private ArrayList _values = new ArrayList();
  private void PopulateArray()
  {
      _values.Add("v1");
      _values.Add("v2");
      _values.Add("v3");
      _values.Add("v4");
  }
</script>

<h2>aspx==class!</h2>
<ul>
<%
  PopulateArray();
  for (int i=0; i<_values.Count; i++)
    Response.Output.Write("<li>{0}</li>", _values[i]);
%>
</ul>
</body> </html>
```

Because our page is now within a class definition, we can do things such as specifying the protection level of fields and methods, using field initializers, and pretty much anything else you might add to a class definition.

In Listing 1-4, we defined a `private` field called `_values` of type `ArrayList`, initialized it to a newly allocated instance, and built a method called `PopulateArray()` to fill the field with values. Then in the body of our page we were able to invoke the `PopulateArray()` method and access the contents of the private `_values` field within a server-side script block. Notice that in this example, all the field and method declarations were placed in a server-side script block, while invocations of methods and access to fields were placed within server-side script tags (`<% %>`). This is important because code placed in each of these two places will be placed in the generated class definition in very different places. Code that falls within a server-side script block (`<script runat=server></script>`) will be placed directly into the class definition. Code that falls within server-side script tags (`<% %>`) will be placed into the body of a function of the class that will be called when the page is rendered. Figure 1-3 shows the relationship between these two server-side code notations and their placement in the generated class definition.

It is important to note this server-side code placement distinction, especially if you are migrating existing ASP pages to ASP.NET. It is no longer possible to include executable code outside the scope of a function within a script block marked as `runat=server`, and conversely, it is no longer possible to define a function within a pair of server-side script tags. Note also that the generated class definition provides a default constructor for you, and if you try to define your own default constructor within your page, it will cause a compiler error. This can be somewhat frustrating if you are trying to properly initialize elements of your class (such as filling up our array of values or subscribing to events). Fortunately, an alternative technique gives you more complete control over the class definition while separating the layout from the page logic. This technique is called code-behind.

1.4 Code-Behind

One of the more frustrating aspects of building traditional ASP pages was the convoluted nature of mixing server-side script with static layout elements. As ASP pages grow in size, they often become harder and harder to understand

```
<!-- SamplePage.aspx -->
<%@ Page Language="C#" %>
<html><body>
<script language="C#" runat=server>
  private ArrayList _values
                    = new ArrayList();
  private void PopulateArray()
  {
      _values.Add("v1");
      _values.Add("v2");
      _values.Add("v3");
      _values.Add("v4");
  }
</script>

<ul>
<%
  PopulateArray();
  for (int i=0; i<_values.Count; i++)
    Response.Output.Write(
         "<li>{0}</li>", _values[i]);
%>
</ul>
</body> </html>
```

```
// Machine-generated source file
// ybngvkuj.0.cs
namespace ASP {
 public class SamplePage_aspx :
          Page, IRequiresSessionState {

   private ArrayList _values
                      = new ArrayList();
   private void PopulateArray()
   {
     _values.Add("v1");
     _values.Add("v2");
     _values.Add("v3");
     _values.Add("v4");
   }
   public SamplePage_aspx() { /*...*/ }

   private void __Render__control1(
           HtmlTextWriter __output,
           Control parameterContainer)
   {
     __output.Write(
        "<!-- SamplePage.aspx -->\r\n");
     __output.Write(
        "\r\n<html><body>\r\n");
     __output.Write("\r\n<ul>\r\n");

     PopulateArray();
     for (int i=0; i<_values.Count; i++)
       Response.Output.Write(
           "<li>{0}</li>", _values[i]);

     __output.Write(
    "\r\n</ul> \r\n</body> </html>\r\n");
   }
   //...
 }
}
```

FIGURE 1-3: Server-Side Code Placement in Page Compilation

as the interplay between server-side script and static HTML becomes more complex. There are ways of dealing with this complexity, including imposing standards mandating scripting techniques and the use of server-side include directives to remove some of the code from a page. ASP.NET adds another, even more appealing option for separating programmatic logic from static page layout with a technique called code-behind.

In our earlier examples, we saw how each page in ASP.NET is compiled into a `Page`-derived class. Code-behind is the technique of creating an intermediate base class that sits between the `Page` base class and the machine-generated class from the .aspx file. This intermediate base class derives directly from `Page`, and the class generated from the .aspx file derives from the intermediate base class instead of directly from `Page`. With this technique, you can add fields, methods, and event handlers in your code-behind class and have these features inherited by the class created from the .aspx file, removing potentially significant amounts of code from the .aspx file. This technique relies on the ability to specify an alternative base class for the autogenerated class, which is done using the `Inherits` attribute of the `Page` directive. Listings 1-5 and 1-6 show our earlier sample page rewritten to use this code-behind technique.

LISTING 1-5: Sample .aspx File Using Code-Behind

```
<!- Codebehind.aspx ->
<%@ Page Language="C#"
    Inherits="EssentialAspDotNet.Architecture.SamplePage"%>
<html><body>

<h2>aspx==class!</h2>
<ul>
<% WriteArray(); %>
</ul>
</body> </html>
```

LISTING 1-6: Sample Code-Behind File

```
// SampleCodeBehind.cs

using System;
using System.Web;
using System.Web.UI;
using System.Collections;

namespace EssentialAspDotNet.Architecture
{
  public class SamplePage : Page
  {
```

continues

```
private ArrayList _values = new ArrayList();
public SamplePage()
{
  _values.Add("v1");
  _values.Add("v2");
  _values.Add("v3");
  _values.Add("v4");
}

protected void WriteArray()
{
  for (int i=0; i<_values.Count; i++)
    Response.Output.Write("<li>{0}</li>",
                          _values[i]);
}
  }
}
```

Note that we were able to move the initialization into the constructor of our class. This code-behind class must be compiled into an assembly and deployed in the /bin directory of this application for this to work (as we will see, all assemblies placed in the /bin directory of an ASP.NET application are implicitly added as references to the page compilation command). The class created from our .aspx file is now derived from SamplePage instead of Page because we are inserting a class into the hierarchy, as shown in Figure 1-4.

As an alternative to precompiling the code-behind file, you can use the src attribute, as shown in Listing 1-7. Any file referenced with the src attribute of the Page directive is compiled into a separate assembly and added to the list of referenced assemblies when the page is compiled. The advantage of using the src attribute for your code-behind files is that you can update a code-behind file just by replacing the file, and the next request that comes in causes ASP.NET to recompile the referenced file. This saves the step of compiling the code into an assembly yourself and updating the physical assembly in the /bin directory. It also ensures that the file will be compiled with the correct version of the .NET libraries, if for some reason you have different versions installed on different machines. On the other hand, if you have a compilation error in your source file, it will not be detected until you deploy the file and the page is accessed again. Precompiling the assembly beforehand guarantees that you will catch all compilation errors before deployment.

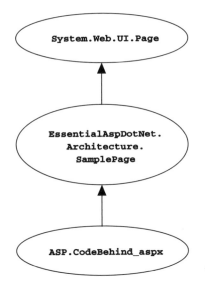

FIGURE 1-4: Class Hierarchy Created Using Code-Behind

LISTING 1-7: Using the src Attribute to Reference a Code-Behind File

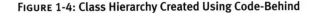

```
<!— Codebehind.aspx —>
<%@ Page Language="C#" src="SampleCodeBehind.cs"
    Inherits="EssentialAspDotNet.Architecture.SamplePage"%>
<!— ... —>
```

1.4.1 Event Handling

The code-behind example shown in the previous section extracted code from the .aspx page by defining methods and fields in the code-behind class, resulting in a "cleaner" page with less code clutter. In addition to methods and fields, code-behind classes can define handlers for events issued by the Page base class, which can be a useful way to manipulate the rendering of a page without adding code to the .aspx file.

The Page base class defines four events (actually, they are inherited from the Control base class) that are called in sequence during its lifetime: Init, Load, PreRender, and Unload, as shown in Listing 1-8. In addition, it defines four virtual function handlers for these events that are invoked when the events are fired, also shown in Listing 1-8. Thus, you can register a handler for any of these events in two ways: by subscribing a delegate to the event manually or by providing an overridden version of the virtual function defined in the base class.

LISTING 1-8: Events Defined in System.Web.UI.Page

```
public class Page : TemplateControl, IHttpHandler
{
  // Events
  public event EventHandler Init;
  public event EventHandler Load;
  public event EventHandler PreRender;
  public event EventHandler Unload;

  // Predefined event handlers
  protected virtual void OnInit(EventArgs e);
  protected virtual void OnLoad(EventArgs e);
  protected virtual void OnPreRender(EventArgs e);
  protected virtual void OnUnload(EventArgs e);
}
```

The Init event occurs before any server-side controls have had their state restored. The Load event occurs after all server-side controls have had their state restored but before any server-side events have been fired. The PreRender event fires after all server-side events have fired but before anything has been rendered—that is, before any HTML has been returned. The Unload event takes place after page rendering has completed.

These events give you fairly complete control over the generation of the page; however, Load is typically the most useful of all of them because it gives you a chance to modify the state of controls before rendering but after their state has been restored. The server-side control model is discussed in detail in the next chapter.

For an example of adding handlers for these events, consider the code-behind class shown in Listing 1-9. This demonstrates a technique used by Visual Studio .NET when working with code-behind files, which is to provide an overridden version of the virtual OnInit method to manually subscribe a delegate to the Load event of the Page class. In this case, the OnInit virtual function is called first, in which the delegate for the Load event is subscribed. When the `Load` event fires, the `MyLoadHandler` is invoked and prints a line of text at the top of the page since it is invoked before the page's rendering process. Note that there is no real advantage or disadvantage to either technique, except that the manual delegate subscription requires an extra step to actually hook it up.

LISTING 1-9: Trapping Page Events in Code-Behind

```
// File: EventsPage.cs
public class EventsPage : Page
{
  // Override OnInit virtual function to manually
  // subscribe a delegate to the Load event
  protected override void OnInit(EventArgs e)
  {
    this.Load += new EventHandler(MyLoadHandler);
  }

  // Load event handler
  protected void MyLoadHandler(object src, EventArgs e)
  {
    Response.Write("<tiny>rendered at top of page</tiny>");
  }
}
```

There is one additional mechanism for subscribing to events issued by the `Page` class called `AutoEventWireup`. This technique works by simply adding a method to your `Page`-derived class, named `Page_Init`, `Page_Load`, `Page_PreRender`, or `Page_Unload`, with the signature required by the `EventHandler` delegate. When the `Page`-derived class is created, one of the initialization steps it goes through uses reflection to look for any functions with these exact names. If it finds any, the initialization routine creates a new delegate initialized with that function and subscribes it to the associated event. Listing 1-10 shows a sample .aspx file that has defined a `Page_Load` method that is wired up using this technique. Note that this function was not a virtual function override nor was it explicitly wired up as an event handler in our code. This technique works similarly in code-behind classes as well.

LISTING 1-10: Using AutoEventWireup to Add an Event Handler

```
<!— AutoEventWireup.aspx —>
<%@ Page Language='C#' %>

<script runat=server>
  protected void Page_Load(object src, EventArgs e)
  {
    Response.Write("<h4>Load event fired!</h4>");
  }
</script>

<html>
<body>
<h1>AutoEventWireup Page</h1>
</body>
</html>
```

Unlike the other two mechanisms for subscribing to events, this mechanism has the disadvantage of relying on runtime type information to look up the method name and perform the event subscription, which is less efficient. If you know you are not going to take advantage of this event subscription technique, you can disable the runtime type lookup by setting the AutoEventWireup attribute of the Page directive to false, as shown in Listing 1-11. If you are building pages with Visual Studio .NET, this flag is set to false in any pages you create with the designer.

LISTING 1-11: Disabling AutoEventWireup

```
<%@ Page Language='C#' AutoEventWireup='false' %>
<!— … —>
```

1.5 Shadow Copying

In our first example of the code-behind technique, we compiled an assembly containing the code-behind class and deployed it in the /bin directory of our ASP.NET application. Our page was then able to reference the class that was added to the assembly via the Inherits attribute of the Page directive. Assemblies deployed in the /bin directory are implicitly available to all pages of that application because they are added to the list of referenced assemblies during page compilation. This is a convenient mechanism not only for deploying code-behind classes, but also for deploying utility or business-logic classes that may be useful across all pages in an application.

To see an example, suppose we have built a utility class to convert temperature from Fahrenheit to centigrade and back again, as shown in Listing 1-12. To deploy this class as a utility class that would be universally accessible among all the pages within our application, we would compile it into an assembly and deploy the assembly in the `/bin` directory of our application. The compilation of every .aspx file in our application would then include an implicit reference to this assembly. Listing 1-13 shows a sample page using our utility class.

LISTING 1-12: Sample Utility Class for Temperature Conversion

```
// File: TempConverter.cs
public class TempConverter
{
  static public double FahrenheitToCentigrade(double val)
  {
    return ((val-32)/9)*5;
  }

  static public double CentigradeToFahrenheit(double val)
  {
    return (val*9)/5+32;
  }
}
```

LISTING 1-13: Sample Page Using the Utility Class

```
<!— File: TempConverter.aspx —>
<%@ Page Language='C#' %>
<html><body>
<h2>32 degrees Fahrenheit is
 <%= TempConverter.FahrenheitToCentigrade(32)%>
  degrees centigrade</h2>
</body></html>
```

In traditional ASP applications, components used by pages and deployed in this fashion were notoriously difficult to update or replace. Whenever the application was up and running, it held a reference to the component file; so to replace that file, you had to shut down IIS (temporarily taking your Web server offline), replace the file, and restart IIS. One of the goals of ASP.NET was to eliminate the need to stop the running Web application whenever components of that application need to be updated or replaced—that is, updating an application should be as simple as using xcopy to replace the components on the Web server with the new updated versions. To achieve this xcopy deployment capability, the designers of ASP.NET had to ensure two things: first, that the running application not hold a reference to the component file; and second, that whenever the component file was replaced with a new version, that new version was picked up with any subsequent requests made to the application. Both of these goals are achieved by using the shadow copy mechanism provided by the Common Language Runtime (CLR).

Shadow copying of assemblies is something you can configure when you create a new application domain in .NET. The AppDomainSetup class (used to initialize an AppDomain) exposes a Boolean property called ShadowCopyFiles and a string property called CachePath, and the AppDomain class exposes a method called SetShadowCopyPath() to enable shadow copying for a particular application domain. The Boolean property turns the mechanism on for a particular application domain, the CachePath specifies the base directory where the shadowed copies should be placed, and the SetShadowCopyPath() method specifies which directories should have shadow copying enabled.

ASP.NET creates a distinct application domain for each application it hosts in its worker process; and for each application domain, it enables shadow copying of all assemblies referenced in the /bin directory. Instead of loading assemblies directly from the /bin directory, the assembly loader physically copies the referenced assembly to a separate directory (also indicated in the configuration settings for that application domain) and loads it from there. This mechanism also keeps track of where the assembly came from, so if a new version of that assembly is ever placed in the original /bin directory, it will be recopied into the "shadow" directory and newly referenced from there. Figure 1-5 shows the shadow copy mechanism in action for an ASP.NET application.

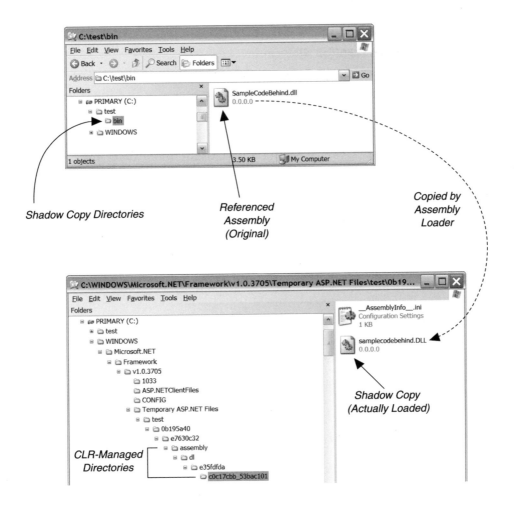

FIGURE 1-5: Shadow Copy Mechanism Used by ASP.NET

In addition to shadow copying of assemblies, ASP.NET needs the ability to create and load assemblies on the fly. The first time an .aspx page is referenced, as we have seen, it is compiled into an assembly and loaded by ASP.NET. What we haven't seen is where those assemblies are located once they are compiled. Application domains also support the concept of a "dynamic directory" specified through the `DynamicBase` property of the `AppDomainSetup` class, which is a directory designed for dynamically generated assemblies that can then be referenced by the assembly loader. ASP.NET sets the dynamic directory of each application it houses to a subdirectory under the system `Temporary ASP.NET Files` directory with the name of the virtual directory of that application. Figure 1-6 shows the location of dynamically generated assemblies for an ASP.NET application with a virtual directory named `test`.

One consequence of both dynamic assembly generation and shadow copying is that many assemblies are copied during the lifetime of an ASP.NET application. The assemblies that are no longer being referenced should be cleaned up so that disk space usage doesn't become a limiting factor in application growth. In the current release of ASP.NET (version 1.0.3705) shadow copied assemblies are removed as soon as possible after a new version of that assembly is copied, and dynamically generated assemblies that are no longer used are cleaned up the next time the ASP.NET worker process is bounced and the particular application associated with the dynamic assemblies is run again. In general, this means that you shouldn't have to worry about unused assemblies generated by ASP.NET wasting space on your machine for very long.

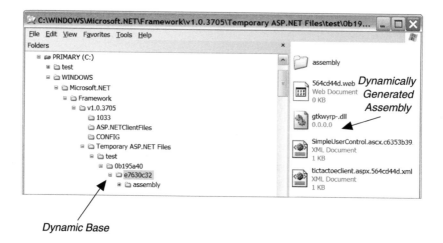

FIGURE 1-6: Dynamic Base Directory Used by ASP.NET

1.6 **Directives**

Throughout this chapter we have used the `@Page` directive to control the default language, code-behind class, and implicit assembly compilation of our .aspx files. In addition to the `@Page` directive, several other directives are available for use in .aspx files, as shown in Table 1-1. Because every .aspx file is compiled into a class, it is important to have control over that compilation, just as you would via compiler switches if you were compiling a class yourself. These directives give you control over many options that affect the compilation and running of your page.

TABLE 1-1: .aspx File Directives

Directive Name	Attributes	Description
`@Page`	See Table 1-2	Top-level page directive
`@Import`	`Namespace`	Imports a namespace to a page (similar to the `using` keyword in C#)
`@Assembly`	`Name` `Src`	Links an assembly to the current page when it is compiled (using `src` implicitly compiles the file into an assembly first)

`@OutputCache`	`Duration`
	`Location`
	`VaryByCustom`
	`VaryByHeader`
	`VaryByParam`
	`VaryByControl`
		Controls output caching for a page (see Chapter 9 for more details)

`@Register`	`Tagprefix`
	`Namespace`
	`Assembly`
	`Src`
	`Tagname`
		Registers a control for use within a page (see Chapter 8 for more details)

`@Implements`	`Interface`	Adds the specified interface to the list of implemented interfaces for this page
`@Reference`	`Page` `Control`	Specifies a page or user control that this page should dynamically compile and link to at runtime

The @Assembly directive provides a way for .aspx files to reference assemblies that are deployed in the global assembly cache or, using the src attribute, to reference a source file that is compiled and referenced implicitly when the page is referenced. The @Import directive serves the same purpose as the using keyword in C#, which is to implicitly reference types within a specified namespace. The @Implements directive gives you the ability to implement an additional interface in your Page-derived class, and the @Reference directive provides a mechanism for referencing the generated assemblies of other pages or user controls.

To see an example of when you might use some of these directives, suppose we decide to deploy the TempConverter class in the global assembly cache so that all the applications on our machine can access its functionality. We also wrap it in a namespace to ensure that there is no clash with other components in our system, and sign it with a public/private key pair. Listing 1-14 shows the source file for our TempConverter component.

LISTING 1-14: Source File for TempConverter Component

```
// File: TempConverter.cs
using System;
using System.Reflection;
[assembly : AssemblyKeyFile("pubpriv.snk")]
[assembly : AssemblyVersion("1.0.0.0")]

namespace EssentialAspDotNet.Architecture
{
  public class TempConverter
  {
    static public double FahrenheitToCentigrade(double val)
    {
      return ((val-32)/9)*5;
    }

    static public double CentigradeToFahrenheit(double val)
    {
      return (val*9)/5+32;
    }
  }
}
```

To reference the TempConverter in one of our pages, we need to reference the TempConverter assembly deployed in the GAC, and we need to fully scope the reference to the class with the proper namespace. To reference a GAC-deployed assembly, we use the @Assembly directive, and to implicitly reference the namespace in which the TempConverter class is defined, we use the @Import directive. A sample page using these directives to work with the TempConverter component is shown in Listing 1-15. Note that to successfully reference a GAC-deployed assembly, you must use the full four-part name of the assembly, including the short name, the version, the culture, and the public key token.

LISTING 1-15: Sample .aspx Page Using the TempConverter Component

```
<!– TempConverter.aspx –>
<%@ Page Language='C#' %>
<%@ Assembly Name="TempConverter, Version=1.0.0.0,
Culture=Neutral,PublicKeyToken=a3494cd4f38077bf" %>
<%@ Import Namespace="EssentialAspDotNet.Architecture" %>
<html>
<body>
<h2>32deg F =
<%=TempConverter.FahrenheitToCentigrade(32)%> deg C</h2>
</body>
</html>
```

The @Page directive has by far the most attributes of any of the directives. Some of these attributes have been brought forward from similar directives in traditional ASP pages, while many are new and unique to ASP.NET. Table 1-2 shows the various @Page directive attributes available, along with their possible values and a description of the attribute usage. The underlined value is the default that will be used if the attribute is left off the @Page directive.

TABLE 1-2: @Page Directive Attributes

Attribute	Values	Description
AspCompat	true | false	Causes this page to run on an STA thread for backward compatibility
AutoEventWireup	true | false	Determines whether events will be auto-wired up (see Chapter 2)

TABLE 1-2: @Page Directive Attributes (continued)

Attribute	Values	Description
`Buffer`	`true	false`	Enables HTTP response buffering
`ClassName`	Any name	Specifies the name of the class to be generated by this file
`ClientTarget`	User agent or alias	Specifies the target user agent to use when accessing this page
`CodePage`	Code page value	Code page value for the response
`CompilerOptions`	String of compiler options	Compiler options to be added to the compilation command when the page is compiled
`ContentType`	Any HTTP type string	MIME type of response for this page
`Culture`	Culture name	Culture to be used when rendering this page
`Debug`	`true	false`	Whether this page is compiled with debug symbols
`Description`	Any text	Not used
`EnableSessionState`	`true	false`	Whether session state is used on this page (see Chapter 10)
`EnableViewState`	`true	false`	Whether view state is enabled for this page (see Chapter 2)
`EnableViewStateMac`	`true	false`	Whether ASP.NET computes a Message Authentication Code (MAC) on the page's view state (to prevent tampering)
`ErrorPage`	Valid URL	Target URL redirection for unhandled exceptions (see Chapter 5)
`Explicit`	`true	false`	For VB.NET, whether explicit declaration of variables is mandated

TABLE 1-2: @Page Directive Attributes (continued)

Attribute	Values	Description
Inherits	Class name	Code-behind class from which this page will inherit
Language	Any .NET language	Default source language of this page
LCID	Locale ID	Locale ID to use for this page
ResponseEncoding	ASCIIEncoding UnicodeEncoding UTF7Encoding UTF8Encoding	Response encoding for the content of this page
Src	Source file name	Source file name of the code-behind class to be dynamically compiled when the page is compiled
SmartNavigation	true | false	Enables smart navigation feature for IE 5 and higher (saves scroll position without flicker)
Strict	true | false	For VB.NET, whether option strict mode is enabled
Trace	true | false	Whether tracing is enabled for this page
TraceMode	SortByTime SortByCategory	When tracing is enabled, how the messages are displayed
Transaction	Disabled NotSupported Supported Required RequiresNew	Whether and how this page participates in a transaction
UICulture	Any valid UI culture	UI culture setting for this page
WarningLevel	0–4	Warning level at which compilation for this page is aborted

One of the attributes that may be of particular interest to developers migrating existing ASP applications is the `AspCompat` attribute. This attribute changes the way a page interacts with COM objects. If you are using COM objects that were written in the single-threaded apartment (STA) model (all VB COM objects fall into this category), there will be additional overhead in invoking methods on that object because ASP.NET pages will by default run in the multithreaded apartment (MTA) when accessing COM objects. If you find that you are writing a page that has a significant number of method calls to STA-based COM objects, you should consider setting the `AspCompat` attribute to true to improve the efficiency of communication with those objects. Be aware that enabling this attribute also creates COM wrappers on top of the `Request` and `Response` objects enabled with `ObjectContext`, adding some overhead to interacting with these classes.

The `ClassName` attribute lets you decide the name of your `Page`-derived class, instead of accepting the default name, which is derived from the .aspx file name. With the `CompilerOptions` attribute you can specify any additional compiler switches you would like to include when your page is compiled. For example, Listing 1-16 shows a page that has requested that warnings be treated as errors when this page is compiled and that the page be compiled with overflow checking enabled for arithmetic operations.

LISTING 1-16: Specifying Additional Compiler Options for a Page

```
<%@ Page Language='C#'
    CompilerOptions="/warnaserror+ /checked+" %>
```

1.7 The New Intrinsics

This chapter ends with a more detailed look at the new classes provided by ASP.NET to replace the old intrinsic objects in ASP. These include the `HttpRequest`, `HttpResponse`, and `HttpServerUtility` classes. While a lot of the contents of these classes will be familiar to developers who have worked with the traditional ASP instrinsics, there are also several new properties and methods with which ASP.NET developers should become acquainted. Listing 1-17 shows the `HttpRequest` class, which takes on the responsibilities of the old `Request` intrinsic in ASP.

LISTING 1-17: HttpRequest Class

```
public sealed class HttpRequest
{
  public string[]              AcceptTypes     {get;}
  public string               ApplicationPath {get;}
  public HttpBrowserCapabilities Browser       {get; set;}
  public HttpClientCertificate  ClientCertificate {get;}
  public Encoding             ContentEncoding {get;}
  public int                  ContentLength   {get;}
  public string               ContentType     {get;}
  public HttpCookieCollection   Cookies         {get;}
  public string          CurrentExecutionFilePath {get;}
  public string               FilePath        {get;}
  public HttpFileCollection    Files           {get;}
  public Stream               Filter          {get; set;}
  public NameValueCollection   Form            {get;}
  public NameValueCollection   Headers         {get;}
  public string               HttpMethod      {get;}
  public Stream               InputStream     {get;}
  public bool                 IsAuthenticated {get;}
  public bool              IsSecureConnection {get;}
  public NameValueCollection   Params          {get;}
  public string               Path            {get;}
  public string               PathInfo        {get;}
  public string          PhysicalApplicationPath {get;}
  public string               PhysicalPath    {get;}
  public NameValueCollection   QueryString     {get;}
  public string               RawUrl          {get;}
  public string               RequestType     {get; set;}
  public NameValueCollection   ServerVariables {get;}
  public int                  TotalBytes      {get;}
  public Uri                  Url             {get;}
  public Uri                  UrlReferrer     {get;}
  public string               UserAgent       {get;}
  public string               UserHostAddress {get;}
  public string               UserHostName    {get;}
  public string[]             UserLanguages   {get;}
    // Methods
  public byte[] BinaryRead(int count);
  public int[]  MapImageCoordinates(string name);
  public string MapPath(string path);
  public void   SaveAs(string filename, bool includeHdrs);
}
```

Many properties of the `HttpRequest` class are type-safe accessors to underlying server variables. Although you can still access all these properties using the `ServerVariables` collection, as you can in traditional ASP, it is usually more convenient and type-safe to access the information using the provided property. For example, the `Url` property is an instance of the `Uri` class that provides an interface to interact with any URI. Several new properties also are available in the `HttpRequest` class, such as the `Browser` property, which provides a collection of information about the capabilities of the current client in the form of the `HttpBrowserCapabilities` class, the full features of which are described in Chapter 8. Another new addition is the `Filter` property exposed by both the `HttpRequest` and `HttpResponse` classes. With the `Filter` property, you can define your own custom `Stream`-derived class through which the entire contents of the request (or response) will pass, giving you the opportunity to change the request or response stream at a very low level. Chapter 4 further discusses request and response filters.

Similarly, the `HttpResponse` class is used to represent the state of the response during the processing of a request. Listing 1-18 shows the main properties and methods available in the `HttpResponse` class.

LISTING 1-18: HttpResponse Class

```
public sealed class HttpResponse
{
    public bool                  Buffer            {get; set;}
    public bool                  BufferOutput      {get; set;}
    public HttpCachePolicy       Cache             {get;}
    public string                CacheControl      {get; set;}
    public string                Charset           {get; set;}
    public Encoding              ContentEncoding   {get; set;}
    public string                ContentType       {get; set;}
    public HttpCookieCollection  Cookies           {get;}
    public int                   Expires           {get; set;}
    public DateTime              ExpiresAbsolute   {get; set;}
    public Stream                Filter            {get; set;}
    public bool                  IsClientConnected {get;}
    public TextWriter            Output            {get;}
    public Stream                OutputStream      {get;}
    public string                Status            {get; set;}
    public int                   StatusCode        {get; set;}
    public string                StatusDescription {get; set;}
    public bool                  SupressContent    {get; set;}
```

```
    // Methods
  public void AddHeader(string name, string value);
  public void AppendCookie(HttpCookie cookie);
  public void AppendHeader(string name, string value);
  public void AppendToLog(string value);
  public void BinaryWrite(byte[] data);
  public void Clear();
  public void ClearContent();
  public void ClearHeaders();
  public void Close();
  public void End();
  public void Flush();
  public void Pics(string value);
  public void Redirect(string url);
  public void SetCookie(HttpCookie cookie);
  public void Write(string value);
  public void WriteFile(string fileName);
}
```

Similar to the request class, the `HttpResponse` class provides all the familiar methods and properties that are exposed by the traditional ASP `Response` object. It also provides new features that fill some holes that existed in the old ASP model. For example, the `Cache` property provides access to an application-wide data cache, the details of which are discussed in Chapter 9.

Finally, the server utility functions are still accessible through the `Server` property of a page, but the functionality is now encapsulated in the `HttpServerUtility` class, shown in Listing 1-19.

LISTING 1-19: HttpServerUtility Class

```
public sealed class HttpServerUtility
{
  public string MachineName {get;}
  public int ScriptTimeout {get; set;}

    // Methods
  public void ClearError();
  public object CreateObject(string obj);
  public object CreateObject(Type objType);
  public object CreateObjectFromClsid(string clsid);
  public void Execute(string url);
  public void Execute(string url, TextWriter output);
  public Exception GetLastError();
```

continues

```
    public string HtmlDecode(string value);
    public string HtmlEncode(string value);
    public string MapPath(string path);
    public void Transfer(string url);
    public string UrlDecode(string url);
    public string UrlEncode(string url);
    public string UrlPathEncode(string url);
}
```

Like the other two intrinsic replacements, the `HttpServerUtility` class provides a mix of familiarity and new features for ASP developers. `HtmlEncode` and `HtmlDecode` provide conversions to and from HTML-compatible strings, translating characters that need escaping, such as "<", into HTML escape sequences such as "<", and back again. Similarly, `UrlEncode` and `UrlDecode` translate characters that need escaping within a URL, such as "?" or "/".

SUMMARY

On the surface, ASP.NET looks much like its predecessor, ASP 3.0. It supports interspersed server-side script, has the same set of intrinsics available, and provides the same ability to mix static HTML layout with dynamic server-side code. Under the covers, however, ASP.NET is dramatically different. Instead of using script interpretation, each page is now compiled in its entirety to a class that derives from `System.Web.UI.Page`. The entire request processing architecture is now based on a set of classes that model each aspect of a request and its response. ASP.NET introduces a new technique called code-behind that involves injecting a class in the hierarchy between the `Page` base class and your .aspx file–generated class, creating a clean separation of page layout from server-side code. Finally, ASP.NET solves the headache of Web application deployment by using the shadow copy mechanism in .NET to load "shadowed" versions of your component assemblies, leaving the original assemblies unlocked and available for replacement without shutting down the Web server.

◼ 2 ◼
Web Forms

A S TECHNOLOGIES MATURE, the programmatic interface to those technologies rises in its level of abstraction. Web applications are finally maturing, and the abstraction level rises with ASP.NET. An analogous transition was made not so long ago with desktop applications. Building an application for a PC used to mean that you had to develop your own interface, including menuing systems, window interaction, mouse and keyboard interaction, and so on. With the advent of platforms such as Macintosh and Windows, the level of abstraction rose. Developers could take advantage of core windowing components that managed menus and windows for them, and it became much rarer for developers to have to render pixels to the screen to interact with the user. Instead, a program now consists of collections of components that are prebuilt to render themselves to the screen and receive input from the user. Developers can then work with these higher-level components to construct applications. Each component has state associated with it, like the text of a menu item or the bitmap image to render to in a window, and it has a mechanism for rendering that state to the target device (usually the screen). Developers construct programs by manipulating the state of these components, and let the objects render themselves automatically, as depicted in Figure 2-1.

Web applications are very different from desktop applications, but analogies can be drawn between the two types of applications. Instead of

Programmatic Elements

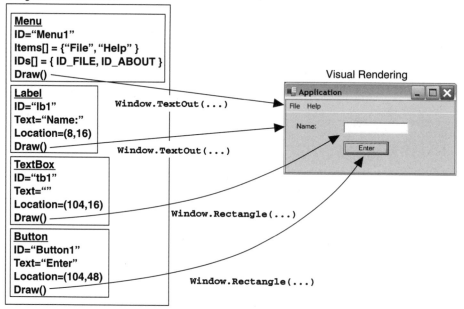

FIGURE 2-1: Conceptual Model for Desktop Applications

rendering by drawing pixels to a display, Web applications render by generating HTML to be processed by a browser. The current state of Web application development is analogous to desktop application development before windowing operating systems were available. Each request is serviced with an HTML response, typically created by performing some data lookup on the server machine and then carefully constructing the HTML to represent that data to the client. While HTML is much higher-level than pixel rendering, the concept of mapping state in an application to HTML for the client to view is similar. That HTML today is rendered primarily by using `printf` or its equivalent to write strings into a response buffer that is carried back to the client.

Now, instead of manually generating the HTML for clients to view the server-side state, we construct a model with a higher level of abstraction, similar to the window component model that windowed operating systems

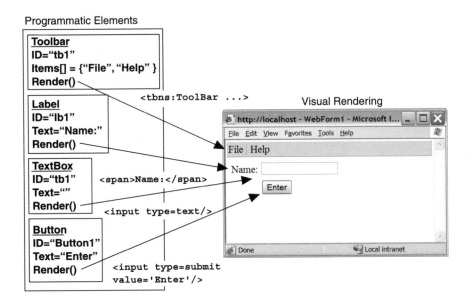

FIGURE 2-2: Conceptual Model for Web Forms Applications

provide. Instead of using windows that know how to render themselves as pixels to a screen, however, we create a set of objects that can render themselves as HTML to the response buffer. This approach potentially can provide similar improvements in developer productivity by removing the details of HTML generation from the hands of developers and letting them focus on the state of a set of components that can render themselves as HTML. This conceptual model is illustrated in Figure 2-2.

2.1 **Server-Side Controls**

Much like desktop application development models, the Web Forms model is constructed from a set of primitive controls. They are referred to as server-side controls in ASP.NET because even though they are rendered to the client as HTML, they exist on the server. The best way to understand server-side controls is to see them in action, so consider the page shown in Listing 2-1.

LISTING 2-1: An ASP.NET Page Using Server-Side Controls

```
<!- WebFormPage1.aspx ->
<%@ Page Language="C#" %>
<html>

<body>
  <form runat=server>
    Enter name: <input type=text id=_name runat=server/>
    <br/>
    Personality: <select id=_personality runat=server>
                   <option>extraverted</option>
                   <option>introverted</option>
                   <option>in-between</option>
                 </select>
    <input type=submit value="Submit" />
    <p>
      <% if (IsPostBack) {%>
        Hi <%=_name.Value%>, you selected
           <%=_personality.Value%>
      <% } %>
    </p>
  </form>
</body>
</html>
```

In many respects, this looks like a traditional ASP page you might write with interspersed server-side code. There are two significant differences, however. First, note that the form, input, and select elements on the page have been marked with a `runat=server` attribute, an attribute usually reserved for differentiating client-side and server-side script blocks. Second, notice that within the paragraph element at the bottom of the page, we were able to reference the value attribute of the input and select elements within server-side evaluation blocks (<%= %>). In a traditional ASP page, these expressions would have no meaning on the server. To retrieve the values of the input and select elements, you would look at the request string for variables whose names matched the identifiers of the two controls. We were also able to test the `Boolean` value `IsPostBack` to find out whether this was an initial GET request issued by the client or a subsequent POST back to our page.

In ASP.NET any HTML element can now have the `runat=server` attribute applied to it. When an element is marked with this attribute, ASP.NET creates a server-side control during page compilation and adds it as a field to the `Page`-derived class. The type of the control depends on the element marked as server-side. Listing 2-2 shows the fields that would be created in the `Page`-derived class created from the .aspx file from Listing 2-1.

LISTING 2-2: Generated Page-Derived Class with Server-Side Controls

```
using System.Web.UI;
using System.Web.UI.HtmlControls;
using System.Web.UI.WebControls;

public class WebFormPage1_aspx : Page
{
  protected HtmlInputText _name;
  protected ListItem      __control3;
  protected ListItem      __control4;
  protected ListItem      __control5;
  protected HtmlSelect    _personality;
  protected HtmlForm      __control2;

  // ...
}
```

These server-side controls added to the `Page`-derived class for our page are initialized with the values entered by the client when a post-back occurs. Furthermore, any modifications to the state of these controls is reflected when the page renders a response to the client. As developers, we can now manipulate controls and their state in a similar fashion to the way desktop controls can be manipulated.

Figure 2-3 enumerates the steps of a client-server interaction when server-side controls are used. Initially (step 1), the client makes a GET request for our page. ASP.NET services this request by creating an instance of our `Page`-derived class. Because this is an initial request for the page and there are no accompanying POST variables with the request, the values of the server-side controls in our page are set to their defaults (empty strings in this case). At step 2, our `Page`-derived class instance renders itself into

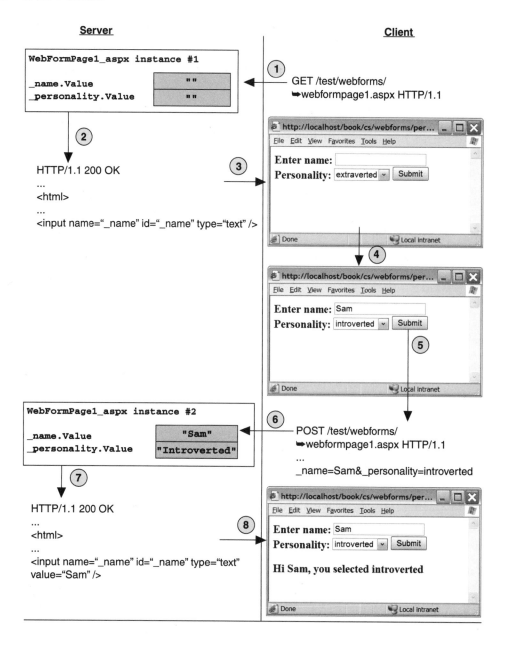

FIGURE 2-3: Client-Server Interaction with Web Forms

the response buffer, and that response is returned to the client in step 3. The client is now presented with our initial form, and can manipulate and add values to all the controls on the form (step 4). When the user presses the Submit button, a POST request is made to the server, with the values of the controls in the form passed as POST variables (step 5). This time, when ASP.NET creates a new instance of our Page-derived class, it notices that the request was a POST request with accompanying POST variables, so it passes the body of the POST request to the page and asks it to restore the state of any server-side controls (step 6). Our Page-derived class extracts the _name and _personality variables from the POST body and initializes the data members of the class corresponding to those variables with the variable values. This time, when the Page-derived class renders itself (step 7) the server-side controls render themselves with their current contents, which are the same as the values submitted by the client in step 5 unless we change them on the server. In step 8, the client receives the response to the POST with the controls rendered with their current state.

One useful facet of this model is that controls marked with the runat=server attribute retain their state across post-backs to the same page. In traditional ASP pages, you must take explicit action to get this behavior, but it falls naturally out of the Web Forms model.

2.2 **ViewState**

In the previous section, we stated that you can mark *any* HTML element with the runat=server attribute to make it accessible programmatically on the server. This at first seems implausible because there are many HTML elements whose values are not sent in the body of a POST request. For example, consider the page shown in Listing 2-3, which shows the implementation of a simple accumulator. When the user posts the page with a numeric value in the input element, the value is added to a running total. The running total is maintained in a server-side span element, whose value is extracted with each post-back and added to the value submitted by the user, and the resultant sum is assigned back into the `InnerText` attribute of the server-side span element.

LISTING 2-3: Accumulator Page

```
<!- Accumulator.aspx ->
<%@ Page Language="C#" %>

<html>
<script runat=server>
protected void Page_Load(object src, EventArgs e)
{
  if (IsPostBack)
  {
    int op1 = int.Parse(_op.Value);
    int op2 = int.Parse(_sum.InnerText);
    _sum.InnerText = (op1+op2).ToString();
  }
}
</script>
<body>
  <form runat=server>
    <h2>ASP.NET accumulator page</h2>
    <input size=2 type=text id=_op runat=server/>
    Sum:<span id=_sum runat=server>0</span>
    <p>
     <input type=submit value="Add" />
    </p>
  </form>
</body>
</html>
```

This page works in spite of the fact that the contents of the span, whose value we depend on for maintaining the total, is not passed back as part of the default post action of the client-side form. The only control in our page's form whose contents is sent back when the form is posted is the _op input element. Or is it?

Listing 2-4 shows the HTML that is rendered the first time this page is requested. Notice that in addition to all the explicit elements that were in our .aspx page, there is a hidden input element named __VIEWSTATE. The value of this element is a base64-encoded string that acts as a state repository for the page. Any elements on a page whose contents are not implicitly posted back via the standard form POST mechanism have their values saved to and restored from this hidden field. It is also used to propagate supplemental state for controls—for example, what prior value was stored in a control so that server-side change notifications can be issued. While the technique of propagating state using hidden input fields is common practice in Web applications, ASP.NET takes it a step further and uses it to unify the server-side control model by ensuring that all elements marked with runat=server retain their state across post-backs.

LISTING 2-4: Accumulator Page Rendering

```
<html>

<body>
  <form name="_ctl0" method="post"
        action="accumulator.aspx" id="_ctl0">
   <input type="hidden" name="__VIEWSTATE"
value="dDwtMTE3NzEwNDc2Njs7PvcRil1nMNe70yha9afq+YEvj46N" />

    <h2>ASP.NET accumulator page</h2>
    <input name="_op" id="_op" type="text" size="2" />
    Sum:<span id="_sum"></span>
    <p>
     <input type=submit value="Add" />
    </p>
  </form>
</body>
</html>
```

Figure 2-4 demonstrates a request sequence for our accumulator page. Each time a request is serviced by the accumulator page, the current value of the _sum span element is restored from the hidden __VIEWSTATE field. And when the page renders its response, the current value of the server-side span element representing the _sum field is placed into the __VIEW-STATE field so that the next time the page is posted back, the value of the _sum can be restored to its most recently displayed value.

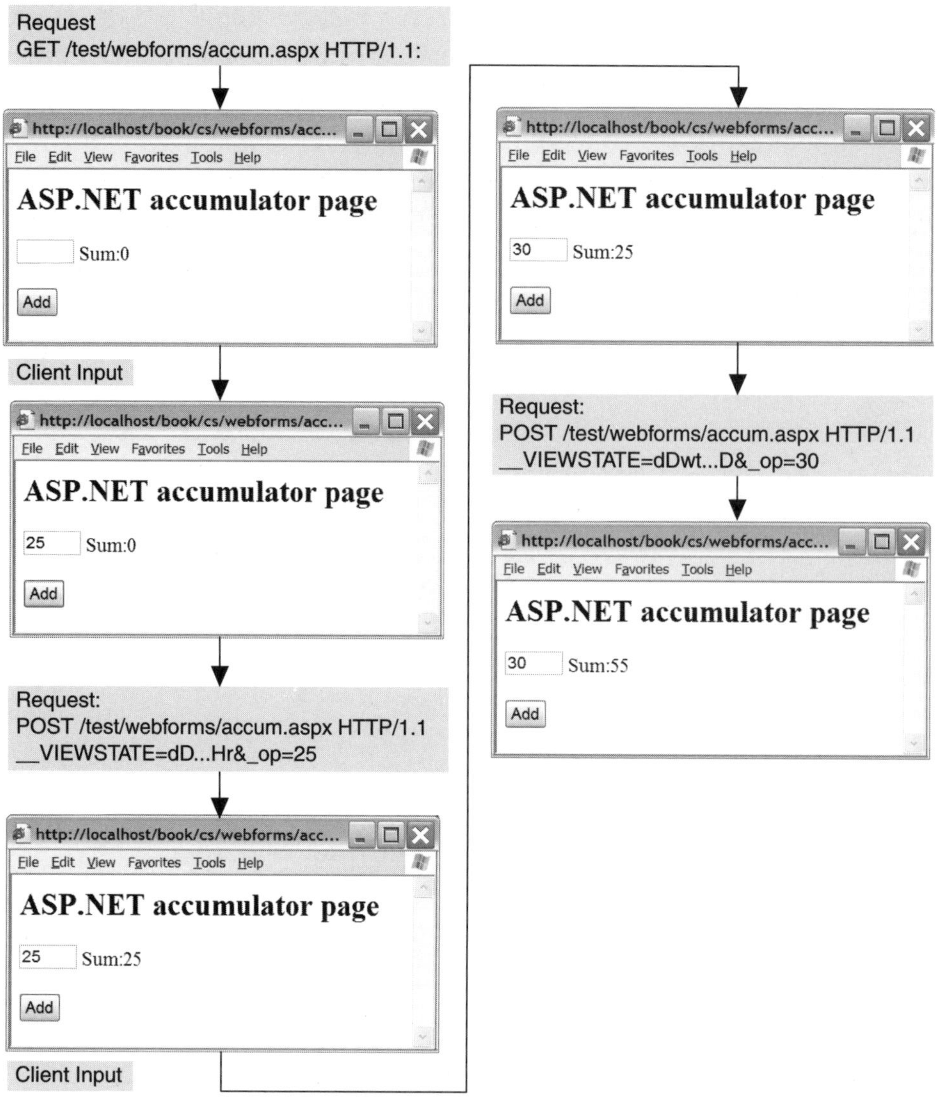

Request
GET /test/webforms/accum.aspx HTTP/1.1:

ASP.NET accumulator page

[   ] Sum:0

[Add]

Client Input

ASP.NET accumulator page

[25] Sum:0

[Add]

Request:
POST /test/webforms/accum.aspx HTTP/1.1
__VIEWSTATE=dD...Hr&_op=25

ASP.NET accumulator page

[25] Sum:25

[Add]

Client Input

ASP.NET accumulator page

[30] Sum:25

[Add]

Request:
POST /test/webforms/accum.aspx HTTP/1.1
__VIEWSTATE=dDwt...D&_op=30

ASP.NET accumulator page

[30] Sum:55

[Add]

FIGURE 2-4: Accumulator Page Request Sequence

2.3 Events

Many of the server-side controls in ASP.NET can generate server-side events in addition to simply acting as state retainers. The server-side control that most obviously generates server-side events is the button. When a client clicks a button in a form, the form is typically submitted back to the server via a POST request, as we have seen in earlier examples in this chapter. What we have not explored yet is the ability to link server-side functions in our Page-derived class.

Server-side events are implemented using the standard event mechanism in the CLR: delegates. Controls that generate server-side events typically expose events of the generic EventHandler delegate type.[5] To register a handler for a server-side event, you must first define a method in your Page-derived class whose signature matches that of the EventHandler delegate. Then you must create a new instance of the EventHandler delegate initialized with your handler and subscribe it to the event exposed by the control. Listing 2-5 shows a sample page that registers an event handler for the ServerClick event of the HtmlInputButton server-side control.

LISTING 2-5: Server-Side Event Handler Using Explicit Delegate Subscription

```
<!— event.aspx —>
<%@ Page Language="C#" %>

<html>
<script runat=server>
protected void OnClickMyButton(object src, EventArgs e)
{
  _message.InnerText = "You clicked the button!";
}

protected void Page_Init(object src, EventArgs e)
{
  _MyButton.ServerClick +=
                     new EventHandler(OnClickMyButton);
}
</script>
<body>
  <form runat=server>

    <h2>ASP.NET event page</h2>
    <p>
    <input type=button id=_MyButton
```

continues

5. Some controls define their own event handler delegates to pass additional information. For example, items within a datagrid expose events using the DataGridItem-EventHandler, which takes a reference to a DataGridItemEventArgs class containing a link to the item for which the event was fired.

```
                value="Click me!" runat=server />
         </p>
         <span id=_message runat=server/>
      </form>
   </body>
</html>
```

Note that in our implementation we provided a handler for the `Init` event of our `Page`-derived class using the `AutoEventWireup` described in Chapter 1 (by simply naming the function `Page_Init`). Within this handler, we explicitly created a new `EventHandler` delegate instance, initialized with the `OnClickMyButton` function, and subscribed that delegate to the `ServerClick` event of the `HtmlInputButton` control on our page. When the button is now clicked in the client browser, our event handler is invoked during the post-back sequence.

An alternative syntax for wiring up event handlers to server-side controls is to add an attribute to the control's tag in the page named `OnEvent`, where `Event` is the name of the event you would like to subscribe to. The value for this attribute should be the name of the server-side method in your `Page`-derived class you would like to have called when the event is fired. For example, instead of explicitly wiring up the delegate as we did in Listing 2-5, we could annotate the input control tag as shown in Listing 2-6.

LISTING 2-6: Server-Side Event Handler Using OnEvent Syntax

```
<!- event.aspx ->
<%@ Page Language="C#" %>

<html>
<script runat=server>
protected void OnClickMyButton(object src, EventArgs e)
{
  _message.InnerText = "You clicked the button!";
}
</script>
<body>
  <form runat=server>
    <h2>ASP.NET event page</h2>
    <p>
    <input type=button id=_MyButton
           value="Click me!"
           OnServerClick="OnClickMyButton" runat=server />
    </p>
```

```
      <span id=_message runat=server/>
    </form>
  </body>
  </html>
```

It is important to understand that server-side events are generated as part of the post-back sequence and are issued through the standard HTTP POST mechanism. Because a given page always issues a generic POST request to the server, it is not obvious how to map a particular post-back request onto server-side events. For example, if we have multiple buttons on a page, each of which has a designated server-side handler, how does ASP.NET know which event to fire when a POST occurs to the page? Listing 2-7 shows a sample page with this problem. There are three separate buttons, and each button has a distinct handler whose implementation changes the color of the server-side div element. If some additional information is not sent through the POST issued by each of these buttons, it will be impossible for ASP.NET to tell which button was pressed and to invoke only the handler for that particular button.

Listing 2-7: Color Page Demonstrating Three Separate Server-Side Event Handlers

```
<!- color.aspx ->
<%@ Page Language="C#" %>

<html>
<script runat=server>
protected void OnRed(object src, EventArgs e)
{
   _color.Style["background-color"] = "Red";
}

protected void OnGreen(object src, EventArgs e)
{
   _color.Style["background-color"] = "Green";
}

protected void OnBlue(object src, EventArgs e)
{
   _color.Style["background-color"] = "Blue";
}

protected void Page_Init(object src, EventArgs e)
{
```

continues

```
    _redButton.ServerClick    += new EventHandler(OnRed);
    _greenButton.ServerClick += new EventHandler(OnGreen);
    _blueButton.ServerClick  += new EventHandler(OnBlue);
  }

  protected void Page_Load(object src, EventArgs e)
  {
    if (!IsPostBack)
    {
      _color.Style["background-color"] = "Red";
      _color.Style["width"] = "100";
      _color.Style["height"] = "100";
    }
  }

</script>
<body>
  <form runat=server>

    <h2>ASP.NET color page</h2>
    <div id=_color runat=server />
    <p>
    <input type=button id=_redButton value="Red"
           runat=server />
    <input type=button id=_greenButton value="Green"
           runat=server />
    <input type=button id=_blueButton value="Blue"
           runat=server />
    </p>
  </form>
</body>
</html>
```

Fortunately, ASP.NET does pass additional information with each POST request when server-side events are issued. In fact, there are two additional hidden fields on a form that uses server-side events like the one shown in Listing 2-7. The first field, __EVENTTARGET, is populated with the identifier of the control that generated the post-back, and the second field, __EVENT-ARGUMENT, is used to pass any parameters necessary to the event. These two hidden fields are populated in the client by using client-side JavaScript to trap the client-side event of the object and then issuing a post-back pro-grammatically. When the POST is processed on the server, ASP.NET checks the contents of the __EVENTTARGET field and fires only events issued by the control whose ID is in that field. Listing 2-8 shows the client-side HTML generated by the color.aspx page shown in Listing 2-7.

LISTING 2-8: Color Page Rendering

```html
<html><body>
  <form name="_ctl0" method="post"
        action="color.aspx" id="_ctl0">
<input type="hidden" name="__EVENTTARGET" value="" />
<input type="hidden" name="__EVENTARGUMENT" value="" />
<input type="hidden" name="__VIEWSTATE" value="dD...==" />

<script language="javascript">
<!--
    function __doPostBack(eventTarget, eventArgument) {
            var theform = document._ctl0;
            theform.__EVENTTARGET.value = eventTarget;
            theform.__EVENTARGUMENT.value = eventArgument;
            theform.submit();
    }
// -->
</script>

    <h2>ASP.NET color page</h2>
    <div id="_color"
       style="background-color:Red;width:100;height:100;"/>
    <p>
    <input language="javascript"
           onclick="__doPostBack('_redButton','')"
           name="_redButton" id="_redButton"
           type="button" value="Red" />
    <input language="javascript"
           onclick="__doPostBack('_greenButton','')"
           name="_greenButton" id="_greenButton"
           type="button" value="Green" />
    <input language="javascript"
           onclick="__doPostBack('_blueButton','')"
           name="_blueButton" id="_blueButton"
           type="button" value="Blue" />
    </p>
  </form>
</body>
</html>
```

The server-side event model completes the Web Forms control model. Through the use of hidden fields, ASP.NET brings a familiar programming model to developers who are used to working with controls that issue events and render their current state, but may not be familiar with the disconnected HTTP protocol over which Web applications communicate.

2.4 **A Day in the Life of a Page**

The analogy between the desktop control model and Web Forms is not complete. Although the fundamental elements behave similarly, such as rendering of state and event propagation, the Web Forms model has an imposed sequencing on the rendering process that does not exist in the desktop model. It is critical for Web developers using ASP.NET to understand this sequencing in order to use the model effectively.

Pages are short-lived objects, as are all the elements they contain. A page is created for the sole purpose of processing a request, and once that request processing has completed, the page is discarded. This means that each request to a page is processed by a new instance of that `Page` class. Moreover, an explicit, deterministic sequence of events takes place after the page is created to service a request. This sequence of events is something that every ASP.NET developer should be aware of, because your pages will not behave the way you expect if you perform things in the wrong order. For example, consider the page shown in Listing 2-9.

LISTING 2-9: Sample Page with Incorrect Control State Manipulation

```
<!- File: sample.aspx ->
<%@ Page Language="C#" %>

<html>

<body>
  <form runat=server>

    <h2>ASP.NET sample page</h2>
    <h3>Page type: <span id=_message runat=server/></h3>
    <%
      // Error - modifying a property of a server-side
      // control within a script block like this can lead
      // to inconsistencies
      _message.InnerText = this.GetType().ToString();
    %>
  </form>
</body>
</html>
```

As noted in the comments, the assignment to the `InnerText` property of the server-side span element has no effect because it falls within a server-side block of code delineated with <%%> tags that is placed after the control that is modified. All server-side code within <%%> tags is added to a Render method of the Page class, as discussed in Chapter 1. By this time, the server-side span has already rendered itself into the response buffer with its inner text set to an empty string, and the assignment has no effect on the output of the page. This is in contrast to a traditional desktop control model, where any modifications made to a control at any time are saved and reflected in that control's rendering.

Figure 2-5 shows the events that occur during a page's lifetime. As a page developer, you have hooks into most of these events, either by defining event handlers for a particular event or by providing overridden versions of virtual functions defined in the Page base class. Most of the programmatic manipulation of server-side controls should occur either in the Load event handler for a page or within a server-side control event

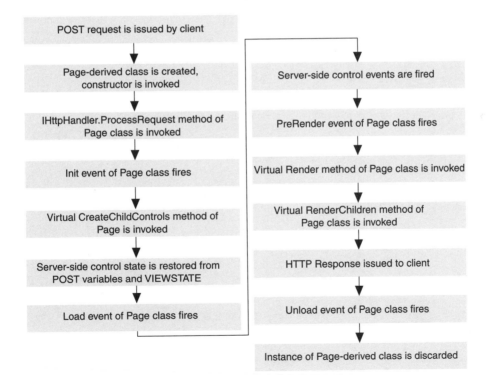

FIGURE 2-5: Page Event Sequence

handler. The Load event fires after the all the server-side contro͏ ͏ave been created and had their state restored from the POST body of the ͏ ͏uest. This gives you an opportunity to both view the values submitted by the client, as well as a chance to populate controls with values you want the client to see in the response to this request.

2.5 Web Forms and Code-Behind

Perhaps the most appealing aspect of the Web Forms model is that in combination with code-behind, it enables true separation of page logic from page layout and rendering. For example, recall the page shown in Listing 2-1, where the input and select elements were marked with the runat=server attribute, enabling state retention and server-side manipulation of those elements. Although this was helpful, our .aspx page was more than pure layout. It included server-side script to print a message, and we statically populated the options of the select element. Using code-behind with Web forms, we can very often remove all code from our .aspx pages, creating a clean partitioning of form logic and form layout. Listing 2-10 demonstrates this technique by showing the same page displayed in Listing 2-1 but now rewritten with a code-behind file, which is shown in Listing 2-11.

LISTING 2-10: Sample Page with Server-Side Controls and Code-Behind

```
<!- WebFormPage2.aspx ->
<%@ Page Language="C#"
        Inherits="EssentialAspDotNet.WebForms.Page2"
        Src="Page2.cs" AutoEventWireUp="false" %>

<html>

<body>
  <form runat=server>
    <h3>Enter name:
        <input type=text id=_name runat=server/></h3>
    <h3>Personality:
        <select id=_personality runat=server /></h3>
     <input type=button id=_enterButton
            value="Enter" runat=server/>
    <p runat=server id=_messageParagraph />
  </form>
</body>
</html>
```

LISTING 2-11: Code-Behind File for Sample Page

```
// Page2.cs

using System;
using System.Web;
using System.Web.UI;
using System.Web.UI.HtmlControls;
using System.Web.UI.WebControls;

namespace EssentialAspDotNet.WebForms
{

public class Page2 : Page
{
  protected HtmlSelect         _personality;
  protected HtmlInputText      _name;
  protected HtmlInputButton    _enterButton;
  protected HtmlGenericControl _messageParagraph;

  override protected void OnInit(EventArgs e)
  {
    // Wire up handler to ServerClick event of button
    _enterButton.ServerClick += new EventHandler(OnEnter);
  }

  override protected void OnLoad(EventArgs e)
  {
    // On initial access, populate select with items
    if (!IsPostBack)
    {
      _personality.Items.Add(new ListItem("extraverted"));
      _personality.Items.Add(new ListItem("introverted"));
      _personality.Items.Add(new ListItem("in-between"));
    }
  }

  protected void OnEnter(object src, EventArgs e)
  {
    // When the user presses enter, print a message
    string msg = string.Format("Hi {0}, you selected {1}",
                   _name.Value, _personality.Value);
    _messageParagraph.InnerText = msg;
  }
}

}
```

Note that we were able to manipulate server-side controls on the form from fields declared in our code-behind class. In fact, looking just at the code-behind file, it appears that we are manipulating uninitialized fields in our class, because the _personality, _name, _enterButton, and _messageParagraph fields are never explicitly created but are definitely used. If you look closely, you will notice that these field names match *exactly* the identifiers of their corresponding server-side controls in the .aspx file. This is an important relationship that you will use almost anytime you work with Web forms and code-behind classes. When you declare a field, either protected or public, with the same name as the identifier of a server-side control in your form, that field is initialized with a reference to that server-side control when the class is created. It is also crucial that the field be of the correct type—in our case we were mapping to four different HTML control types and had to carefully declare each field with the correct type, matching it to the element on the form to which it corresponds. We discuss this mapping of server-side HTML elements to classes in more detail in the upcoming HtmlControls section.

This process of associating server-side controls with fields in a Page-derived class occurs during the parsing of the .aspx page. The parser must be careful not to redefine fields in the class that is generated from the .aspx file, because this would mask any fields declared with the same name in the code-behind base class. Instead, the parser uses reflection to query the code-behind base class during the parsing of the .aspx file. If there is a public or protected field declared in the code-behind base class whose name matches the identifier of the server-side control, it will not generate a field for that control in the generated class. If there is no such field in the code-behind base class, it will create a field in the newly generated class. This guarantees that all server-side controls have a corresponding field in the generated class, either inherited from the code-behind base class or declared directly in the generated class. This is also why the code-behind base class must declare these fields as either public or protected, so that the derived class can access them and assign the newly created control references to them.

Figure 2-6 shows this field binding. In this example, the Test.aspx file contains three server-side controls: the form, which has no explicit identifier,

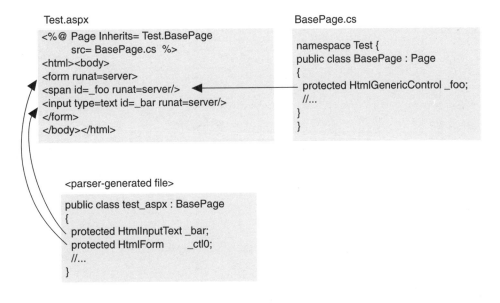

Test.aspx
```
<%@ Page Inherits= Test.BasePage
       src= BasePage.cs  %>
<html><body>
<form runat=server>
<span id=_foo runat=server/>
<input type=text id=_bar runat=server/>
</form>
</body></html>
```

BasePage.cs
```
namespace Test {
public class BasePage : Page
{
  protected HtmlGenericControl _foo;
  //...
}
}
```

<parser-generated file>
```
public class test_aspx : BasePage
{
  protected HtmlInputText _bar;
  protected HtmlForm       _ctl0;
  //...
}
```

FIGURE 2-6: Binding Fields to Server-Side Controls

the server-side span element named _foo, and the server-side input element named _bar. The code-behind class, BasePage, contains a single protected field named _foo of type HtmlGenericControl, which is what a span element maps to. Thus, when the parser generates the class from the Test.aspx file, it adds two fields to the derived class: one for the form control with an artificially generated identifier (_ctl0) and the other using the _bar identifier assigned in the page.

2.6 Root Path Reference Syntax

Many of the server-side controls contain URL properties, such as the src attribute of the img control or the href property of the a control. There is a convenient syntax that you can use within a URL property of a server-side control to reference the root of your application directory to avoid hard-coding relative paths in your application's directory structure. The syntax is to precede the path with the tilde character (~), which at compile time is resolved to a reference to Request.ApplicationPath, as shown in

Listing 2-12. Note that this syntax works only with server-side controls and cannot be used with regular HTML elements.

LISTING 2-12: Using Root Path Reference Syntax

```
<!- RootPathSyntax.aspx ->
<html>
<body>
<h1>Root path reference test page</h1>
<form runat="server">
<a href="~/otherpages/hi.aspx" runat="server">
<img runat="server" src="~/images/hi.gif"/>
</a>
</form>

</body> </html>
```

2.7 HtmlControls

Throughout this chapter, the examples have referenced control classes such as `HtmlInputText` and `HtmlGenericControl`, simply stating that they were examples of server-side controls. This section more formally introduces these classes and their compatriots in the `HtmlControl` hierarchy. It is classes from this hierarchy that your page will work with if you elect to use server-side controls by adding `runat=server` attributes to existing HTML elements in a form (in contrast to using the syntactically different `WebControls`, discussed in the next section).

You can mark literally *any* HTML element in an .aspx file with the `runat=server` attribute to obtain a server-side version. When you do this, the server-side control that is created to correspond to the client-side HTML element comes from the `HtmlControl` hierarchy. This hierarchy is shown in Figure 2-7.

Note that all these classes derive from a common base class, `System.Web.UI.Control`, and, more specifically, from `System.Web.UI.Html-Controls.HtmlControl`. The `Control` base class contains functionality and state common to all server-side controls, the details of which are discussed in Chapter 8, where we look at building your own server-side controls. The `HtmlControl` base class further adds properties and methods

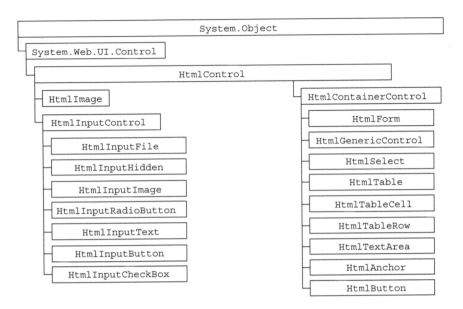

FIGURE 2-7: HtmlControl Hierarchy

common to all HtmlControls. This includes properties such as Style and Disabled. When you create an .aspx file with HTML tags attributed with runat=server, the class chosen from this hierarchy depends on the tag. Table 2-1 lists the various HTML tags and their corresponding Html-Control-derived classes.

TABLE 2-1: Tag Mappings for HtmlControls

Tag	HtmlControl Class
`<img runat=server/>`	HtmlImage
`<input type=file runat=server/>`	HtmlInputFile
`<input type=hidden runat=server/>`	HtmlInputHidden
`<input type=image runat=server/>`	HtmlInputImage
`<input type=radio runat=server/>`	HtmlInputRadioButton
`<input type=text runat=server/>`	HtmlInputText

TABLE 2-1: Tag Mappings for HtmlControls (continued)

Tag	HtmlControl Class
`<input type=checkbox runat=server/>`	`HtmlInputCheckBox`
`<form runat=server>`	`HtmlForm`

`<span runat=server>`
`<div runat=server>`
`<p runat=server>`
etc. (all other elements)
	`HtmlGenericControl`

`<select runat=server/>`	`HtmlSelect`
`<table runat=server/>`	`HtmlTable`
`<td>` (within a server-side table) `<th>` (within a server-side table)	`HtmlTableCell`
`<tr>` (within a server-side table)	`HtmlTableRow`
`<textarea runat=server/>`	`HtmlTextArea`
`<a runat=server/>`	`HtmlAnchor`
`<input type=button runat=server />`	`HtmlInputButton`
`<input type=submit runat=server />`	`HtmlInputButton`
`<input type=reset runat=server />`	`HtmlInputButton`

Note that while many of the HTML elements have unique mappings, there is a class of tags that all map to a single control: `HtmlGenericControl`. The `HtmlGenericControl` class represents controls that have no unique server-side behavior, such as the span, body, and p elements. This class simply contains a `TagName` property in addition to the properties it inherits from the `HtmlControl` base class. The `TagName` is set to the name of the tag that should be rendered by the control (such as span, body, or p), and the inherited attribute collection (`Attributes`) is a generic set of name/value pairs that will be rendered as attributes for the tag. Note also that this control derives from the `HtmlContainerControl`, meaning that it can contain other controls and literal HTML within its tag.

The remainder of the `HtmlControls` have properties, methods, and events similar to their HTML counterparts, so anyone used to working with HTML should feel comfortable with these controls. For details on each control, refer to the online documentation available through MSDN.[6]

2.8 **WebControls**

Web Forms with HTML server-side controls is a compelling model in and of itself, but the `HtmlControls` are true to their browser counterparts and retain the many idiosyncrasies of HTML elements. Even more compelling would be a set of server-side controls that were not one-to-one mappings of HTML elements but programmatically friendlier controls that took care of mapping to the appropriate HTML elements. Enter `WebControls`.

Most of the HTML elements you might place on a page can also be rendered by classes in the `WebControl` hierarchy. This is a set of classes parallel to the `HtmlControl` classes that provide a simplified, more uniform programming model and many more advanced composite controls, such as the `DataGrid`, `Xml`, `Calendar`, and `Validation` controls. Figure 2-8 shows the complete hierarchy of `WebControls` available in ASP.NET.

This example shows the idiosyncratic nature of the HTML controls. To set the background color of an `HtmlTable` class to gray, you would assign `gray` to the `BgColor` property of the class. To set the background color of a span element via its server-side equivalent, the `HtmlGenericControl`, you would need to set the `Style` attribute to `background-color:gray;`. The analogous classes in the `WebControls` hierarchy would be `Table` and `Label`, both of which have a `BackColor` attribute that stores not a string but an instance of the `System.Color` class. So in each case, you would set the `BackColor` property to `Color.Gray`. This consistency in naming and sharing of common properties is found throughout the `WebControls` hierarchy.

---

6. MSDN documentation is available through Visual Studio .NET or at http://msdn.microsoft.com.

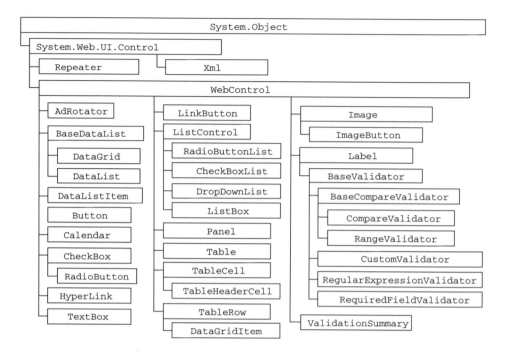

FIGURE 2-8: WebControl Hierarchy

In addition to increased uniformity, the WebControls provide many more complex controls that render not as single HTML elements but as combinations of HTML elements based on control state. Many of these controls are discussed in detail in future chapters, including the validation and data binding controls. Other interesting controls that we look at now include the list controls, the Xml control, the Panel control, and the AdRotator control.

2.8.1 List Controls

ASP.NET introduces several new list controls, all of which derive from the common base class ListControl. Each list control supports a collection of items (of type ListItemCollection) and properties to set and retrieve the selected item (or index), data binding, and the ability to issue a POST back to the form when the selection is changed. Listing 2-13 shows the common properties of the `ListControl` class.

LISTING 2-13: ListControl Properties

```
public class ListControl : WebControl
{
  public virtual bool      AutoPostBack            {get; set;}
  public virtual string    DataMember              {get; set;}
  public virtual object    DataSource              {get; set;}
  public virtual string    DataTextField           {get; set;}
  public virtual string    DataTextFormatString    {get; set;}
  public virtual string    DataValueField          {get; set;}
  public virtual ListItemCollection Items          {get; set;}
  public virtual int       SelectedIndex           {get; set;}
  public virtual ListItem SelectedItem             {get;}

  public event EventHandler SelectedIndexChanged;
  //...
}
```

Two of the list controls should be familiar to anyone with HTML experience: `DropDownList` and `ListBox`. Each of these controls renders as HTML `Select` elements; the only difference is that `ListBox` renders with a `Size` attribute set to `4` (by default), so that it appears as a fixed list. The other two list controls are examples of controls that exist only as server-side controls: `CheckBoxList` and `RadioButtonList`. These controls give you a programmatic interface on the server similar to that of `DropDownList` and `ListBox`, but when they render to the client, they render as tables (or as spans if `RepeatLayout` is set to `Flow`) with embedded input elements, because they have no direct equivalent in HTML. Figure 2-9 shows the rendering of two instances of these controls.

Several additional controls in the `WebControls` hierarchy provide interesting alternatives to hand-rendering HTML techniques. The `Xml` control provides a mechanism for performing XSL transforms on XML input as part of a page's output. The `AdRotator` control uses an XML file as input to render an image that changes with each post-back, which is useful for randomly displaying images, often for advertisements. Finally, the `Panel` control, which renders as a `DIV` element, is useful for containing groups of

Renders as →

```
<asp:CheckBoxList id=_cb1 runat= server >
 <asp:ListItem Value= 1 >Item 1</asp:ListItem>
 <asp:ListItem Value= 2 >Item 2</asp:ListItem>
 <asp:ListItem Value= 3 >Item 3</asp:ListItem>
</asp:CheckBoxList>
```

```
<table id= _cbl1  border= 0 >
<tr>
<td><input id= _cbl1_0  type= checkbox
name= _cbl1:0  />
  <label for= _cbl1_0 >Item 1</label></td>
</tr><tr>
<td><input id= _cbl1_1  type= checkbox
name= _cbl1:1  />
  <label for= _cbl1_1 >Item 2</label></td>
</tr><tr>
<td><input id= _cbl1_2  type= checkbox
name= _cbl1:2  />
  <label for= _cbl1_2 >Item 3</label></td>
</tr>
</table>
```

Renders as →

```
<asp:RadioButtonList id=_rbl1 runat= server >
 <asp:ListItem Value= 1 >Item 1</asp:ListItem>
 <asp:ListItem Value= 2 >Item 2</asp:ListItem>
 <asp:ListItem Value= 3 >Item 3</asp:ListItem>
</asp:RadioButtonList>
```

```
<table id= _rbl1  border= 0 >
<tr>
<td><input id= _rbl1_0  type= radio
name= _rbl1  value= 1 />
  <label for= _rbl1_0 >Item 1</label></td>
</tr><tr>
<td><input id= _rbl1_1  type= radio
name= _rbl1  value= 2 />
  <label for= _rbl1_1 >Item 2</label></td>
</tr><tr>
<td><input id= _rbl1_2  type= radio
name= _rbl1  value= 3 />
  <label for= _rbl1_2 >Item 3</label></td>
</tr>
</table>
```

FIGURE 2-9: Rendering of CheckBoxList and RadioButtonList Controls

controls whose alignment or visibility you need to change programmatically. Listing 2-14 shows a sample .aspx page that uses all these controls together.

LISTING 2-14: Sample Use of Xml, AdRotator, and Panel Controls

```
<!— File: XmlAdPanel.aspx —>
<%@ Page language="c#" %>
<HTML>
```

```
<body>
<form runat="server">
<asp:Xml id=_xml1 runat="server"
        DocumentSource="sample.xml"
        TransformSource="sampleTransform.xsl">
</asp:Xml><br/>
<asp:AdRotator id=_ar1 runat="server"
      Width="468px" Height="60px"
      AdvertisementFile="pics.xml"></asp:AdRotator>

<asp:Panel id=_p1 runat=server HorizontalAlign='center'
                  Visible='true' bgColor='cornsilk'>
  <asp:Label id=_l1 runat=server>Panel label</asp:Label>
  <br/>
  <asp:TextBox id=_tb1 runat=server/>
  <br/>
  <asp:Button Text='Push me!' runat=server/>
</asp:Panel>
</FORM>

  </body>
</HTML>
```

2.9 **WebControls versus HtmlControls**

One of the first questions many people ask when they see that ASP.NET provides two sets of controls is, Which set of controls should I use? The answer depends on your needs. For most developers, it will be simpler to work with the WebControls hierarchy of controls because they are most like the desktop equivalents that most programmers are familiar with. They are also more uniform in their treatment of attributes. For example, every WebControl exposes a CssClass attribute providing a hook to a style-sheet style, but none of the HtmlControls expose such an attribute. Thus, to associate a style-sheet class with an HtmlControl, you must program-matically populate the Attributes collection with a name/value pair con-sisting of the string "class" and the name of the style-sheet class.

The two primary reasons for using HtmlControls are porting and using alternate designers. It may be simpler to port existing ASP or plain HTML pages to ASP.NET by selecting a subset of the elements on a form to run on the server by just adding the runat=server attribute. A designer other than Visual Studio .NET may be simpler to work with if the Html-Controls are used instead of the WebControls, because the designer is more likely to recognize familiar HTML elements. However, many of the most popular designers, including FrontPage and Dreamweaver, have announced support for ASP.NET WebControl elements. It is also not a matter of either/or, because WebControls can be freely mixed with HtmlControls, so if it makes more sense to use WebControls in one place and HtmlControls in another, feel free to do so.

2.10 Building Web Forms with Visual Studio .NET

All the topics discussed in this chapter are directly applicable to building Web forms with the Visual Studio .NET designer; however, there are some subtleties to the way the designer works that you should be aware of.

Figure 2-10 shows a sample ASP.NET Web application in Microsoft Visual Studio .NET. In this example, a pair of server-side controls has been added with the designer, and a handler has been associated with the Click event of the server-side button. There are two important Page attributes to notice in the generated .aspx file. First, note the Codebehind attribute, whose value is set to the source file for the code-behind. This is *not* equivalent to the src attribute discussed in Chapter 1, but is a tag used exclusively by Visual Studio .NET to associate source files with .aspx pages (so that they show up as connected in the Solution Explorer and so that the code-behind file can be brought up for any .aspx page by using the F7 key). ASP.NET does not recognize this attribute and ignores it altogether. For the code-behind class to be referenced by a Visual Studio .NET–created page, it must be compiled into an assembly and placed in the /bin directory of the virtual root for that application. This is exactly what Visual Studio .NET does for you. In fact, all code files within a Web application project are compiled into a single assembly, which is placed in the /bin directory of the virtual root associated with that project. The second important attribute to note is AutoEventWireup, which is set to false. This means that your page and code-behind class may not use the automatic event wire-up

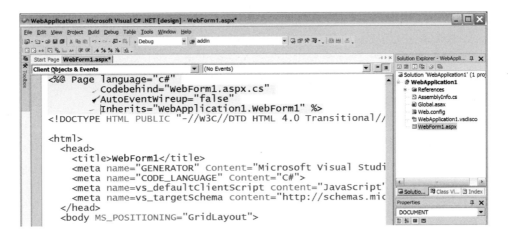

FIGURE 2-10: Visual Studio .NET Web Form Application

mechanism for `Page` events. Instead, you must explicitly register delegates for any events you want to handle.

To complete the picture, Listing 2-15 shows the code-behind file, `Web-Form1.aspx.cs`, that is referenced by the .aspx page in our sample project. Note that when the designer is used to place a server-side control on a form, it takes care to place a protected data member of the appropriate type in the code-behind file. Also note that because `AutoEventWireup` is disabled from the .aspx page, the code-behind generated by Visual Studio .NET is careful to explicitly wire up the `Load` event handler of the `Page` class. The `Init` event of the `Page` class is used as the bootstrap to initialize all the other events by calling the helper function, `InitializeComponent`. Notice that the designer explicitly added an event handler for the `Click` event of the server-side button in the `InitializeComponent` implementation. In general, anytime you add a handler for a server-side event in the designer, it explicitly subscribes to that event in this method. The `Init` event is handled by overriding the virtual `OnInit` method inherited from the `Page` base class, which is registered as an event handler for the `Init` event in the `Page` class's constructor.

Listing 2-15: Visual Studio .NET–Generated Code-Behind File

```
using System;
using System.Collections;
using System.ComponentModel;
using System.Data;
using System.Drawing;
using System.Web;
using System.Web.SessionState;
using System.Web.UI;
using System.Web.UI.WebControls;
using System.Web.UI.HtmlControls;

namespace WebFormsApp
{
  public class WebForm1 : Page
  {
    protected Button _PushMe;
    protected TextBox _Name;

    private void Page_Load(object sender, EventArgs e)
    {
     // Put user code to initialize the page here
    }

#region Web Form Designer generated code
    override protected void OnInit(EventArgs e)
    {
      InitializeComponent();
     base.OnInit(e);
    }

    private void InitializeComponent()
    {
      _PushMe.Click +=
                new System.EventHandler(Button1_Click);
      this.Load += new System.EventHandler(this.Page_Load);
    }
#endregion
    private void Button1_Click(object sender, EventArgs e)
    {
    }
  }
}
```

There are several mistakes people often make when they begin working with Visual Studio .NET because of some of these default settings. The first mistake is to assume that the Codebehind attribute implicitly compiles the code-behind file when the page is accessed. This is not true, and the code-behind file must be explicitly compiled and then deployed to the /bin directory of the application. Another mistake is to remove the AutoEvent-Wireup attribute (or set it to true) without removing the explicit event wire-up in the code-behind file. Removing this attribute causes ASP.NET to automatically add an event handler for any function in the code-behind file or in the .aspx file that matches one of the hard-coded event handlers. In most cases, this will be the Page_Load method defined in the code-behind file, and the symptom will be that the Load event appears to fire twice for each Page creation. In reality, the Load event is firing only once, but there are now two handlers registered for the event.

SUMMARY

ASP.NET brings control-based programming to Web application development with Web forms. Borrowing from the familiar desktop application control model, ASP.NET defines a number of control classes to represent elements on a Web form. These controls render themselves as HTML as part of a response to an HTTP request. Any modification made to the state of these controls on the server is reflected in the subsequent rendering to the client, letting the developer focus more on structuring the application and less on the details of rendering to a browser. To make this control-based programming model work for all elements on a page, ASP.NET introduces ViewState as a means of transferring the state of controls that are not propagated as part of a standard POST request. Server-side events complete the control model.

Two sets of server-side control classes are available: HtmlControls and WebControls. The HtmlControl classes closely mirror their HTML tag counterparts and are convenient to use when converting an existing HTML page to ASP.NET. The WebControls provide a more uniform programmatic interface and will be used by most developers building ASP.NET pages from scratch.

■ 3 ■
Configuration

A SK ANY THREE traditional ASP developers what they like *least* about building applications in ASP and you will always get three different answers. Of course, it will always be the same three different answers. One of the developers will claim that debugging is absolutely the worst part of ASP development. A second developer will state emphatically that deployment is by far the worst part of ASP development. And the third developer will claim that no *one* thing is the worst, but the combination of debugging and deployment is the worst part of ASP development.

When the ASP.NET team set out to design the next version of ASP, many of their top priorities were to remedy the most glaring deficiencies of ASP. The debugging of ASP.NET applications is covered in Chapter 5, but fear not, it does improve. As for deployment improvements, Chapter 1 discussed the solution to one of the most frustrating aspects of deployment with ASP applications: the fact that you had to stop IIS to replace any DLLs (usually COM libraries) that were used by your application. ASP.NET remedies this by introducing the shadow copy mechanism for all referenced assemblies placed in the /bin directory of the application, so neither the ASP.NET worker process nor IIS has to be stopped to replace components associated with an application. This feature is often categorized as part of the xcopy deployment feature of ASP.NET—the fact that for most ASP.NET applications, installing or upgrading an application is as simple as using xcopy (or a similar copy utility) to place new files on the server.

The xcopy deployment of ASP.NET would not be complete, however, if it were not also possible to configure ASP.NET applications by copying a file. For a traditional ASP application, all the configuration settings are stored in the IIS metabase, which is a binary repository managed through a set of COM APIs. Installing an ASP application on a server means that the metabase must be updated to reflect the configuration settings of the application, which means that a person with adequate privileges must run a script on the server. Similarly, updating an ASP application requires running a script on the server to update the metabase. In addition, it is not trivial to discover what the current settings for an application are, because the metabase is stored in the registry in a proprietary binary format, unreadable by any means except the COM APIs.

In keeping with ASP.NET's goal of supporting xcopy deployment, the configuration for an ASP.NET application is specified through an XML file, named web.config, placed at the top of the virtual root for the application. In fact, this file uses the same configuration layout that all .NET applications use, where the configuration file is named after the application, such as myapp.exe.config. The web.config file is just a specially named file whose settings apply to the pages and classes within that directory for an ASP.NET application, since ASP.NET applications are housed in the larger aspnet_wp.exe containing process. Because the web.config XML file is stored as plain text, it is easy to view with any text editor or to manipulate programmatically with any XML API. It is also easy to deploy, simply by copying a new version of the text file to the server. When the next request is serviced, ASP.NET will notice that the timestamp on the web.config file has changed and will immediately apply the new settings to that request and all subsequent requests.

3.1 **web.config**

If you have configured a Web application with IIS before, many of the configuration settings available in web.config will be familiar to you. To begin with, let's see how to use the web.config file to configure something simple, such as changing the session state timeout for an application. At the top of your virtual root directory, you would create a new text file named web.config, the contents of which specify a new value for the timeout attribute of the sessionState element, as shown in Listing 3-1.

LISTING 3-1: Sample web.config File Changing the Session State Timeout

```
<configuration>
  <system.web>
    <sessionState mode='Inproc' timeout='10' />
  </system.web>
</configuration>
```

Note that the format of this file is standard XML, with a single top-level element named configuration. Most of the settings applied to ASP.NET applications are elements within the <system.web> element, so that is the next element specified. The sessionState element has a number of attributes, and even though in this case, we care about only the timeout attribute, we also have to specify the mode attribute because it is required for this element. Once this file is placed at the root of our virtual directory, any subsequent requests will pick up the settings we have specified, which in our case means that the session state timeout would be set to 10 minutes, instead of the default 20 minutes. A complete list of all the top-level elements that apply to ASP.NET applications and their purpose is shown in Table 3-1.

TABLE 3-1: Top-Level Configuration Elements Available in web.config

Element	Purpose
<authentication>	Specify the client authentication mode to use
<authorization>	Allow or deny users or roles access
<browserCaps>	Specify browser capabilities based on user agent
<clientTarget>	Define client targets
<compilation>	Control page compilation and assembly references
<customErrors>	Control error page display and define custom error pages
<globalization>	Set the request and response encoding

TABLE 3-1: Top-Level Configuration Elements Available in web.config (continued)

Element	Purpose
`<httpHandlers>`	Add or remove HTTP handlers
`<httpModules>`	Add or remove HTTP modules
`<httpRuntime>`	Control aspects of HTTP request processing
`<identity>`	Specify impersonation for this application
`<machineKey>`	Control the validation and decryption key
`<pages>`	Set defaults for page attributes globally
`<processModel>`	Control the behavior of the worker process
`<securityPolicy>`	Define trust levels with associated policy files
`<sessionState>`	Control session state
`<trace>`	Enable application-wide tracing
`<trust>`	Select which trust level to use
`<webServices>`	Specify Web service protocols and extensions
`<appSettings>`	Add application-specific data elements

3.1.1 Configuration Hierarchy

While it is most common to deploy a web.config file at the root of your virtual root directory for an ASP.NET application, there are several additional places where web.config files can be placed. ASP.NET supports the hierarchical application of configuration settings in a top-down fashion. Configuration files can be placed in four locations: machine, site, application, and subdirectory.

At the top of the hierarchy is a single, machine-wide configuration file called machine.config, which contains the default settings for all ASP.NET applications on that machine. This file can be found in your $FRAMEWORK\ CONFIG directory, where $FRAMEWORK is the path to the .NET installation (typically something like c:\winnt\Microsoft.NET\Framework\v1.0.3705).

The machine.config file is the only *required* configuration file; all web.config files are optional and are necessary only if you want to change some of the default settings defined in machine.config for your application.

The next configuration file to be consulted is the web.config file placed in the root directory of the Web site. Any configuration settings in this file are applied to all ASP.NET applications running on that site.

After that, the web.config file at the root of the virtual directory of an ASP.NET application is consulted, and any configuration settings are applied to all pages and directories within that application.

Finally, you can also place web.config files within subdirectories under the virtual root. Any configuration settings in a subdirectory configuration file apply to all pages within that subdirectory or any subdirectories below it. It is important to note that the subdirectory structure used to apply configuration settings is the one specified in the URL path, not the physical directory path on disk (although typically they mirror each other).

Figure 3-1 shows the hierarchy of configuration files for an ASP.NET application. This example demonstrates all the configuration files that would affect the ASP.NET application living under the myvdir virtual directory, which is defined within the default site on the machine. Note that when a request maps into a subdirectory of the application, additional web.config files may be applied to the processing for that request.

One of the advantages of this hierarchical composition of configuration settings is the level of granularity it allows. You can, for example, localize the configuration settings for a collection of pages within your application that reside in a particular subdirectory, without having to alter the top-level configuration file for that application. If you ever decide to move that subdirectory of pages to another application, their configuration settings will follow them. The disadvantage of this model is that you can never be sure exactly what configuration settings are being applied to a particular page in your application without inspecting all configuration files that apply. As you begin to work with ASP.NET configuration files, keep this in mind, and be sure to check all four configuration file locations if you see any unexpected behavior.

For example, consider the application of the three configuration files shown in Figure 3-2. The top-level machine.config file contains an

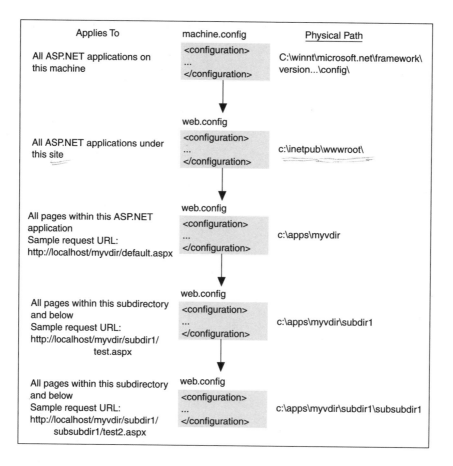

FIGURE 3-1: Hierarchy of Configuration Files

`httpHandlers` element that maps requests for files ending in `.ashx` to a class called `SimpleHandlerFactory`. On a virtual directory on the machine (`c:\inetpub\wwwroot\foo`) is another configuration file, with no additional settings, so requests made for `.ashx` files at this location are forwarded to the `SimpleHandlerFactory` class. However, in a subdirectory (`c:\inetpub\wwwroot\foo\bar`) a third configuration file explicitly removes the `.ashx` handler from the list of handlers. If a request for an `.ashx` file is made to this subdirectory, it will *not* be forwarded to the `SimpleHandlerFactory` class as it would have just a directory above. Although it may be convenient to use elements with this subtractive capability, it is often difficult to predict their behavior at a particular point on the disk without knowing all other configuration files that may affect their behavior.

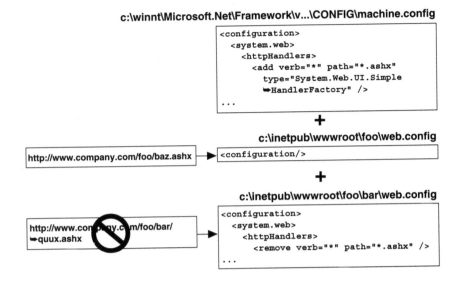

FIGURE 3-2: Hierarchical Configuration Settings Example

3.1.2 **Location Element**

Depending on your application design, you may find it more convenient to specify configuration settings for subdirectories and files in a single configuration file instead of spreading multiple configuration files throughout your directory structure. Among other things, this approach makes it easier to see exactly what settings apply to what files by looking at a single configuration file. ASP.NET supports multiple configuration settings in a single file using the `location` element. The `location` element takes an attribute named `path`, which can be a path to a file or a directory, and acts as a mini configuration file within the primary configuration file. To see an example, we could write a single top-level `web.config` file using the `location` element to perform the equivalent of what the two configuration files shown in Figure 3-2 performed, as shown in Listing 3-2.

LISTING 3-2: Using the location Element

```
<configuration>
  <location path="bar">
    <system.web>
```

continues

```
    <httpHandlers>
      <remove verb="*" path="*.ashx" />
    </httpHandlers>
   </system.web>
  </location>
 </configuration>
```

This technique is particularly useful when granting and revoking authorization rights to various sections of your application, as we will see in Chapter 11.

3.1.3 Element Placement

Most of the configuration elements available can be defined in any of the four configuration file locations: machine, site, application, and subdirectory. However, a subset of settings have restrictions on where they can be used. The `authentication`, `sessionState`, `trust`, and `httpModules`[7] elements can be defined only at the machine, site, or application levels, *not* at the subdirectory level. These elements all affect how the application behaves overall, and it would not make sense to apply them to only a subset of pages in the application. The `processModel` element is even more restricted and can exist only at the machine level. As we will see, this element controls the machine-wide process management for ASP.NET and thus cannot be applied anywhere but at the machine level.

3.1.4 Impact of Configuration Changes

Any changes made to a `web.config` file are detected by ASP.NET on the next request, and the application domain for that application is reloaded. Among other considerations, it is important to note that this causes any in-process session state and any application state to be lost. Because of this, changes to a configuration file should be kept to a minimum on a live server, and if in-process session state or application state is being used, be sure the configuration files are updated at a time that will not inconvenience users of the application. Any changes to the `processModel` element in the `machine.config` file are an additional special case. These changes will not be applied until the worker process is terminated and restarted,

---

7. In the current release, `httpModules` are allowed in subdirectory configuration files, but they do not take effect. In a future release, they will not even be allowed.

either by performing an IIS reset, by manually killing the `aspnet_wp.exe` process, or through the worker process bouncing itself for any number of reasons. Terminating the worker process loses session and application state not only for that application but for all ASP.NET applications running on that machine. For this reason, changes to the process model for a machine should happen extremely infrequently on a production machine.

3.1.5 **IIS and web.config**

In the current release of ASP.NET, IIS is always listening for requests and dispatching them to the ASP.NET worker process if they are ASP.NET requests. This important to realize because the configuration settings in the IIS metabase are applied *before* the request to the ASP.NET worker process is dispatched.

One important example of this is security. Security is configurable through the metabase for any Web application hosted with IIS. ASP.NET also has a number of configuration settings related to security, but the IIS settings are applied before the ASP.NET settings. For example, if you specify in the IIS metabase that users must be authenticated using Windows authentication, but in your ASP.NET application `web.config` file you have granted anonymous access, users will always be required to authenticate before they can access pages in your application. For this reason, it is a good practice to leave the IIS metabase settings at their defaults and to specify all application configuration through the ASP.NET `web.config` file. This strategy also simplifies installation because the only thing you need to set up in the IIS metabase is the virtual directory pointing to the ASP.NET application.

3.2 **Configuration Data**

When Web applications are deployed, there are often constant data values that need to be modified so that the application runs properly on the deployment server. Examples of such values include database connection strings and preferences or settings that influence the appearance or behavior of the application. ASP.NET configuration files provide a specific element for storing generic name/value pairs, called `appSettings`, which is ideal for storing these types of settings. It supports a subelement called `add`, which takes a key and value pair of attributes, as shown in Listing 3-3.

LISTING 3-3: Specifying Application-Specific Configuration Data

```
<!- File: web.config ->
<configuration>
  <appSettings>
    <add key="DSN"
         value="server=localhost;uid=sa;pwd=;database=pubs"
    />
    <add key="bgColor" value="white" />
  </appSettings>
</configuration>
```

In this example, we have chosen to store two pieces of application-specific data: a data source connection string and a background color. Placing data like this in a configuration file makes it very easy to customize these values by simply changing them in the configuration file. This is especially appealing for data that may change from one site installation to another. It is also an efficient mechanism for storing and retrieving small amounts of data, because the entire contents of the configuration file are loaded into memory when the application starts, so there is no file access involved with retrieving the values once they have been loaded. Once key/value pairs have been added to the appSettings element, you can extract them from any page or object in your application using the Configuration Settings class, as shown in Listing 3-4.

LISTING 3-4: Retrieving appSettings Configuration Data

```
<!- File: samplepage.aspx ->
<%@ Page Language='C#' %>
<%@ Import Namespace='System.Configuration' %>

<script runat=server>
protected void Page_Load(object src, EventArgs e)
{
  string dsn = ConfigurationSettings.AppSettings["DSN"];
  // use dsn to connect to a database...

  string bgColor =
          ConfigurationSettings.AppSettings["bgColor"];
  // use retrieved background color...
}
</script>

<!- remainder of page not shown ->
```

Note in Listing 3-4 that the namespace System.Configuration was imported, because that is where the ConfigurationSettings class resides. This class provides a static indexer called AppSettings that is used to retrieve the values indexed by their key in the appSettings element of a configuration file. The keys used to index the appSettings element are not case sensitive, so be aware that bgColor and BgColor, for example, will map to the same element.

One frequently asked question is, What prevents someone from directly accessing the web.config file in my application, potentially revealing the database login information and other data that should be protected? Fortunately, ASP.NET has a built-in handler called the HttpForbiddenHandler that is designed to restrict access to particular files. Among the files designated to use this handler are any files ending with the extension .config (also protected are .cs, .vb, .asax, .resx, and others). When this handler is invoked by an attempt to access any file with a forbidden extension, it returns an HTTP error code of 403, indicating that the access is forbidden; so by default, configuration settings are inaccessible to external clients.

3.3 Process Model

One of the most interesting configuration elements available is the processModel element. It is different from all the other configuration elements in several ways.

- It can be placed only in the systemwide machine.config file.
- Changes to this element do not take effect until the worker process is restarted.
- The configuration settings defined in this element are read in by the unmanaged aspnet_isapi.dll ISAPI extension DLL instead of the managed mechanism used by the other settings.

This element controls various aspects of the ASP.NET worker process (aspnet_wp.exe), including its lifetime, how many instances are created at a time, what security identity it runs under, and how large a thread pool it should use to service requests. Table 3-2 shows the attributes available with this element.

TABLE 3-2: Attributes of the processModel Element

Attribute	Values	Default	Description
Enable	true | false	true	Whether ASP.NET is hosted in an external worker process (`true`) or directly in `inet-info.exe` (`false`)
timeout	Infinite | HH:MM:SS	Infinite	Total life of a process—process bounced after timeout
idleTimeout	Infinite | HH:MM:SS	Infinite	Total idle life of a process—process bounced when reached
shutdown-Timeout	Infinite | HH:MM:SS	0:00:05	Time given to process to shut down before being killed
requestLimit	Infinite | number	Infinite	Total number of requests to serve before bouncing process
request-QueueLimit	Infinite | number	5000	Number of queued requests allowed before bouncing process
restart-QueueLimit	Infinite | number	10	Number of requests kept in queue while process is restarting
memoryLimit	Number	60	Percentage of physical memory process is allowed to use before bouncing process
webGarden	true | false	false	Whether process should be affinitized with a particular CPU (for multi-CPU machines)

TABLE 3-2: Attributes of the processModel Element (continued)

Attribute	Values	Default	Description
cpuMask	Bitmask	0xffffffff	Controls number of CPUs available for ASP.NET worker processes (webGarden must be true)
userName	SYSTEM | MACHINE | username	MACHINE	Windows identity to run the worker process in (MACHINE uses low-privileged ASPNET account)
Password	AutoGenerate | password	Auto-Generate	Password for username
logLevel	All | None | Errors	Errors	Event types logged to event log
client-Connected-Check	HH:MM:SS	0:00:05	Time a request is left in the queue before a client-connected check is performed
comAuthen-tication-Level	Default | None | Connect | Call | Pkt | PktIntegrity | PktPrivacy	Connect	Level of authentication for DCOM security
comImperson-ationLevel	Default | Anonymous | Identify | Impersonate | Delegate	Imper-sonate	Authentication level for COM security
response-Restart-Deadlock-Interval	Infinite | HH:MM:SS	00:09:00	Time to wait between restarting worker process because of responseRestart-DeadlockInterval

TABLE 3-2: Attributes of the processModel Element (continued)

Attribute	Values	Default	Description
response-Deadlock-Interval	Infinite | HH:MM:SS	00:03:00	For deadlock detection, timeout for responses when there are queued requests
maxWorker-Threads	Number	25	Maximum number of I/O threads per CPU in the thread pool
maxIoThreads	Number	25	Maximum number of I/O threads per CPU in the thread pool
serverError-MessageFile	File name	" "	Customization for "Server Unavailable" message

Most of the attributes shown in Table 3-2 affect the lifetime of the worker process. At first, it may seem illogical to have such precise control over how long the worker process lives. After all, why not just have it live forever, and be done with it? The sheer number of ways you can request that the worker process self-terminate and restart indicates that the ASP.NET team recognized that sometimes things go wrong—resources leak, deadlocks occur, memory limits are reached, and so on. Some of these things may be beyond your control, and the best choice in those cases is often to simply terminate the worker process and restart it. In many cases, this will have little impact on the servicing of clients because of the disconnected nature of the HTTP protocol. The primary drawbacks of a process bounce are the loss of in-process session state, application state, and entries in the data cache.

This practice of bouncing the process servicing requests is not as uncommon as you may think—many high-volume Web servers today make it a regular practice to bounce the server process periodically. The ASP.NET team recognized this in the beginning and built in a number of safeguards to ensure that the process bounce would occur smoothly and under the right conditions. This was so important in their list of goals that internally they liked to use the slogan "ASP.NET—Designed for Failure," which of course did not go over very well with the marketing people and was therefore left as an internal slogan only.

As mentioned, the conditions under which you can elect to have the server process bounce are numerous. By default, only two conditions cause the process to bounce: 1) if the total memory utilization of the process exceeds 60% of the physical memory on the machine (specified by the `memoryLimit` attribute) and 2) if more than 5,000 requests are queued. Both of these conditions are abnormal and should not be encountered under normal operating conditions; but if they do occur, it is likely that something is wrong and that bouncing the process may very well cure it. You can add conditions that will bounce the process, including an explicit timeout (`timeout`), an idle timeout (accumulated time spent idle—`idleTimeout`), and an upper bound on the number of requests serviced by a worker process (`requestLimit`).

You also have some amount of control over CPU utilization through the `processModel` element. For example, if your server has multiple CPUs, you can enable the `webGarden` attribute, to request that a dedicated worker process run on each CPU. You can also restrict which CPUs are used to host worker processes if you don't want to use them all, through the `cpuMask` attribute. For example, if you have a 4 CPU machine, but you want to use only processors 0, 1, and 2 to host ASP.NET worker processes, you specify `webGarden` as `true` and `cpuMask` as `0x00000007`, which corresponds to the binary bitmask `0...0111`, as shown in Listing 3-5.

LISTING 3-5: Specifying Multiple Worker Processes on a Multi-CPU machine

```
<processModel enable="true"
              timeout="Infinite"
              idleTimeout="Infinite"
              shutdownTimeout="0:00:05"
              requestLimit="Infinite"
              requestQueueLimit="5000"
              restartQueueLimit="10"
              memoryLimit="60"
              webGarden="true"
              cpuMask="0x00000007"
```

continues

```
userName="machine"
password="AutoGenerate"
logLevel="Errors"
clientConnectedCheck="0:00:05"
comAuthenticationLevel="Connect"
comImpersonationLevel="Impersonate"
responseRestartDeadlockInterval="00:09:00"
responseDeadlockInterval="00:03:00"
maxWorkerThreads="25"
maxIoThreads="25" />
```

Be aware that if you enable the `webGarden` attribute on a multi-CPU machine, session state, application state, and the global data cache are not shared between worker processes. Chapter 10 discusses ways of dealing with state sharing between processes.

The other way you have control over CPU utilization is through the number of worker and I/O threads used within the worker process to service requests. The distinction between the two types of threads is that I/O threads are bound to I/O completion ports and are used to access a particular I/O object (such as a stream or a pipe), and worker threads are traditional unrestricted threads. Currently, ASP.NET processes requests primarily on I/O threads[8] because requests are initiated through an asynchronous write to a named pipe from IIS, the details of which we discuss in Chapter 4. These threads are drawn from the process-wide thread pool maintained for every .NET application. By default, these pools are initialized with 25 threads per CPU on the machine, which is generally a sufficient number of threads to keep the CPU utilization high. If for some reason the requests to your application end up doing a lot of waiting (for external resources, perhaps), limiting the process to 25 threads may be too constraining, in which case you could increase the number to anything less than 100. Be advised, however, that it is generally uncommon for this to be the case, and leaving the thread pools at their default of 25 should almost always be adequate.

---

8. This changes in Windows Server 2003 with IIS 6.0. Because ASP.NET is directly integrated into IIS 6.0, there is no longer any need to dispatch requests to ASP.NET over named pipes, so requests are processed on worker threads instead of I/O threads.

The remaining attributes in the `processModel` element are related to security and are discussed further in Chapter 11.

3.3.1 **Accessing Process Information**

In addition to controlling various aspects of the process model, you can access information about the worker processes on a machine programmatically. The `ProcessModelInfo` class provides a pair of static methods to retrieve information about the current worker process and past worker processes that may have terminated recently. Each of these functions returns a reference to a `ProcessInfo` class populated with information about the worker process, including its age, the maximum amount of memory it has used, its process ID, how many requests it has serviced, when it was started, its status, and why it was shut down (if it was). Listing 3-6 shows the `ProcessModelInfo` and `ProcessInfo` classes. Figure 3-3 shows sample output from calling `ProcessModelInfo.GetHistory(10)`.

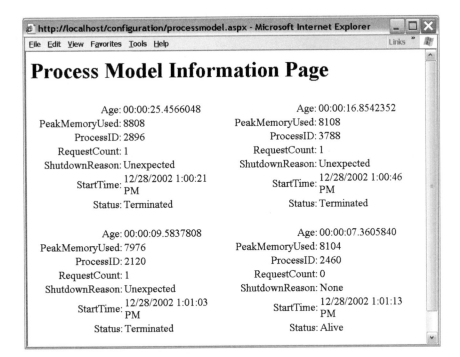

FIGURE 3-3: Sample ProcessModelInfo Output

LISTING 3-6: ProcessModelInfo and ProcessInfo Classes

```
public class ProcessModelInfo
{
  public static ProcessInfo GetCurrentProcessInfo();
  public static ProcessInfo[] GetHistory(int num);
}

public class ProcessInfo
{
  public TimeSpan Age {get;}
  public int PeakMemoryUsed {get;}
  public int ProcessID {get;}
  public int RequestCount {get;}
  public ProcessShutdownReason ShutdownReason {get;}
  public DateTime StartTime {get;}
  public ProcessStatus Status {get;}
}
```

3.3.2 IIS 6.0 Process Model Changes

With the release of IIS 6.0 in Windows Server 2003, the process model changes dramatically. To begin with, the processModel element in machine.config is ignored because it is replaced with equivalent settings in the IIS metabase, which is now stored in XML format in the metabase.xml file. ASP.NET is no longer hosted in aspnet_wp.exe but in one or more instances of w3wp.exe. Even more significantly, you are no longer constrained to just one worker process per CPU on a particular machine. Instead, you can configure what are called application pools, which contain collections of virtual directories that all share the same worker process. The properties of each application pool control how that particular worker process behaves, including even more settings than are available in the processModel element. Some of the new process model settings include the ability to set specific times of the day when the process should recycle; separate memory limits for virtual memory and actual used memory; CPU usage monitoring with the ability to recycle the process if utilization is too high; rapid-fail protection by disabling the application pool if it encounters a fixed number of failures within a particular time limit; and start-up and shutdown time limits.

The other significant change is that HTTP requests are now handled in kernel mode through the `http.sys` service. This service listens for HTTP requests and places them in the appropriate application queue. This means that `inetinfo.exe` is no longer the front end for HTTP requests, so the advantage of servicing requests in-process is gone. All requests are routed through the kernel-mode HTTP listener and dispatched to some process for servicing. Moving HTTP request queuing into the kernel means that faults in user-mode processes cannot adversely affect the HTTP listener, and even if a crash occurs in the user-mode request processing infrastructure, the kernel service will continue to accept and queue up requests until either the queues completely fill up or the service is shut down.

If you are moving an ASP.NET application to IIS 6.0, but you still want to use the process model and configuration settings of IIS 5.0, you can set a backward-compatibility flag in IIS 6.0 that causes it to run in IIS 5.0 isolation mode. This must be applied at the machine level, because it affects how all requests are processed on a given machine.

3.4 Additional Settings

The best way to familiarize yourself with the various settings available for ASP.NET applications is to open the `machine.config` file on your system and peruse the elements. Each element is carefully documented with available child elements and attributes, and many examples are included. It is also in this file that you can find out what the defaults are for all of the ASP.NET applications on your machine. We discuss some of the additional elements in later chapters, where they are more directly relevant to the topic at hand.

As you begin to develop ASP.NET applications, you should be aware of two additional configuration elements: the `assemblies` element and the `pages` element. If you find you are using the `@Assembly` directive to add a reference to a GAC-deployed assembly to several pages in an application, you can instead reference that assembly once globally in the application's `web.config` file using the `assemblies` element. For example, suppose you have built a utilities assembly called `Util` that contains a number of utility classes used throughout the applications on your server. If you decide to deploy this assembly in the GAC, you can add an implicit reference to the assembly to all pages in your application by adding it to the `assemblies` element in your root `web.config` file, as shown in Listing 3-7.

LISTING 3-7: Adding an Application-wide Reference to a GAC-Deployed Assembly

```
<configuration>
  <!- ... ->
  <system.web>
  <compilation>
    <assemblies>
      <add assembly="Util, Version=1.0.0.0, Culture=neutral,
PublicKeyToken=a77a5c561934e089" />
    </assemblies>
  </compilation>
  </system.web>
</configuration>
```

Similarly, if you find that you are repeating the same @Page directives for many of the pages in your application, you can instead use the `pages` element in your application-wide `web.config` file to change the default for many of the @Page directive attributes. For example, suppose you wanted to disable view state for all pages in your application by default. Listing 3-8 shows the configuration file necessary to do this.

LISTING 3-8: Using the pages Element

```
<configuration>
  <!- ... ->
  <system.web>
  <pages enableViewState='false' />
  </system.web>
</configuration>
```

3.5 Reading Configuration Information

We have already seen how to retrieve values stored in the `AppSettings` element by calling `ConfigurationSettings.AppSettings["xxx"]`, where xxx is the key we used to index the value. This static indexer is actually a convenience wrapper around a more general way of retrieving any configuration setting element through the `ConfigurationSettings.GetConfig()` method, as shown in Listing 3-9.

LISTING 3-9: Reading Configuration Settings

```
object settings =
            ConfigurationSettings.GetConfig("appSettings");
NameValueCollection nvc = settings as NameValueCollection;
if (nvc != null)
{
  string val = (string)nvc["xxx"];
}
```

Any configuration element (except the `processModel` element) can be retrieved using this technique. Internally, this maps into a request for the cached settings of the configuration file for that element, and if they have not yet been cached, a request to read them. At the lowest level of the configuration hierarchy, the physical XML files on disk are read by a class called `ConfigurationRecord`, using the `XmlTextReader` class to efficiently pull in the configuration data. Configuration information is parsed and stored on demand, so if a particular configuration element is never requested, it will never be read and loaded into memory. The job of parsing individual sections of the configuration file falls to configuration section handlers.

Conceptually, all ASP.NET configuration files are divided into two sections: the configuration section handlers and the configuration data. Until now, we have been adding information to the configuration data section only and have not even included the configuration section handler portion in our `web.config` files. If you look at the `machine.config` file on your system, however, you will see that the top of the file includes a number of configuration section handlers.

The job of a configuration section handler is to parse a portion of the configuration file, which makes this configuration file format extremely extensible. The classes responsible for reading in portions of the file are not established until the file is actually read, at which point instances of each parser object are created and passed the portion of the file they are

machine.config

```
<configuration>
  <configSections>
    <sectionGroup name="system.web">
      <section name="compilation"
          type="System.Web.UI.CompilationConfigurationHandler,
System.Web, Version=1.0.3300.0, Culture=neutral,
PublicKeyToken=b03f5f7f11d50a3a" />
        <!-- ... -->
    </sectionGroup>

    <section name="appSettings"
          type="System.Configuration.NameValueFileSectionHandler, System,
Version=1.0.3300.0, Culture=neutral, PublicKeyToken=b77a5c561934e089" /
>
    <!-- ... -->
  </configSections>

  <system.web>
    <compilation>
      <assemblies>
        <add assembly="mscorlib" />
      </assemblies>
    </compilation>
  </system.web>
  <appSettings>
    <add key="BkgdColor" value="Tan" />
  </appSettings>
</configuration>
```

FIGURE 3-4: Configuration Section Handlers in machine.config

responsible for. Figure 3-4 shows this relationship in a portion of the sys-temwide machine.config file. Note that the compilation section of the configuration file is parsed by a class called CompilationConfigura-tionHandler, specified under the configSections element. It also falls under a sectionGroup element, which further scopes the name of the section it will parse—in this case, to be under an element named sys-tem.web. The other configuration section handler shown in this sample is the one for appSettings. Notice that this element is parsed by a class called NameValueFileSectionHandler and is a top-level element in the configuration file.

Each class added in the configSections element must implement the IConfigurationSectionHandler interface, shown in Listing 3-10, which has a single method called Create. The Create method is called by the top-level configuration file parser (the ConfigurationRecord class) when a tag designated for that handler is read in the configuration file. When the Create method is called for a handler, it is passed the parent configuration section (if there is one), the current HttpConfigurationContext object (through the input parameter), and most importantly, a reference to the XmlNode to be parsed by the handler. In most cases, the handler simply walks through the child nodes and attributes of the XmlNode passed in. The return value from this function is an object containing whatever state the handler wishes to retain in the running program, and it is cached and available anywhere in the application through the ConfigurationSettings.GetConfig() method.

LISTING 3-10: IConfigurationSectionHandler Interface

```
public interface IConfigurationSectionHandler
{
    object Create(object parent, object input, XmlNode node);
}
```

Most of the ASP.NET configuration section handlers define a corresponding state retainer class that acts as a repository for the configuration settings associated with that handler. For example, a CompilerConfiguration class stores the contents of the compilation element, a PagesConfiguration class stores the contents of the pages element, and so on. Thus, for any active ASP.NET application, there are a number of in-memory instances of configuration classes populated with configuration state. These instances are stored in a hash table that is global to the application, and all calls to the ConfigurationSettings.GetConfig() method are simply accesses into this global hash table, as shown in Figure 3-5.

Be aware that most of the configuration classes used by ASP.NET are internal classes and are thus not accessible. ASP.NET uses the configuration classes to set the defaults and other values in the classes it creates.

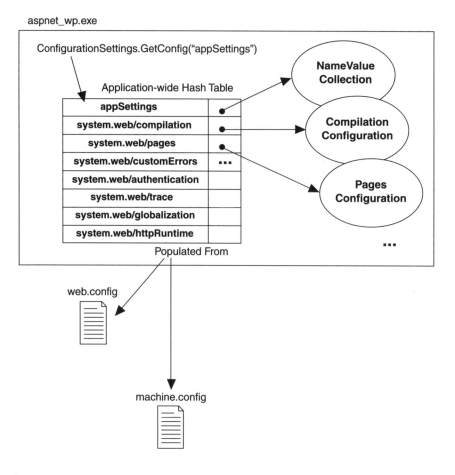

FIGURE 3-5: In-memory Configuration Settings Layout

3.6 Building a Custom Configuration Section Handler

Although most commonly used application-specific settings can be stored in the appSettings element, you may sometimes want to augment the set of available configuration elements with your own custom one. Even if you never need to do this, it is still instructive to walk through an implementation of a custom configuration section handler to better understand how the web.config file is parsed.

To see an example of building a custom configuration section handler, suppose we want our applications to be able to specify custom elements using an element called `acme`, contained in a new section called `acmeGroup`, as shown in Listing 3-11. The elements we are interested in are `font`, `backgroundColor`, `underlineLinks`, `horizontalWidth`, and `verticalWidth`, presumably to customize the way our application appears on a particular installation site.

LISTING 3-11: Sample Custom Configuration Element

```
<!— File: web.config —>
<configuration>
  <acmeGroup>
    <acme>
      <font>Courier New</font>
      <backgroundColor>Green</backgroundColor>
      <underlineLinks>true</underlineLinks>
      <horizontalWidth>600</horizontalWidth>
      <verticalWidth>800</verticalWidth>
    </acme>
  </acmeGroup>
</configuration>
```

To begin with, we must come up with some mechanism for saving the state associated with this configuration. There are many ways of doing this, but to keep things simple, let's take the approach of defining a class with public data members corresponding to the configuration elements we have defined. The `AcmeSettings` class shown in Listing 3-12 should be suitable.

LISTING 3-12: Sample Custom Configuration Settings State Class

```
// File: AcmeSettings.cs
namespace EssentialAspDotNet.Config
{
  public class AcmeSettings
  {
    public string Font;
    public string BackgroundColor;
    public bool   UnderlineLinks;
    public int    HorizontalWidth;
    public int    VerticalWidth;
  }
}
```

Next, we need to build a class that implements IConfigurationSec-tionHandler to parse our section of the configuration file and store the contents into our new AcmeSettings class, shown in Listing 3-13.

LISTING 3-13: Sample Custom Configuration Section Handler

```
// File: AcmeConfigHandler.cs
namespace EssentialAspDotNet.Config
{
  public class AcmeConfigHandler :
                              IConfigurationSectionHandler
  {
    public object Create(object parent, object input,
                      XmlNode node)
    {
      AcmeSettings aset = new AcmeSettings();

      foreach (XmlNode n in node.ChildNodes)
      {
        switch (n.Name)
        {
          case ("font"):
            aset.Font = n.InnerText;
            break;
          case ("backgroundColor"):
            aset.BackgroundColor = n.InnerText;
            break;
          case ("underlineLinks"):
            aset.UnderlineLinks = bool.Parse(n.InnerText);
            break;
          case ("horizontalWidth"):
            aset.HorizontalWidth = int.Parse(n.InnerText);
            break;
          case ("verticalWidth"):
            aset.VerticalWidth = int.Parse(n.InnerText);
            break;
        }
      }
      return aset;
    }
  }
}
```

The final step is to tell the configuration file to use this class to parse the acme element in our configuration files. As shown in Listing 3-14, we do this by adding a section element to the configSections portion of our configuration file—this could be in the systemwide machine.config file, the sitewide `web.config`, or the application-wide `web.config`, and it will apply to all configuration files parsed after that one is read.

LISTING 3-14: Installing a Custom Configuration Section Handler

```
<!— File: web.config —>
<configuration>
  <configSections>
    <sectionGroup name="acmeGroup">
      <section name="acme"
        type="EssentialAspDotNet.Config.AcmeConfigHandler,
AcmeConfigHandler"
      />
    </sectionGroup>
  </configSections>
  <!— ... —>
</configuration>
```

Any page or piece of code in our application could now access this configuration information using the `ConfigurationSettings.GetConfig()` method, passing in the section group and section name we created, and casting the result to our `AcmeSettings` class, as shown in Listing 3-15.

LISTING 3-15: Accessing Custom Configuration Information

```
// File: TestAcmeSettings.aspx
protected void Page_Load(object src, EventArgs e)
{
  AcmeSettings set;
  set = ConfigurationSettings.GetConfig("acmeGroup/acme")
      as AcmeSettings;

  // use set here (like set.Font, set.BackgroundColor,
  // etc.)
}
```

3.6.1 Using the NameValueFileSectionHandler

If you want a custom configuration section, but you don't want to go to the trouble of writing your own class that implements the `IConfigurationSectionHandler` interface, you can create a new section that reuses the same class as the `appSettings` element. You are limited to using the `add` element with key/value pairs for adding new configuration elements, but if this is tolerable, adding a new configuration section becomes even easier. For example, Listing 3-16 shows how to add a new section called myGroup to a configuration file and populate it with values similar to our custom acmeGroup shown earlier. Notice that the type specified in the section element refers to a class found in the system assembly called NameValueFileSectionHandler. Instances of this class store the key/value pairs in a NameValueCollection for later access. Listing 3-17 shows how you would access this collection from within an .aspx page in the application.

LISTING 3-16: Adding a Custom Configuration Section with a Prebuilt Handler

```
<!— File: web.config —>
<configuration>
  <configSections>
    <section name="myGroup"
    type="System.Configuration.NameValueFileSectionHandler, System,
Version=1.0.3300.0, Culture=neutral,
PublicKeyToken=b77a5c561934e089"/>

  </configSections>

  <myGroup>
    <add key="font" value="Courier New"/>
    <add key="backgroundColor" value="Green"/>
    <add key="underlineLinks" value="true"/>
    <add key="horizontalWidth" value="600"/>
    <add key="verticalWidth" value="800"/>
  </myGroup>
  <!— ... —>
</configuration>
```

LISTING 3-17: Accessing Custom Configuration Information with NameValueCollection

```
// File: TestAcmeSettings.aspx
protected void Page_Load(object src, EventArgs e)
{
  NameValueCollection set;
  set = ConfigurationSettings.GetConfig("myGroup")
      as NameValueCollection;

  // use set here (like set["Font"],
  // set["BackgroundColor"], etc.)
}
```

SUMMARY

ASP.NET applications are configured using a set of XML configuration files named `web.config`. These configuration files replace the role of the metabase in IIS and enable configuration changes by simply copying new files onto the server. Configuration files can be placed in several places on a Web server. There is always a top-level `machine.config` file that contains the default settings for all ASP.NET applications deployed on that machine. You can place a `web.config` file in the root directory of a site that applies to all applications deployed on that site. You can also place `web.config` files at the top level of a virtual directory or in any subdirectory of an application, and the settings are applied hierarchically, with local configuration files overriding higher-level ones.

In addition to the typical Web application settings, several new elements are available. The `appSettings` element is useful for storing generic name/value pairs of data for retrieval during application execution. The `processModel` element gives you very precise control over how the lifetime of the ASP.NET worker process is managed. Finally, you can also create your own configuration sections by authoring a class that implements `IConfigurationSectionHandler` or by using the provided `NameValue-FileSectionHandler` class.

■ 4 ■
HTTP Pipeline

A SP.NET IS BUILT on top of an extensible HTTP request processing architecture known as the HTTP pipeline. Every time you author a new .aspx page, you are defining a new endpoint to service a request. The page, however, is just the last class in a series of classes that are used to process each request.

This chapter covers the details of the HTTP pipeline, beginning with a detailed look at how a request is routed through the various pieces of the architecture and ultimately dispatched to your page. We then look at the three primary points of extensibility in the pipeline: defining custom application classes, building custom modules, and writing custom handlers. The chapter concludes with a look at threading and pooling in the pipeline, discussing both the resource management of ASP.NET and the implications of threading for your applications.

4.1 **A Day in the Life of a Request**

The best way to understand the internals of the request processing architecture in ASP.NET is to trace the path of a request from its initial entry into a server all the way to its ultimate dispatching to the `ProcessRequest` method of your `Page` class. We begin with a high-level overview of how requests are routed on a machine processing requests with ASP.NET, and then take a more detailed look at the internals of the pipeline.

4.1.1 **Ten Thousand–Foot View of Request Processing**

Typically, ASP.NET requests initiate from IIS.[9] When an HTTP request comes in from a client, typically on port 80, the IIS process (`inetinfo.exe`) receives the request and attempts to locate an extension mapping for the URL requested. If the request is for an ASP.NET page (it ends with .aspx), IIS loads the `aspnet_isapi.dll` ISAPI extension DLL and passes the request on to it. Once the `aspnet_isapi.dll` receives the request, it attempts to locate the ASP.NET worker process, housed in `aspnet_wp.exe`. If it is not running, it is started, and several named pipe connections are established between the ISAPI DLL and the worker process. Once these connections are established, the request is sent across a named pipe to the ASP.NET worker process for handling. Inside the worker process, ASP.NET routes the request to a designated `AppDomain` and dispatches it to the HTTP pipeline in that `AppDomain`. The end result of the request passing through the pipeline is the compilation (first time only) and creation of a class that implements the `IHttpHandler` interface, typically your `Page`-derived class. This handler acts as the endpoint of the request, populates the response buffer, and delivers the response back through the same channels it came from until IIS ends up sending back the response buffer. Figure 4-1 depicts this high-level view of request processing in ASP.NET.

4.1.2 **Inside the Pipeline**

Once the request makes it into the worker process, it goes through a series of steps and classes before it arrives at the ultimate handler. To begin with, each ASP.NET application is housed within an `AppDomain` in its worker process. `AppDomains` are a CLR construct that provides processlike memory and security isolation, without the overhead of actually creating separate processes. ASP.NET uses `AppDomains` to separate applications from each other so that if one application has a problem, it can safely be removed without affecting the remaining applications. Figure 4-2 depicts the various

---

9. It is possible to host ASP.NET using another mechanism for dispatching and processing requests. Microsoft has produced a sample called Cassini, which demonstrates hosting ASP.NET in a custom Web server application. For more details, see http://www.asp.net.

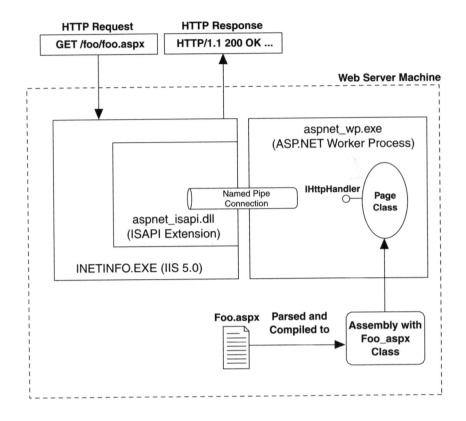

HTTP Request
GET /foo/foo.aspx

HTTP Response
HTTP/1.1 200 OK ...

Web Server Machine

aspnet_wp.exe
(ASP.NET Worker Process)

Named Pipe
Connection

IHttpHandler

Page Class

aspnet_isapi.dll
(ISAPI Extension)

INETINFO.EXE (IIS 5.0)

Foo.aspx   **Parsed and Compiled to**   **Assembly with Foo_aspx Class**

FIGURE 4-1: High-Level View of Request Processing in ASP.NET

pipeline classes that live within an application's AppDomain and shows how they interact to service a request.

The first thing that happens when a request is dispatched to an application is that an instance of the HttpWorkerRequest class is created (1), which contains all the information about the current request, including the requested URL, the headers, and so on. Once the HttpWorkerRequest class is created, it is passed into the static ProcessRequest method of the HttpRuntime class, which is executed in the AppDomain of the application, initiating the processing of the request (2). The first thing the HttpRuntime class does is to create a new instance of the HttpContext class, initialized with the HttpWorkerRequest class (3). The HttpContext class is the

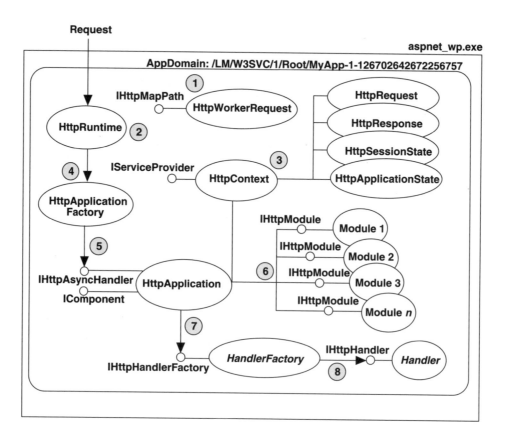

FIGURE 4-2: Classes in the HTTP Pipeline

"glue" of the pipeline, since it holds all the classes together by keeping all
the relevant information about the current request in one location. When
the HttpContext class is first created, it allocates new instances of the
HttpRequest and HttpResponse classes and stores them as fields. It also
provides property accessors to the application and session state bags. Once
the HttpContext class is created, the HttpRuntime class requests an
instance of the HttpApplication-derived class for this application by calling the static GetApplicationInstance method of the HttpApplica-
tionFactory class (4). GetApplicationInstance either creates a new
instance of the HttpApplication (or a derivative) class or pulls one from

a pool of application objects if one is available (5). Once the `HttpApplication` class is created or retrieved, it is initialized, and during its initialization it allocates any modules that are defined for this application (6). Modules are classes that implement the `IHttpModule` interface and serve to pre- and postprocess requests.

Once the modules have been created, the `HttpRuntime` class asks its newly retrieved `HttpApplication` class to service the current request by calling its `BeginProcessRequest` method (7), defined by the `IHttpAsyncHandler` interface implemented by the application class. The `HttpApplication` class then takes over the request processing and locates the appropriate handler factory for the current request, based on the URL path. For example, if the request is for an .aspx page, it uses the `PageHandlerFactory` class. Once it locates the appropriate factory, it invokes the `GetHandler` method on the `IHttpHandlerFactory` interface to retrieve a fresh copy of the appropriate handler class. Handler classes serve as the endpoint for requests and very often are simply the `Page`-derived class that is created from an .aspx file. In general, handlers are classes that implement the `IHttpHandler` interface and populate the response buffer when asked to process a request. Once the handler is created, its `ProcessRequest` method is called (8), passing in the current `HttpContext` class so that it has access to the `Request`, the `Response`, and all the other request-specific pieces of information necessary. Once the `ProcessRequest` method returns, the request is complete.

4.2 Context

One of the most important classes in the pipeline is the `HttpContext` class. This class maintains all the request-specific data and is accessible to most elements within the pipeline. The context class shows up as a parameter to many methods, including the `ProcessRequest` method of handlers, and it is directly accessible via the `Context` property of both the `Page` class and the `HttpApplication` class. Table 4-1 shows the set of properties available on the `HttpContext` class.

TABLE 4-1: Properties of HttpContext

Name	Type	Description
Current (static)	HttpContext	Context for the request currently in progress
Application	HttpApplication-State	Application-wide property bag
ApplicationInstance	HttpApplication	Active application instance
Session	HttpSessionState	Per-client session state
Request	HttpRequest	HTTP request object
Response	HttpResponse	HTTP response object
User	IPrincipal	Security ID of the caller
Handler	IHttpHandler	Handler for the request
Items	IDictionary	Per-request property bag
Server	HttpServer-Utility	HTTP server object
Error	Exception	Unhandled exception object
Cache	Cache	Application-wide cache
Trace	TraceContext	Trace class for diagnostic output
TraceIsEnabled	Boolean	Whether tracing is currently enabled
WorkerRequest	HttpWorkerRequest	The current worker request object
IsCustomError-Enabled	Boolean	Whether custom error pages are currently enabled
IsDebuggingEnabled	Boolean	Whether the current request is in debug mode
IsInCancellable-Period	Boolean	Whether the current request can still be cancelled

The `Items` property bag is a particularly useful collection to be aware of because it lets you store and retrieve request-specific data from anywhere in the pipeline. This can be useful if you are building custom modules, for example, and want to save information at one point during the request to read again later in the request. The interface to the `Items` collection is similar to all the other property-bag collections, using a string-based indexer to store an object reference.

Another useful property to know about is the static `Current` property of the `HttpContext` class. This property always points to the current instance of the `HttpContext` class for the request being serviced. This can be convenient if you are writing helper classes that will be used from pages or other pipeline classes and may need to access the context for whatever reason. By using the static `Current` property to retrieve the context, you can avoid passing a reference to it to helper classes. For example, the class shown in Listing 4-1 uses the `Current` property of the context to access the `QueryString` and print something to the current response buffer. Note that for this static property to be correctly initialized, the caller must be executing on the original request thread, so if you have spawned additional threads to perform work during a request, you must take care to provide access to the context class yourself.

LISTING 4-1: Using the Current Property of HttpContext

```
public class MyClass
{
  void SomeFunction()
  {
    HttpContext ctx = HttpContext.Current;
    ctx.Response.Write("Hello, ");
    string name = ctx.Request.QueryString["name"];
    ctx.Response.Output.WriteLine(name);
  }
}
```

4.3 Applications

The first point of extensibility in the HTTP pipeline that we explore is the application class. In any ASP.NET application, the `HttpApplication` class plays a vital role in nearly every aspect of processing requests. It acts as the initial entry point for a request to a particular application; it serves as a repository of globally available resources in an application, such as application state, the cache, and session state; and it provides access to many important events that occur during the lifetime of an application. You can make use of many of these features by simply using the `HttpApplication` instance that is created implicitly for you when your application starts. It is accessible through the `HttpContext` class and the `Page` class via their `ApplicationInstance` properties.

You can also customize the application class associated with your application by creating a class that derives from `HttpApplication` and intercepting events or adding whatever supplemental functionality you desire. For ASP.NET to know about and use your application class, you must create a file called `global.asax`, located at the top of the virtual directory associated with your application. Like .aspx files, this file is parsed and compiled into an assembly when the application is first accessed. In this case, the class created derives from `HttpApplication`. Listing 4-2 shows a sample `global.asax` file with several commonly defined event handlers. Note that the `Application` directive is used at the top of the file instead of the `Page` directive used by .aspx files. Also notice that the page consists primarily of a server-side script block, which contains of a number of method definitions. These methods are specially named such that when the class is created, they are automatically wired up as handlers to the corresponding events.

LISTING 4-2: A Sample global.asax File

```
<%! file: global.asax %>
<%@ Application Language="C#" %>

<script runat=server>
protected void Application_Start(object src, EventArgs e)
{ }

protected void Session_Start(object src, EventArgs e)
{ }

protected void Application_BeginRequest(object src,
```

```
                                        EventArgs e)
  { }

  protected void Application_EndRequest(object src,
                                        EventArgs e)
  { }

  protected void Application_AuthenticateRequest(object src,
                                                 EventArgs e)
  { }

  protected void Application_Error(object src, EventArgs e)
  { }

  protected void Session_End(object sender, EventArgs e)
  { }

  protected void Application_End(object src, EventArgs e)
  { }
  </script>
```

As with .aspx files, you can use code-behind for `global.asax` files if you prefer to precompile your `HttpApplication`-derived class. If you are working with Visual Studio .NET, you will notice that when you create a new ASP.NET Web application project, it creates a new `global.asax` file for you with an associated code-behind class. Listing 4-3 shows a `global.asax` file that uses code-behind, which is shown in Listing 4-4. Also, as with the `Page` directive, you can elect either to precompile the code-behind class or to use the `src` attribute to have ASP.NET automatically compile the file into a class for you. You may notice that Visual Studio .NET again uses the `CodeBehind` attribute on the `Application` directive, even though technically this is not an attribute recognized by ASP.NET. This attribute is used exclusively by Visual Studio .NET to create the association between the .asax file and its code-behind file in the designer. As with pages, Visual Studio .NET uses the precompiled model when working with application classes.

LISTING 4-3: Using Code-Behind with global.asax

```
<%! file: global.asax %>
<%@ Application Inherits="MyApp" %>
```

LISTING 4-4: Code-Behind File for global.asax

```
//file: myapp.cs
using System;
using System.Web;
using System.Web.UI;

public class MyApp : HttpApplication
{
  //...
}
```

Typically, you would create a custom application class to add handlers to application-level events that occur during request processing. For example, you may want to trap the BeginRequest and EndRequest notification events issued for every request that is handled by an application, perhaps to calculate the time it takes to process each request. Listing 4-5 shows a sample global.asax file that traps the BeginRequest and EndRequest events to calculate the time taken to process each request. In the EndRequest handler, once the time has been calculated, it prints out a footer to the response buffer to show the time it took at the bottom of each page.

LISTING 4-5: Tracking Request Time in a global.asax File

```
<%! file: global.asax %>
<%@ Application Language="C#" %>

<script language="C#" runat=server>
protected void Application_BeginRequest(object sender,
                                        EventArgs e)
{
  this.Context.Items["startTime"] = DateTime.Now;
}

protected void Application_EndRequest(object sender,
                                      EventArgs e)
{
  DateTime dt = (DateTime)this.Context.Items["startTime"];
  TimeSpan ts = DateTime.Now - dt;
  this.Context.Response.Output.Write(
    "<br/><font size=1>request processing time: {0}</font>",
    ts);
}
</script>
```

It is worth noting the usage of the `Items` collection of the `HttpContext` class shown in the previous example. As mentioned earlier, the `Items` collection is a generic property bag of data that is maintained by the `HttpContext` class on a per-request basis. It can be used as a place to save data that is used by elements in the pipeline for a particular request. It is critically important that you not store data like this in fields of your `HttpApplication`-derived class, because as we will see in more detail later in this chapter, each request to a particular application may have a distinct instance of the application class created (or more likely, drawn from a pool). As soon as you begin adding state to your application class, it can quickly become confusing as one request is handed an application class with state initialized from a previous one. So as a general rule, never store instance-state in an `HttpApplication`-derived class, or if you do, take care to reinitialize that state with each request. Alternatively, you can rely on one of the many state repositories available to you in the pipeline, such as the `Items` collection of the `HttpContext` class, the application-wide `Cache` object, or the per-client session state bag.

4.3.1 **Application Events**

A number of events are available in the `HttpApplication` class. Table 4-2 shows the events that are exposed by `HttpApplication`, most of which are issued with each request that is processed by your application, the two exceptions being the `Error` and `Disposed` events. To add a handler for any one of these events, you can either explicitly wire up a delegate to the event during the initialization of your application, or you can define a method whose name is of the form "Application_*event*," and it will be wired up automatically at runtime.

TABLE 4-2: Events Exposed by HttpApplication

Event	Reason for Firing	Order
BeginRequest	New request received	1
AuthenticateRequest	Security identity of the user has been established	2
AuthorizeRequest	User authorization has been verified	3

TABLE 4-2: Events Exposed by HttpApplication (continued)

Event	Reason for Firing	Order
ResolveRequestCache	After authorization but before invoking handler, used by caching modules to bypass execution of handlers if cache entry hits	4
AcquireRequestState	To load session state	5
PreRequest-HandlerExecute	Before request sent to handler	6
PostRequest-HandlerExecute	After request sent to handler	7
ReleaseRequestState	After all request handlers have completed, used by state modules to save state data	8
UpdateRequestCache	After handler execution, used by caching modules to store responses in cache	9
EndRequest	After request is processed	10
Disposed	Just before shutting down the application	-
Error	When an unhandled application error occurs	-
PreSendRequest-Content	Before content sent to client	-
PreSendRequest-Headers	Before HTTP headers sent to client	-

In addition, you can wire up handlers to a number of events that occur at different times during the lifetime of an application. The only way to wire up handlers to these particular events is to define methods with the names that match the events, because they are invoked internally by other classes in the pipeline and are not exposed directly as events on the HttpApplication class. Table 4-3 shows the list of additional events, none of which are issued on a per-request basis, for which you can add handlers.

TABLE 4-3: Additional Events Available through global.asax

Event	Reason for Firing
Application_Start	Application starting
Application_End	Application ending
Session_Start	User session begins
Session_End	User session ends

In addition to the events exposed by the `HttpApplication` class and `global.asax`, several properties and methods are worth noting. Listing 4-6 shows the class with some of its more commonly used members. Note that there are property accessors to all the core elements of the pipeline, including the application state bag, the context, the request, the response, the session state, and the server. The virtual `Init()` method can be overridden in derived classes to perform initialization and is called once in the lifetime of your `HttpApplication`-derived class, after all modules for that application have been added. Another interesting method is `CompleteRequest()`, which can be called at any time during request processing to preemptively terminate a request.

LISTING 4-6: Members of the HttpApplication Class

```
public class HttpApplication : IHttpAsyncHandler, IComponent
{ // Properties
  public HttpApplicationState Application {get;}
  public HttpContext          Context     {get;}
  public HttpModuleCollection Modules     {get;}
  public HttpRequest          Request     {get;}
  public HttpResponse         Response    {get;}
  public HttpServerUtility    Server      {get;}
  public HttpSessionState     Session     {get;}
  public IPrincipal           User        {get;}
  // Methods
  public virtual void Init();
  public void CompleteRequest();
  // ...
}
```

4.3.2 Declarative Object Creation

In addition to defining methods within server-side script blocks in `global.asax` files, you can also define instances of classes by using the `object` tag. You can use the `object` tag to create either .NET classes or COM classes (accessed via interoperability) and can select the scope (either session or application) at which you would like the object to live. Listing 4-7 shows a sample `object` declaration within a `global.asax` file.

LISTING 4-7: Using the object Tag in global.asax

```
<%! File: global.asax %>

<object id="MyGlobalCollection" runat="server"
  scope="application" class="System.Collections.ArrayList" />
```

Using the `object` tag in `global.asax` does two things for you. First, it creates a read-only property using the name specified with the `id` attribute in your `HttpApplication`-derived class, which on first access instantiates the class and stores it in either the `HttpApplicationState.Static-Objects` or the `HttpSessionState.StaticObjects` collection, depending on the scope. The second thing it does is to add a read-only property to every `Page`-derived class created by .aspx file compilation, so that you can easily reference the object from every page in your application.

The declarative object creation syntax is in place largely to ensure that traditional ASP applications that use this same syntax will still work the same way. In the new ASP.NET world of class-based programming, the idea of implicitly adding properties to access a global object to every page is somewhat distasteful and should probably be avoided. Prefer instead to work directly with the session state bag, discussed in detail in Chapter 10, or for application-wide objects, the `Cache`, discussed in detail in Chapter 9.

4.4 Custom Handlers

The second and most commonly used point of extensibility in the pipeline is the handler. Every time you author a new .aspx file, you are creating a new `Page`-derived class, which acts as an endpoint to a request, or a **handler**. To act as a handler within the pipeline, a class must implement the IHttpHandler interface, shown in Listing 4-8.

LISTING 4-8: The IHttpHandler Interface

```
public interface IHttpHandler
{
  void ProcessRequest(HttpContext ctx);
  bool IsReusable {get;}
}
```

The Page class implements this interface, and in its implementation of the ProcessRequest method, it populates the response buffer by rendering all the controls contained within the page. When you create a new .aspx file, your only concern is to create controls on the page, which are in turn rendered at the appropriate time by the Page base class from which you derive.

Suppose, however, that you want to build a class that services requests but doesn't take advantage of the Page control-based rendering mechanism. You could create a page that contained nothing but code, or you could take more complete control over the request processing mechanism and author your own handler directly. You may also want to use the HTTP pipeline to service requests that are made to non-ASP.NET extensions. In either case, you can construct a custom handler by creating a class that implements the IHttpHandler interface directly, and then adding information to your configuration file indicating when that handler should be used.

To see an example, suppose we wanted to create a simple calculator handler that accepted GET requests, with an accompanying query string providing the parameters and operation, as shown in Listing 4-9.

LISTING 4-9: GET-Based Calculator Request

```
http://localhost/httppipeline/calc.calc?a=3&b=4&op=multiply
```

The first step is to create a new class that implements the IHttpHandler interface. In our implementation of ProcessRequest, we look for the a, b, and op variables passed through the query string, perform the calculation, and write the result back to the response object. The read-only property, IsReusable, decides whether a new instance of this class will be created for each request or shared, pooled instances of this class will be used. The CalcHandler class is shown in Listing 4-10.

LISTING 4-10: Sample Calc Handler Class

```
// File: CalcHandler.cs

public class CalcHandler : IHttpHandler
{
  public void ProcessRequest(HttpContext ctx)
  {
    int a = int.Parse(ctx.Request["a"]);
    int b = int.Parse(ctx.Request["b"]);

    switch (ctx.Request["op"])
    {
      case "add":
        ctx.Response.Write(a+b);
        break;
      case "subtract":
        ctx.Response.Write(a-b);
        break;
      case "multiply":
        ctx.Response.Write(a*b);
        break;
      default:
        ctx.Response.Write("Unrecognized operation");
        break;
    }
  }

  public bool IsReusable { get { return true; } }
}
```

The next step is to make ASP.NET aware that we would like our class to be used as the endpoint for any GET requests made to our application with the endpoint of calc.calc. To do this, we need to add an entry to our configuration file within the httpHandlers element, as shown in Listing 4-11. Note that for the verb, we restrict requests to be GET requests only. You could also specify "*" here if you didn't want to restrict the types of requests serviced by your handler. The `path` attribute indicates the end-point name you want mapped onto this handler, and the `type` attribute defines the type and assembly from which the type should be loaded to service requests.

LISTING 4-11: web.config Entry for Calc Handler

```
<!- file: web.config ->
<configuration>
  <system.web>
    <httpHandlers>
      <add verb="GET" path="calc.calc"
          type="CalcHandler, CalcHandler" />
    </httpHandlers>
  </system.web>
</configuration>
```

The last step in wiring up a handler is to let IIS know that you would like requests of a given extension to be mapped into the ASP.NET worker process. By default, only ASP.NET-specific extensions (.aspx, .ascx, .ashx, and so on) are mapped to the ASP.NET worker process. Figure 4-3 shows a sample extension mapping created through the Internet Information Services utility.

FIGURE 4-3: Extension Mapping in IIS

4.4.1 **Custom Handlers for File Processing**

One common example of when you might want to implement a custom handler is when you have existing (non-HTML) files on your system that you would like to expose as pages in a Web application. Instead of converting the files to an HTML format, you could write a handler that would read the files at request time and dynamically generate "HTMLized" content.

To see an example, suppose we want to display source code files with syntax coloring. That is, every time someone navigates to a .cs file in our application, we render it not as plain text but as HTML-enhanced text to show the keywords in blue and the comments in green, much as the Visual Studio .NET editor does. The first step is to construct a new class that implements the `IHttpHandler` interface. In our implementation of `Process-Request`, we open the requested file, parse its contents, and populate the response buffer with a syntax-colorized version of the code. The shell of such a class is shown in Listing 4-12.

LISTING 4-12: A Custom Handler for Viewing .cs Source Files

```
// File: CsSourceHandler.cs
public class CsSourceHandler : IHttpHandler
{
  public void ProcessRequest(HttpContext ctx)
  {
    try
    {
      StreamReader sr =
              new StreamReader(ctx.Request.PhysicalPath);
      // write out html and body elements first
      context.Response.Output.Write("<html><body>");

      // extract short file name to print at top of file
      string filename = context.Request.PhysicalPath;
      int idx = filename.LastIndexOf("\\");
      if (idx >= 0)
        filename = filename.Substring(idx+1,
                                    filename.Length-idx-1);
      context.Response.Output.Write("//File: {0}<br>",
                                    filename);

      string str;
      do
      {
        str = sr.ReadLine();
        if (str != null)
```

```
                context.Response.Output.Write("{0}<br/>",
                    /*convert str to colorized html here*/ );
        } while (str != null);
        context.Response.Write("</body></html>");
    }
    catch (FileNotFoundException )
    {
        context.Response.Write("<h2>Missing file</h2>");
    }
  }

  public bool IsReusable
  {
    get {return false; }
  }
}
```

The code for colorizing the source code text is not shown here but is included in the set of samples for this book.[10] Once we add the mapping for .cs files to our handler in our `web.config` file, clients can view any .cs files with syntax coloring. If a request for a file ending with the .cs extension comes into our application, a new instance of our `CsSourceHandler` class is created, and its `ProcessRequest` method is invoked. The only remaining concern is that we must ensure that IIS passes requests for .cs extensions to ASP.NET, which will then route the request appropriately. Typically, the last step in hooking up a custom handler, therefore, is to map the desired extension to the ASP.NET ISAPI extension DLL, as shown in the previous example in Figure 4-3. Note that in this particular case, this step is unnecessary because when ASP.NET is installed, it associates all .NET source code files with ASP.NET, which in turn maps requests for source code files to the `HttpForbiddenHandler` class, preventing users from accessing any source files in your application by default. The entry in our local `web.config` file for .cs extensions overrides the one found in `machine.config`, and our handler is called.

4.4.2 .ashx
In addition to creating custom handlers by building classes and configuring them through `web.config` and IIS, you can create them without the

---

10. Samples for this book are available at http://www.develop.com/books/essentialasp.net.

configuration steps by using the .ashx extension. Any file ending with .ashx (where the "h" stands for "handler") goes through the same parsing and compilation phase that .aspx files go through, but the resulting class must implement the `IHttpHandler` interface directly instead of deriving from `Page`. The format of .ashx files begins with a `WebHandler` directive, followed by a class definition much like one you would place directly in a source file. The class you would like to serve as the endpoint for requests made to this file is indicated through the `Class` attribute of the `WebHandler` directive, and the class must implement `IHttpHandler`. Using .ashx files to define custom handlers is convenient because there is no need to go through the process of registering a new extension, nor do you have to add any configuration elements to your `web.config` file. Listing 4-13 shows a sample .ashx file that implements the same calculator handler shown earlier, and Listing 4-14 shows a request to perform a calculation using this file as an endpoint.

LISTING 4-13: Building a Custom Handler with .ashx Files

```
<!- file: calc.ashx ->
<%@ WebHandler Language="C#" Class="CalcHandler" %>

using System;
using System.Web;

public class CalcHandler : IHttpHandler
{
  public void ProcessRequest(HttpContext ctx)
  {
    int a = int.Parse(ctx.Request["a"]);
    int b = int.Parse(ctx.Request["b"]);

    switch (ctx.Request["op"])
    {
      case "add":
        ctx.Response.Write(a+b);
        break;
      case "subtract":
        ctx.Response.Write(a-b);
        break;
      case "multiply":
        ctx.Response.Write(a*b);
        break;
      default:
```

```
        ctx.Response.Write("Unrecognized operation");
        break;
    }
  }

  public bool IsReusable { get { return false; } }
}
```

LISTING 4-14: Calculator Request for .ashx Handler

```
http://localhost/httppipeline/calc.ashx?a=3&b=4&op=multiply
```

4.4.3 Handler Pooling

You may have noticed that the `IHttpHandler` interface supports a read-only property called `IsReusable`, used to indicate whether instances of a particular handler can be safely pooled. If you build a custom handler and return `true` from this property, ASP.NET pools instances of your handler as they are used to service requests. If you return `false`, a new instance of your handler is created each time a request is serviced. In general, it typically doesn't make that much difference whether your handlers are pooled or not, because the instantiation mechanism in the CLR and the garbage collector are quite efficient, so typically little is gained by doing pooling on your handler classes. The one case you might consider enabling pooling is if it takes significant time to set up the handler. For example, if your handler retrieved information from a database to perform its request processing, and that information did not change from one request to the next, it might make sense to request pooling on your handler. Handler pooling is never used by the standard handlers provided by ASP.NET. The `Page` class, which is by far the most common handler, returns `false` from `IsReusable`, and the factory class that allocates pages does not even perform pooling. The same goes for .ashx handlers—they are never pooled.

4.4.4 Custom Handler Factories

If you want more control over the creation of your handler, you can write a custom handler factory—a class that implements the `IHttpHandlerFactory` interface, as shown in Listing 4-15. The first method, `GetHandler()`, is called when a new instance of the requested handler is needed. The `ReleaseHandler()` method is called when the pipeline is finished processing a request with a handler, placing the control of handler creation and destruction in your hands. The deployment of a handler factory is identical to that of a custom handler, but instead of specifying a class that implements `IHttpHandler`, you specify a class that implements `IHttpHandlerFactory`. When a handler is requested, the runtime queries the class listed in the configuration file, and if it supports the `IHttpHandlerFactory` interface, it uses the factory to create an instance of the handler. Otherwise, it queries the class for its `IHttpHandler` interface and creates it directly.

LISTING 4-15: IHttpHandlerFactory Interface

```
public interface IHttpHandlerFactory
{
   IHttpHandler GetHandler(HttpContext ctx, string
            requestType, string url, string translatedPath);
   void ReleaseHandler(IHttpHandler handler);
}
```

You may want to consider implementing your own custom handler factory if you want to build your own pooling mechanism, or if you want to initialize your handlers with some data as they are being created by passing data into a nondefault constructor of your handler class. Listing 4-16 shows a slightly more involved example with a class called `PooledCalc-Factory` that implements a pooling handler for the calculator handler class we wrote earlier. The pooling implementation uses a static instance of the `Stack` collection class with a limited size of ten. Note that every access to the shared stack object is protected by a lock on the `Type` object of the `PooledCalcFactory` class. This guarantees that no more than one instance will ever manipulate the stack shared by all instances of the class.

LISTING 4-16: A Custom Pooling Factory for the Calc Handler

```
// File: PoolingFactory.cs
public class PooledCalcFactory : IHttpHandlerFactory
{
   const int cPoolSize = 10;
   // Static stack of CalcHandler instances
```

```
  private static Stack _handlers = new Stack(cPoolSize);

  // GetHandler returns a CalcHandler instance from
  // the static stack, if available, or a new instance
  public IHttpHandler GetHandler(HttpContext ctx,
      string requestType, string url, string translatedPath)
  {
    IHttpHandler handler = null;

    // Acquire a lock on the SyncBlock associated with our
    // Type object to prevent concurrent access to our
    // static stack
    lock (this.GetType())
    {
      // if handler is available on stack, pop it
      if (_handlers.Count > 0)
        handler = (IHttpHandler) _handlers.Pop();
    }

    // if no handler was available, create new instance
    if (handler == null)
      handler = new CalcHandler();

    return handler;
  }

  // ReleaseHandler puts a handler back on the static
  // stack, if the handler is reusable and the stack
  // is not full
  public void ReleaseHandler(IHttpHandler handler)
  {
    if (handler.IsReusable)
      lock(this.GetType())
      {
        if (_handlers.Count < cPoolSize)
          _handlers.Push(handler);
      }
  }
}
```

As mentioned earlier, the deployment of this factory class, along with the calculator handler, is nearly identical to the way we deployed the calculator handler initially. This time, however, we specify the type and assembly of our factory class instead of the handler class directly, as shown in Listing 4-17.

LISTING 4-17: Configuration File for Specifying a Custom Handler Factory

```
<!— File: web.config —>
<configuration>
  <system.web>
    <httpHandlers>
      <add verb="GET" path="calc.calc"
           type="PooledCalcFactory, PoolingFactory" />
    </httpHandlers>
  </system.web>
</configuration>
```

4.5 Custom Modules

The last and perhaps most powerful point of extensibility in the HTTP pipeline is the module. Modules live at the application scope and can tap into any of the HttpApplication events. They are created the first time the application is created and exist throughout the lifetime of the application. Modules are typically used to perform pre- or postprocessing on requests, similar in many ways to ISAPI filters in IIS. ASP.NET itself uses modules for a number of application-level features, including authentication, authorization, output caching, and out-of-process session state management. Table 4-4 shows the various system-provided modules and the services they provide.

TABLE 4-4: Modules Defined in ASP.NET

Module	Purpose
OutputCacheModule	Page-level output caching
SessionStateModule	Out-of-process session state management
WindowsAuthenticationModule	Client authentication using integrated Windows authentication
FormsAuthenticationModule	Client authentication using cookie-based forms authentication
PassportAuthenticationModule	Client authentication using MS Passport
UrlAuthorizationModule	Client authorization based on requested URL
FileAuthorizationModule	Client authorization based on requested file

Note that all these services require hooks into the pipeline before the request is issued to a handler. This is a common requirement of a module, to be able to tap into the request processing pipeline and potentially alter, abort, or otherwise change the current request.

To construct your own module, you begin by building a class that implements the IHttpModule interface, shown in Listing 4-18. This interface consists of two methods, Init() and Dispose(). The Init method is called when the module is first created, and it takes as a parameter a reference to the current HttpApplication object. Typically, a module uses the application class to register delegates to some of the events exposed by HttpApplication. The Dispose method is called when the application is being closed, giving modules an opportunity to perform any cleanup necessary.

LISTING 4-18: IHttpModule Interface

```
public interface IHttpModule
{
  void Dispose();
  void Init(HttpApplication context);
}
```

To see an example, let's build a module that tracks the request processing time for all requests serviced by an application. The logic for this class is identical to our earlier implementation of tracking request time through the global.asax file, and in fact, the capabilities of global.asax and modules largely overlap. We discuss how best to choose which technique to use in the next section. Listing 4-19 shows our TimerModule class, which will keep track of the start request time in the Items collection of the Http-Context class, as we did in our global.asax example. This time, for variety, instead of printing the timing results to the response buffer, we create a custom header that contains the timing information.[11]

LISTING 4-19: Sample Module to Collect Request Timing Information

```
// File: TimerModule.cs
//
public class TimerModule : IHttpModule
```

continues

---

11. Thanks go to Aaron Skonnard, who first showed me this timer module example.

```
{
  public void Dispose() {}

  public void Init(HttpApplication httpApp)
  {
    // subscribe delegates to the BeginRequest and
    // EndRequest events of the HttpApplication class
    httpApp.BeginRequest +=
            new EventHandler(this.OnBeginRequest);
    httpApp.EndRequest +=
            new EventHandler(this.OnEndRequest);
  }

  public void OnBeginRequest(object o, EventArgs ea)
  {
    HttpApplication httpApp = o as HttpApplication;

    // record time that event was handled in
    // per-request Items collection
    httpApp.Context.Items["sTime"] = DateTime.Now;
  }

  public void OnEndRequest(object o, EventArgs ea)
  {
    HttpApplication httpApp = o as HttpApplication;

    DateTime dt = (DateTime)httpApp.Context.Items["sTime"];

    // measure time between BeginRequest event
    // and current event
    TimeSpan ts = DateTime.Now - dt;

    httpApp.Context.Response.AddHeader("RequestTiming",
                                       ts.ToString());
  }
}
```

Now, to deploy this module, the class must be compiled into an assembly, deployed in the /bin directory of the application (or in the GAC), and an entry must be made in the web.config file of the application under the httpModules element. Listing 4-20 shows a sample web.config file that would register this module, assuming we compiled the class into an assembly named TimerModule. Note that the add element takes a name and a type for attributes, where the name is some application-unique string identifying the module, and the type is the class name (fully namespace qualified) followed by the assembly name.

LISTING 4-20: Timer Module Configuration

```
<!- File: web.config ->
<configuration>
  <system.web>
    <httpModules>
      <add name="Timer"
           type="TimerModule, TimerModule" />
    </httpModules>
  </system.web>
</configuration>
```

4.5.1 Modules as Filters

In addition to monitoring requests and supplementing responses, modules can be used to filter both requests and responses. Filtering is useful if you want to modify the incoming request before it reaches its handler or to change the outgoing response as it is being written. Filters can be useful for adding things like common footers to all pages processed by an application or even stripping off portions of a response before sending it back to the client.

To build a module that acts as a filter, you need to construct a new `Stream`-derived class and at the beginning of each request (`Application_BeginRequest`), create a new instance of your `Stream`-derived class and assign it to the `Filter` property of either the `Request` or the `Response` object. From this point on, all writes to the `Response` stream (or reads from the `Request` stream) will use your new stream class. The tricky part in getting a filter working properly is that you need to keep the old `Request` or `Response` stream around, cached in your custom stream, so that you can read from or write to the actual request or response stream when you need to. Your new stream class thus acts as a filter sitting between the original stream and any reads or writes. This relationship is shown in Figure 4-4.

To see an example of building a filtering module, suppose we wanted to alter the outgoing response of all requests made to an application by stripping off some portion of the response and logging it to a file. As we will see in the next chapter, there is a compelling reason to build such a filtering module. One of the diagnostic features of ASP.NET, called tracing, augments the output of any given page with supplemental information about

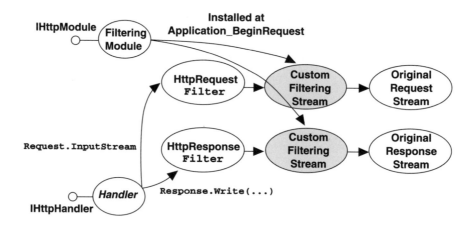

FIGURE 4-4: Filtering with HttpModules

the request. This is extremely useful information, but there is no way to tell ASP.NET to write that trace information to a file instead of directly to the Response stream. So for our example, we will build an HttpModule that monitors all responses, looking for the beginning of the trace output of a response (if there is one). Once the trace output is detected, we will stop passing it along to the Response stream and instead redirect the output to a file stream to store on disk.

Our first task is to build the custom stream class that sits between any calls to Response.Write() and the actual Response stream. This class, which we call TraceRedirectStream, is shown in Listing 4-21. The first thing to note about this custom stream class is that it encapsulates two streams as data members. The first, called _primaryStream, is initialized to the actual Response stream. The second, called _otherStream, is initialized to a file stream to which the trace information is to be written. The constructor of our custom stream class takes the two streams as parameters, as well as the request URL so that it can document what request generated the trace information. Many of the Stream functions of this class simply forward along to the _primaryStream data member, so that it behaves like the standard Response stream in most ways. The interesting functions are Write and FindTraceStartTag. The purpose of FindTraceStartTag is to scan the text being written for the string that indicates the beginning of the trace output. This function is then used within the `Write` method to determine which stream to write to. The first time the trace start tag is encountered, we write out a header to the file stream to document the request URL, and then all subsequent writes to our stream are sent to the file stream and not to the original `Response` stream.

LISTING 4-21: Custom Stream Class to Redirect Trace Output

```
public class TraceRedirectStream : Stream
{
  private Stream  _primaryStream;
  private Stream  _otherStream;
  private bool    _inTrace = false;
  private string  _requestUrl;
  // Signals the start of the trace information in a page
  private const string _cStartTraceStringTag =
                        "<div id=\"__asptrace\">";

  public TraceRedirectStream(Stream primaryStream,
                             Stream otherStream,
                             string requestUrl )
  {
    _primaryStream = primaryStream;
    _otherStream   = otherStream;
    _requestUrl    = requestUrl;
  }

  private void WriteLine(Stream s, string format,
                         params object[] args )
  {
    string text = string.Format(format +
                                Environment.NewLine, args);
    byte[] textBytes = Encoding.ASCII.GetBytes(text);
    s.Write(textBytes, 0, textBytes.Length);
  }

  public override bool CanRead
  {
    get { return(_primaryStream.CanRead); }
  }

  public override bool CanSeek
  {
    get { return(_primaryStream.CanSeek); }
```

continues

```
    }

    public override bool CanWrite
    {
      get { return(_primaryStream.CanWrite); }
    }

    public override long Length
    {
      get { return(_primaryStream.Length); }
    }

    public override long Position
    {
      get { return(_primaryStream.Position); }

      set
      {
        _primaryStream.Position = value;
        _otherStream.Position = value;
      }
    }

    public override long Seek(long offset,
                              SeekOrigin direction)
    {
      return _primaryStream.Seek(offset, direction);
    }

    public override void SetLength(long length)
    {
      _primaryStream.SetLength(length);
    }

    public override void Close()
    {
      _primaryStream.Close();
      _otherStream.Close();
    }

    public override void Flush()
    {
      _primaryStream.Flush();
      _otherStream.Flush();
    }

    public override int Read( byte[] buffer, int offset,
                              int count )
    {
```

```
    return _primaryStream.Read(buffer, offset, count);
}

public override void Write( byte[] buffer, int offset,
                            int count )
{
  if (_inTrace)
  {
    // if we are writing out trace information,
    // it is always the last part of the output stream,
    // so just continue writing to the log file until
    // the request completes.
    _otherStream.Write(buffer, offset, count);
  }
  else
  {
    // We are not currently writing out trace information,
    // so as we write response information, look for the
    // trace start string, and begin writing to the trace
    // log if we encounter it. Scan the entire buffer
    // looking for the trace start tag.
    int idx = FindTraceStartTag(buffer, offset, count);

    if (idx > 0) // if non-negative, start tag found
    {
      WriteLine(_otherStream,
                "<hr/><h3>Request URL: {0}</h3>",
                _requestUrl);
      _inTrace = true;

      // write non-trace portion of buffer to primary
      // response stream
      _primaryStream.Write(buffer, offset, idx);
      // write trace portion to other stream (log)
      _otherStream.Write(buffer, idx+offset, count - idx);
    }
  }
}

public override int ReadByte()
{
  int b = _primaryStream.ReadByte();
  _otherStream.Position = _primaryStream.Position;
  return(b);
}

public override void WriteByte( byte b )
```

continues

```
        {
          if (this._inTrace)
            _otherStream.WriteByte(b);
          else
            _primaryStream.WriteByte(b);
        }

        private int FindTraceStartTag(byte[] buffer, int offset,
                                     int count)
        {
          int bufIdx = offset;
          int ret = -1;

          while ((bufIdx < count+offset) && (ret < 0))
          {
            if (buffer[bufIdx] ==
                    TraceRedirectStream._cStartTraceStringTag[0])
            {
              int i=1;
              while ((i <
                  TraceRedirectStream._cStartTraceStringTag.Length)
                    && (bufIdx+i < count+offset))
              {
                if (buffer[bufIdx+i] !=
                      TraceRedirectStream._cStartTraceStringTag[i])
                  break;
                i++;
              }
              if (i >=
                  TraceRedirectStream._cStartTraceStringTag.Length)
                ret = bufIdx;
            } // if (buffer[bufIdx]...
            bufIdx++;
          } // while (bufIdx < ...

          return ret;
        } // private int FindTraceStartTag...

      } // public class TraceRedirectStream...
```

Now we are left with the task of installing this stream in place from a module. Our custom HttpModule adds handlers for the BeginRequest and EndRequest events so that our custom stream can be installed and closed when the request is complete. The installation of the stream involves creating a new instance and assigning it to the Filter property of the

Response object with each new request. This custom module is shown in Listing 4-22.

LISTING 4-22: TraceDumpModule Class

```
public class TraceDumpModule : IHttpModule
{
  private TraceRedirectStream  _responseStream;
  private string              _logFileName;

  public void Init( HttpApplication httpApp )
  {
    _logFileName = @"C:\temp\tracelog.htm";

    httpApp.BeginRequest +=
            new EventHandler(OnBeginRequest);
    httpApp.EndRequest += new EventHandler(OnEndRequest);
  }

  void OnBeginRequest( object sender, EventArgs a )
  {
    HttpApplication httpApp = sender as HttpApplication;

    FileInfo fiLogFile;
    if( File.Exists(_logFileName) )
      fiLogFile = new FileInfo(_logFileName);

    // Open the log file (for appending) and log
    // any trace output made to that request.
    //
    Stream responseLog = File.Open( _logFileName,
                      FileMode.Append, FileAccess.Write );

    long pos = httpApp.Request.InputStream.Position;
    CopyStream(httpApp.Request.InputStream, responseLog);

    httpApp.Request.InputStream.Position = pos;

    // Set the response filter to refer to the trace
    // redirect stream bound to the original response
    // stream and the log file. As this stream processes
    // the response data, it will selectively send non-
    // trace output to the original stream, and trace
    //output to the log file
    //
    _responseStream =
```

continues

```
                   new TraceRedirectStream(httpApp.Response.Filter,
                       responseLog, httpApp.Request.Url.ToString());
        httpApp.Response.Filter = _responseStream;
    }

    void OnEndRequest( object sender, EventArgs a )
    {
        if( _responseStream != null )
            _responseStream.Close();
    }

    void CopyStream( Stream inStream, Stream outStream )
    {
        byte[] buf = new byte[128];
        int bytesRead = 0;
        while ((bytesRead=inStream.Read(buf, 0, buf.Length))
                > 0 )
        {
            outStream.Write(buf, 0, bytesRead);
        }
    }

    public void Dispose()
    {}
}
```

4.5.2 Module Pooling

Unlike handlers, which are pooled only when you create custom handlers whose IsReusable property returns true, modules are always pooled. Each time a new instance of the HttpApplication-derived class is created, a new set of modules is created to accompany it. Thus, the advice given earlier for application classes holds true for custom modules as well—save no state between requests.

4.5.3 Modules versus global.asax

As noted earlier, all the functionality of a module can also be implemented in the application-specific global.asax file. The converse is not true, however, because global.asax provides several additional events and features that are not available to modules, such as the session start event or the ability to use the object tag to declare application or session scoped objects. For many tasks at the application level, however, it is not always clear whether the feature should be implemented in a module or in the `global.asax` file. Table 4-5 provides a comparison of various features supported by modules and the `global.asax` file.

TABLE 4-5: Module versus global.asax

Feature	Module	global.asax
Can receive event notifications for all `HttpApplication`-generated events	Yes	Yes
Can receive event notifications for `Session_Start/_End`, `Application_Start/_End`	No	Yes
Can be deployed at the machine level	Yes	No
Supports declarative object instantiation	No	Yes

Note that the one significant advantage of modules is that they can be deployed at the machine level. By deploying your module's assembly in the GAC, you can add that module either directly to the machine-wide `machine.config` file or individually to multiple applications' `web.config` files, without having to recopy the assembly to each application's `/bin` directory. The one significant advantage of the `global.asax` file is that it supports additional events issued when the application starts and ends and when each session starts and ends. The `global.asax` file also supports declarative object instantiation, but as we have seen, this is a feature most developers are unlikely to make much use of anyway.

As a general guideline, it is usually wise to place any application-specific features that are unlikely to be useful in other applications in `global.asax`. If you find yourself building a feature, such as a response timer, that might be useful to more than one application, consider building it as a module instead of coding it directly into `global.asax`.

4.6 Threading in the Pipeline

To efficiently service multiple client requests, Web servers make extensive use of concurrency, by launching multiple processes and/or spawning multiple threads to service requests and perform work. As we have seen, ASP.NET creates a distinct `AppDomain` for each application housed in its worker process, but what has not yet been mentioned is how threads are allocated and dispatched to service those requests.

For the most part, ASP.NET developers need not concern themselves with the multitude of issues that come with developing in a multithreaded environment. `Page` requests are always serviced on the same thread, and a distinct instance of the `Page` class is always created to service any new requests. Distinct instances of application and module objects are also used to service each request. It is important, however, to understand how threads are used to service requests, so that you don't make any incorrect assumptions about concurrent access to any of the state in your applications.

To begin with, ASP.NET uses the process-wide CLR thread pool to service requests. The size of this pool is configurable in the `processModel` element of `machine.config`, discussed in Chapter 3, and is set to a default of 25 worker threads and 25 I/O threads. When running on Windows 2000 or Windows XP, ASP.NET services requests primarily on I/O threads from the CLR thread pool. This is done for efficiency because each request is initiated by an asynchronous write to a named pipe from the ISAPI extension DLL, `aspnet_isapi.dll`, within the IIS process (`inetinfo.exe`). When the asynchronous write is received by the ASP.NET worker process (`aspnet_wp.exe`), it is processed on an I/O thread, so to avoid thread switching, the request is usually serviced directly on that thread. Note that this behavior changes with Windows Server 2003 and IIS 6.0 because ASP.NET is more tightly integrated. In IIS 6.0, there is no dedicated worker process for ASP.NET since it is integrated into the process model exposed by IIS 6.0, which lets you designate whether a particular virtual directory lives in a distinct worker process (`w3wp.exe`) or in a worker process shared by other virtual directories. In this scenario, ASP.NET services requests on worker threads drawn from the process-wide CLR thread pool.

For each request that comes in, a new instance of the appropriate `HttpApplication`-derived class is created, as are the associated modules for that application. To avoid reallocating applications and modules too often, each `AppDomain` maintains a pool of applications and modules. The maximum size of the application pool is the same as the size of the thread pool, so by default, up to 25 requests per worker process can be processed concurrently, each with its own application and module set. Figure 4-5 shows a possible snapshot in time of the ASP.NET worker process. In this

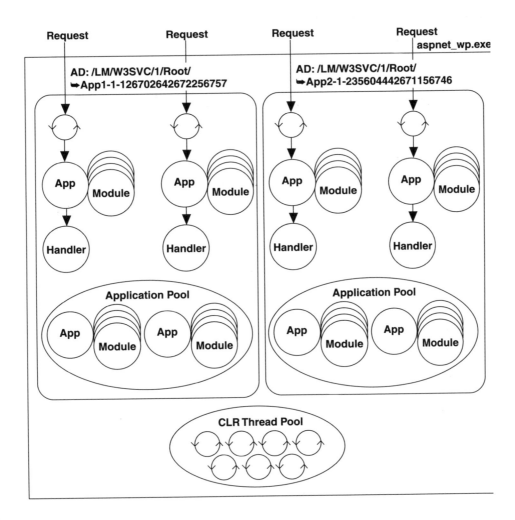

FIGURE 4-5: Threading and Pooling in the HTTP Pipeline

scenario, there are two active applications in the worker process, each with a dedicated `AppDomain`. Each application is currently processing two requests, and each is using two threads from the ASP.NET thread pool to service those requests.

Several aspects of this architecture may influence the way you construct your ASP.NET applications. First of all, the fact that applications and modules are instantiated multiple times for a particular application means that you should never rely on adding fields or other state to your application or module classes, because it is replicated and not shared across multiple requests as you might think. Instead, use one of the many state repositories available in the pipeline, such as the application-wide cache, the session state bag, the application state bag, or the per-request items collection of the `HttpContext` class. Also, by default, most handlers created to service requests are not pooled. As we have seen, you can pool handlers and even control pooling on a per-handler basis via the `IsReusable` property of `IHttpHandler`, but the only handlers that are pooled implicitly are custom handlers that you write with no designated handler factory. The `Page-HandlerFactory` class does not perform pooling, nor does the factory `SimpleHandlerFactory` class, which instantiates .ashx-defined handlers. Typically, therefore, each request is serviced by a freshly allocated instance of the appropriate handler class, which is discarded after the request completes.

4.6.1 Asynchronous Handlers

When we discussed implementing custom handlers earlier in the chapter, the call to the `ProcessRequest` method of the handler was always made synchronously in the context of the thread executing the request in the pipeline. There may be occasions where you would like this invocation to be asynchronous, allowing the primary request processing thread to be returned to the thread pool while your handler performs its work. For these occasions, there is another handler interface, derived from `IHttpHandler`, called `IHttpAsyncHandler`, shown in Listing 4-23.

LISTING 4-23: The IHttpAsyncHandler Interface

```
public interface IHttpAsyncHandler : IHttpHandler
{
  IAsyncResult BeginProcessRequest(HttpContext ctx,
                                   AsyncCallback cb,
                                   object obj);
  void EndProcessRequest(IAsyncResult ar);
}
```

Handlers that implement this interface must implement two additional methods beyond the standard methods of IHttpHandler. The first method is BeginProcessRequest, which the application class calls instead of directly calling ProcessRequest. It is then up to the handler to launch a new thread to process the request, and return immediately from the Begin-ProcessRequest method, passing back a reference to a class that implements IAsyncResult so that the runtime can detect when the operation is complete. The other method, EndProcessRequest, is called when the request processing is complete, and can be used to clean up any allocated resources if necessary.

The most straightforward ways to implement an asynchronous handler would be either to use an asynchronous delegate invocation or to call ThreadPool.QueueUserWorkItem with the method to perform the request processing. Unfortunately, using either of these two techniques would completely defeat the purpose of building an asynchronous handler, because they both draw from the same process-wide CLR thread pool that ASP.NET uses to service requests. While the primary request thread would indeed be freed up and returned to the thread pool, another thread would be drawn out of the pool to perform the asynchronous delegate execution (or work item completion), resulting in a net gain of zero threads for servicing additional requests and thus rendering the asynchronous nature of the handler useless.

To build a truly effective asynchronous handler, therefore, you must spawn an additional thread by hand in response to BeginProcessRequest (or even better, use a thread from a different thread pool, discussed later).

There are three important aspects to building a successful asynchronous handler:

- Constructing a class that supports `IAsyncResult` to be returned from `BeginProcessRequest`
- Spawning the thread to perform your request processing asynchronously
- Notifying ASP.NET that you are finished processing the request and are ready to return the response

We begin the construction of an asynchronous handler by building a class that supports `IAsyncResult`. This class will be returned from the call to `BeginProcessRequest` and later will be passed into our implementation of `EndProcessRequest`, so among other things, this class is a useful place to store request-specific state that we may need to use during the processing of a request. The `IAsyncResult` interface is shown in Listing 4-24.

LISTING 4-24: The IAsyncResult Interface

```
public interface IAsyncResult
{
  public object      AsyncState           { get; }
  public bool        CompletedSynchronously { get; }
  public bool        IsCompleted          { get; }
  public WaitHandle  AsyncWaitHandle      { get; }
}
```

In our example, we store a reference to the `HttpContext` object associated with this request, a reference to the `AsyncCallback` delegate passed into `BeginProcessRequest` (which we must later invoke to complete the request), and a generic object reference for extra data that may be used by the caller of `BeginProcessRequest`. The other element that must be implemented in this class is a synchronization object that threads can wait on to be signaled when the operation completes. We use the common technique of supplying a `ManualResetEvent` that fires when our request is complete, but we allocate it only if someone requests it. Finally, our class has a convenience method called `CompleteRequest` that triggers the `Manual-ResetEvent` if it was created, invokes the `AsyncCallback` delegate, and sets our `IsCompleted` flag to `true`. The complete class definition for `AsyncRequestState` is shown in Listing 4-25.

LISTING 4-25: The AsyncRequestState Class Definition

```
class AsyncRequestState : IAsyncResult
{
  public AsyncRequestState(HttpContext ctx,
                           AsyncCallback cb,
                           object extraData )
  {
    _ctx = ctx;
    _cb = cb;
    _extraData = extraData;
  }

  internal HttpContext _ctx;
  internal AsyncCallback _cb;
  internal object _extraData;
  private bool _isCompleted = false;
  private ManualResetEvent _callCompleteEvent = null;

  internal void CompleteRequest()
  {
    _isCompleted = true;
    lock (this)
    {
      if (_callCompleteEvent != null)
        _callCompleteEvent.Set();
    }
    // if a callback was registered, invoke it now
    if (_cb != null)
      _cb(this);
  }

  // IAsyncResult interface property implementations
  public object AsyncState
  { get { return(_extraData);    } }
  public bool CompletedSynchronously
  { get { return(false);         } }
  public bool IsCompleted
  { get { return(_isCompleted); } }
  public WaitHandle AsyncWaitHandle
  {
    get
    {
      lock( this )
```

continues

```
          {
            if( _callCompleteEvent == null )
              _callCompleteEvent = new ManualResetEvent(false);

            return _callCompleteEvent;
          }
        }
      }
    }
```

The next step is to spawn a new thread on which we will process our request. The method we call on this new thread will need access to the state we cached in the `AsyncRequestState` class shown in Listing 4-25, but unfortunately the `ThreadStart` delegate used to spawn new threads in .NET does not take any parameters. To get around this, we create another class with the necessary state cached as data members (in this case, simply a reference to the `AsyncRequestState` object for this request) and with an instance method that can be used to initialize the `ThreadStart` delegate. Listing 4-26 shows the definition of this class, called `AsyncRequest`. Note that the `ProcessRequest` method we define in this class is the method that will be called from our manually created thread, and when it completes, it signals that the request processing is complete by invoking `CompleteRequest` on the `AsyncRequestState` object.

LISTING 4-26: The AsyncRequest Class Definition

```
class AsyncRequest
{
  private AsyncRequestState _asyncRequestState;

  public AsyncRequest(AsyncRequestState ars)
  {
    _asyncRequestState = ars;
  }

  public void ProcessRequest()
  {
    // This is where your non-CPU-bound
    // activity would take place, like accessing a Web
    // service, polling a slow piece of hardware, or
    // performing a lengthy database operation.
    // We put the thread to sleep for 2 seconds to simulate
    // a lengthy operation.
    Thread.Sleep(2000);
```

```
    _asyncRequestState._ctx.Response.Write(
            "<h1>Async handler responded</h1>");

    // tell asp.net we are finished processing this request
    _asyncRequestState.CompleteRequest();
  }
}
```

Finally, we are ready to build the asynchronous handler class itself. This class, which we just call AsyncHandler, must implement all the methods of the IHttpAsyncHandler interface shown earlier, which derives from IHttpHandler, for a total of four methods. The ProcessRequest method is not used and will never be called, because we implement Begin-ProcessRequest. In BeginProcessRequest, we create a new instance of our AsyncRequestState class, initializing it with the HttpContext object, the AsyncCallback delegate, and the generic object reference passed in as parameters. We then prepare a new AsyncRequest object, initialized with the freshly created AsyncRequestState object, and launch a new thread. Our implementation of EndProcessRequest does not do anything in this example, but it can be used in general to perform any cleanup or last-minute response additions. The AsyncHandler class definition is shown in Listing 4-27.

LISTING 4-27: The AsyncHandler Class Definition

```
public class AsyncHandler : IHttpAsyncHandler
{
  public void ProcessRequest(HttpContext ctx)
  {
    // not used
  }

  public bool IsReusable
  {
    get { return false;}
  }

  public IAsyncResult BeginProcessRequest(HttpContext ctx,
                                AsyncCallback cb,
                                object obj)
  {
```

continues

```
            AsyncRequestState reqState =
                          new AsyncRequestState(ctx, cb, obj);
            AsyncRequest ar = new AsyncRequest(reqState);
            ThreadStart ts = new ThreadStart(ar.ProcessRequest);
            Thread t = new Thread(ts);
            t.Start();

            return reqState;
        }


        public void EndProcessRequest(IAsyncResult ar)
        {
            // This will be called on our manually created thread
            // in response to our calling ASP.NET's AsyncCallback
            // delegate once our request has completed processing.
            // The incoming
            // IAsyncResult parameter will be a reference to the
            // AsyncRequestState class we built, so we can access
            // the Context through that class if we like.
            // Note - you *cannot* access the current context
            // using the HttpContext.Current property, because we
            // are running on our own thread, which has not been
            // initialized with a context reference.
            AsyncRequestState ars = ar as AsyncRequestState;
            if (ars != null)
            {
                // here you could perform some cleanup, write
                // something else to the Response, or do whatever
                // else you needed
            }
        }
    }
}
```

If we now build this handler and register it as an endpoint (as we did with our earlier handlers), it will successfully process requests asynchronously from the calling request thread of ASP.NET. Figure 4-6 shows the sequence of events that take place when a request mapped onto our asynchronous handler is made. First, the application class notices that our handler implements IHttpAsyncHandler, so instead of calling the synchronous ProcessRequest method, it invokes BeginProcessRequest on our handler, passing in the current context and an asynchronous callback delegate for our handler to invoke when it is complete. Our handler then creates a new AsyncRequestState object, initialized with the parameters passed into BeginProcessRequest. Next, our handler creates a new

`AsyncRequest` object, initialized with the `AsyncRequestState` object, and launches a new thread using the `AsyncRequest.ProcessRequest` method as the entry point. Our handler then returns the `AsyncRequestState` object to the application object, and the calling thread is returned to the thread pool while our hand-created thread continues processing the request.

Once the `ProcessRequest` method of our `AsyncRequest` object has finished performing its lengthy tasks, it calls the `CompleteRequest` method of our `AsyncRequestState` class. This in turn fires the `AsyncCallback` delegate originally passed into our `BeginProcessRequest` method, signaling

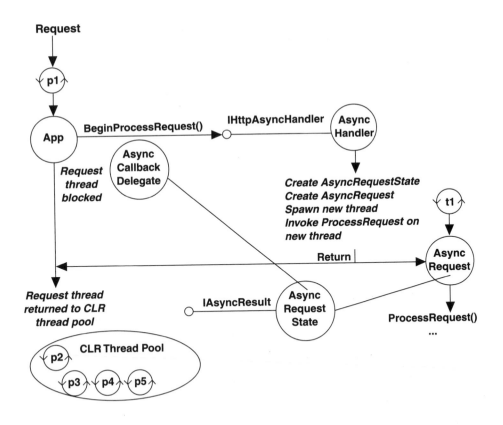

FIGURE 4-6: Asynchronous Handler Operation—Phase 1: The Handoff

that the response has been prepared and is ready for return. The first thing the `AsyncCallback` delegate does is to call the `EndProcessRequest` method on our asynchronous handler class. Once that returns, it triggers the completion of the request by sending back the prepared response. Note that all of this processing happens on the secondary thread that we created in our handler, not on a thread pool thread. Figure 4-7 shows the steps for completing the request to our asynchronous handler.

One problem remains with our asynchronous handler implementation—it has the potential to create an unbounded number of threads. If many requests are made to our asynchronous handler, all of which take a significant amount of time to service, we could easily end up creating more threads than the underlying operating system could handle. To deal with this, we need to provide a secondary thread pool to service our asynchronous requests in a bounded fashion. The mechanics of creating custom

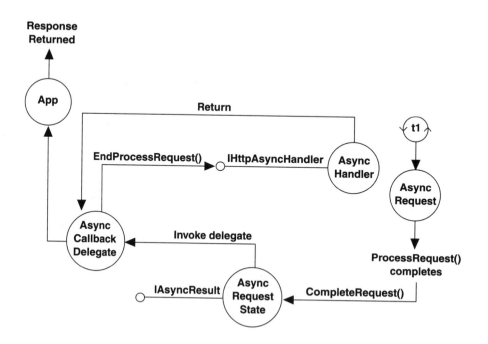

FIGURE 4-7: Asynchronous Handler Operation—Phase 2: Request Completion

thread pools are beyond the scope of this chapter, but a fully operational asynchronous handler using a supplemental thread pool is available for download in the online samples for this book.

Building asynchronous handlers instead of synchronous ones can add considerable complexity to a design, so you should take care when determining whether you really need the asynchronous capability of these types of handlers. The purpose of an asynchronous handler is to free up an ASP.NET thread pool thread to service additional requests while the handler is processing the original request. This makes sense to do only if the work of servicing the request requires a significant amount of non-CPU-bound time to complete. For example, if the completion of a request depended on the completion of several remote procedure calls or perhaps Web service invocations, that would be a candidate to implement an asynchronous handler. Building asynchronous handlers to service CPU-intensive requests only adds threads to compete with the ASP.NET thread pool threads and may slow down the overall processing time for the request.

SUMMARY

Requests in ASP.NET are serviced by a collection of classes referred to as the HTTP pipeline. This pipeline has three primary points of extensibility: custom applications, custom handlers, and custom modules. A custom application is built by creating a new class that derives from `HttpApplication`, which happens automatically when you author a `global.asax` file. Custom applications can be used to perform application-level tasks by trapping events and responding to them. A custom handler is built by creating a new class that implements the `IHttpHandler` interface and registering that class in your application's configuration file. Custom handlers can be used as endpoints to a request in lieu of `Page` classes if the baggage of the `Page` processing architecture is not necessary. A custom module is built by creating a new class that implements the `IHttpModule` interface and adding event handlers to that class for any of the application-level events. Custom modules are useful for performing generic filtering and monitoring in ASP.NET applications.

Most development in ASP.NET can take place without concern for multithreading issues, because most of the classes in the pipeline are used by only one thread at a time at the instance level. It is important to understand, however, that both modules and application classes are pooled, so it is not wise to store any cross-request state in either. In some cases, it may be necessary to build asynchronous handlers to avoid clogging the ASP.NET worker thread pool with requests that take a long time to complete.

■ 5 ■
Diagnostics and Error Handling

T RADITIONALLY, ONE OF the most frustrating aspects of building ASP-based Web applications has been the inconsistent debugging and diagnostic support. The script debuggers for diagnosing server-side VBScript or JavaScript errors are notoriously unreliable, and the most commonly used diagnostic tool used for analyzing ASP applications is `Response.Write()`. Contrast these tools with the rich debugging and diagnostic facilities that both C++ and Visual Basic developers have had for years, and it is obvious why ASP developers have been frustrated with debugging.

Fortunately, ASP.NET changes all that. To begin with, because ASP.NET pages are now compiled into complete assemblies before execution, they can be debugged with the same debugging facilities available to component and application developers, including the full-featured Visual Studio .NET debugger. Second, the diagnostics for building ASP.NET applications have also improved significantly, including a tracing facility that lets you print diagnostic messages that display only when tracing is enabled, and a number of new performance monitor counters to track everything from worker process lifetime to requests processed per second.

In addition to diagnostic support, ASP.NET provides comprehensive error handling and recovery support. You can provide custom error pages to be displayed when specific error codes are returned, and because all of ASP.NET is built on top of the CLR, the native exception handling mechanism in .NET is used to transmit unexpected errors.

5.1 Diagnostics in ASP.NET

ASP.NET offers several tools for diagnosing problems in your applications. Tracing provides a welcome alternative to printing diagnostic messages to your pages using `Response.Write`, which ASP developers have always relied on heavily. Application-level tracing is useful for tracking down problems that occur across multiple pages in an application. And more than 50 new performance monitor counters provide detailed diagnostic information about ASP.NET's behavior on your server.

5.1.1 Page Tracing

One of the most useful, and easiest-to-use, diagnostic features of ASP.NET is page tracing. Simply adding `Trace=true` to your `@Page` directive causes ASP.NET to generate diagnostic information at the end of your normal page rendering, containing everything you would ever want to know about the request and its response. Page-level tracing is extremely convenient because just by placing one additional attribute on your .aspx page, you can quickly collect information about the any request made to that page. Figure 5-1 shows an example of a page that has enabled tracing and the resulting output generated when that page is rendered.

Enabling page tracing displays six pieces of information for a page, as listed in Table 5-1. The request details section shows the session ID, the time of the request, the encoding types of the request and response, and the resulting status code. The trace information section contains the output of trace statements made either by system libraries or by the page. The control tree section displays all the controls that were created to render the page along with how many rendering bytes they occupied and how much information they stored in the view state cache. The cookies collection shows the names and values of all cookies sent by a client. The headers collection shows all the header information presented by the client at the time of the request. Finally, the server variables section shows all the intrinsic server variables available to page scripts, and their values.

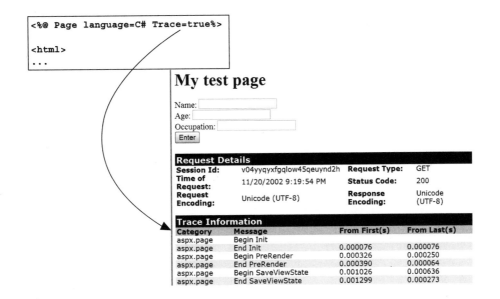

FIGURE 5-1: Enabling Trace on a Page

TABLE 5-1: Contents of Page Trace Information

Section	Description
Request details	Details of the request, including the session ID, the time the request was made, the request and response encodings, the request type, and the return status code
Trace information	Output of any `Trace.Write` or `Trace.Warn` statements
Control tree	Hierarchical display of all server-side controls in the requested page
Cookies collection	All cookies accompanying the request
Headers collection	All headers accompanying the request
Server variables	All the server variables and their values at the time of the request

5.1.2 **Writing Trace Messages**

The goal of enabling tracing on a page is to be able to see at a glance all the relevant data associated with a particular request, to easily diagnose any problems that might have occurred. Many of the methods in ASP.NET classes generate some output to the trace stream, as you will see if you enable tracing on a page. In addition to the ASP.NET-generated output, however, it is often even more useful to have custom output from your own classes and pages printed to the trace output stream. To do this, you can access the `Trace` property of your `Page` class that references an instance of the `TraceContext` class. You can use the `Write` method to send information to the trace information region of the trace output. If instead you use the `Warn` method, the trace statement is printed in red to indicate it is a warning. Finally, you can check to see whether tracing is enabled by querying the `IsEnabled` property of the `TraceContext` object if your trace operation involves any additional code that should be avoided when tracing is disabled, as shown in Figure 5-2.

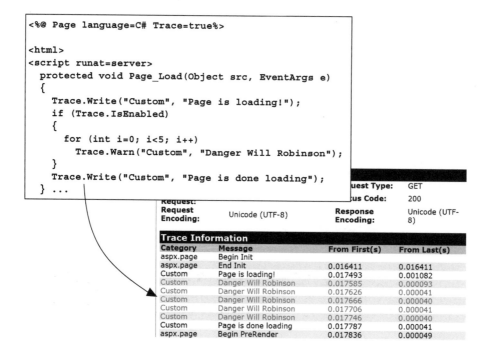

FIGURE 5-2: Writing Custom Trace Messages

It is good practice to add trace output to most of your pages and classes, even if you see no immediate need for the information. When something goes wrong on a page, you are better off having more diagnostic information to help resolve the problem quickly. Tracing is appealing because it does not generate any output or occupy any additional computation time unless you explicitly enable it, so there is no cost in liberally adding trace messages to your pages.

5.1.3 Application-Level Tracing

It is often useful, when you are trying to track down a problem, to be able to save several page traces for later review and analysis. You can do this by enabling tracing at the application level instead of the page level. When you enable tracing in your application-wide configuration file, ASP.NET saves the trace output of every page visited until you disable it. Figure 5-3 shows an example of enabling trace at the application level and the corresponding output generated by navigating to the `trace.axd` URL at any location in your application.

The attributes for the `trace` element are shown in Table 5-2. In addition to simply enabling, `trace` accepts `requestLimit` as an attribute to control how many pages to trace (which defaults to 10), `pageOutput` to control whether page-level tracing is shown as well, `traceMode` to control the

web.config

```
<configuration>
  <system.web>
    <trace enabled='true' />
  </system.web>
</configuration>
```

Application Trace
Book/CS

[clear current trace]

Physical Directory: C:\users\fo\asp\book\samples\cs\

Requests to this Application				Remaining: 4
No. Time of Request	File	Status Code	Verb	
1 11/20/2002 9:30:11 PM	/diagnostics/tracesample.aspx	401	GET	View Details
2 11/20/2002 9:30:11 PM	/diagnostics/tracesample.aspx	200	GET	View Details
3 11/20/2002 9:31:07 PM	/diagnostics/default.aspx	401	GET	View Details
4 11/20/2002 9:31:07 PM	/diagnostics/default.aspx	200	GET	View Details

FIGURE 5-3: Enabling Application-Level Tracing

sorting of the trace output, and `localOnly` to control whether remote access to the site can see the trace output. Once tracing has been enabled for an application, all requests made for pages in that application are traced and stored in-memory in the worker process. To view the page traces, navigate to `trace.axd` at the root of the application, for which a special `HttpHandler` is defined, and ASP.NET displays a list of all the traces stored since application-level tracing was enabled.

TABLE 5-2: trace Element Attributes

trace Attributes	Values	Description
enabled	true | false	Whether application-level tracing is enabled or disabled
localOnly	true | false	Show trace output on the localhost only
pageOutput	true | false	Display trace output on individual pages in addition to caching application-level traces
requestLimit	Number	How many traces to store in memory before removing earlier traces (defaults to 10)
traceMode	SortByTime | SortByCategory	How to sort the trace output

5.1.4 Performance Monitor Counters

In addition to the page-level diagnostic features, ASP.NET provides many counters for the performance monitoring utility to track the performance and behavior of your applications. More than 50 counters are available, ranging from how many times the worker process has restarted to how many requests are processed per second. A partial list of the available counters is shown in Table 5-3.

TABLE 5-3: Performance Counters Available for ASP.NET

Counter	Description
Application Restarts	Number of times the application has been restarted during the Web server's lifetime
Applications Running	Number of currently running Web applications
Request Execution Time	Number of milliseconds it took to execute the most recent request
Requests Queued	Number of requests waiting to be processed
Requests Rejected	Number of requests rejected because the request queue was full
Worker Process Restarts	Number of times a worker process has restarted on the machine
Anonymous Requests/Sec	Number of anonymous requests per second
Cache API Entries	Number of user-added entries in the cache
Cache API Hit Ratio	Ratio of hits called from user code
Compilations Total	Number of .asax, .ascx, .ashx, or .aspx source files dynamically compiled
Errors During Execution	Number of errors that have occurred during the processing of a request
Output Cache Hit Ratio	Ratio of hits to requests for output cacheable requests
Pipeline Instance Count	Number of active pipeline instances
Requests Succeeded	Number of requests that executed successfully
Requests/Sec	Number of requests executed per second
Sessions Active	Number of currently active sessions
Sessions Total	Number of sessions since the application was started

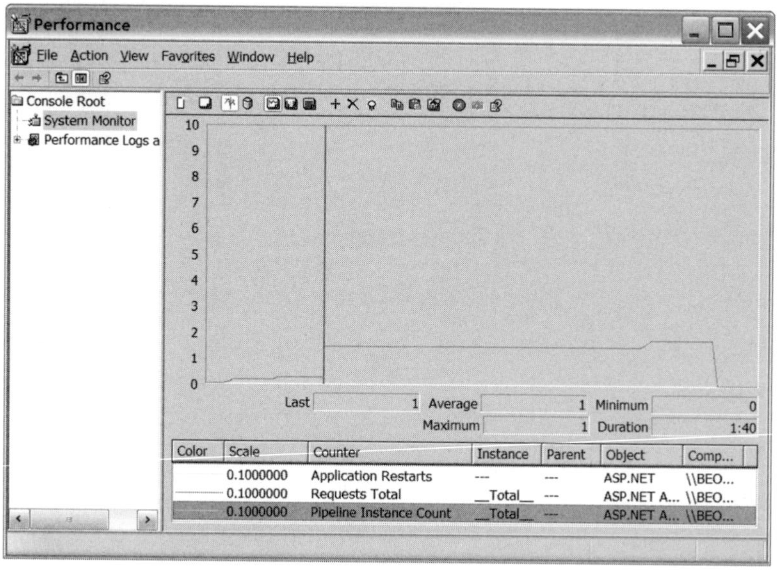

FIGURE 5-4: Performance Monitor

When you install ASP.NET, these counters should be installed on the same machine. To use any of the counters, bring up the Performance administrative tool (perfmon.exe), and choose to add a counter. You should see two categories of ASP.NET performance objects, one simply labeled ASP.NET and the other labeled ASP.NET Applications. Figure 5-4 shows a sample instance of the Performance tool with three of the ASP.NET performance counters activated.

5.2 Debugging

Because ASP.NET pages are compiled into assemblies, you can debug them in much the same way you might debug any other .NET component. First, you must be sure you compile your pages with debug symbols. To do this on a per-page basis, set the Debug attribute on the Page directive to true, as shown in Listing 5-1.

LISTING 5-1: .aspx Page with Debug Compilation

```
<%@ Page Language="C#" Debug="true" %>
<!- ... ->
```

Alternatively, you can enable debug compilation for all the pages in your application by adding the compilation element to your web.config file with debug set to true, as shown in Listing 5-2.

LISTING 5-2: web.config with Debug Compilation

```
<configuration>
  <system.web>
    <compilation debug='true' />
  </system.web>
</configuration>
```

Also keep in mind that any code-behind assemblies that you precompile must be built with debug symbols enabled in order to debug them with source display. Once debug symbols have been generated for your page assemblies, you can use the Visual Studio .NET debugger to step through any server-side or client-side code. If you are building a Web application with Visual Studio .NET, the simplest way to execute your program is with Debug/Start. If, on the other hand, you are trying to debug an application that is already running or that was not built with Visual Studio .NET, you can use the alternative technique of attaching to the ASP.NET worker process. To do this, select Debug/Processes from the menu within Visual Studio .NET. When presented with a dialog, select the aspnet_wp.exe process to attach. This will bring up a second dialog, displaying all the active AppDomains in the worker process. Select the AppDomain that has your virtual directory name in it, and attach. You can now open any source files from your application that you would like to debug, and place break-points as desired. Figure 5-5 shows the dialogs you are presented with when you attach to the process.

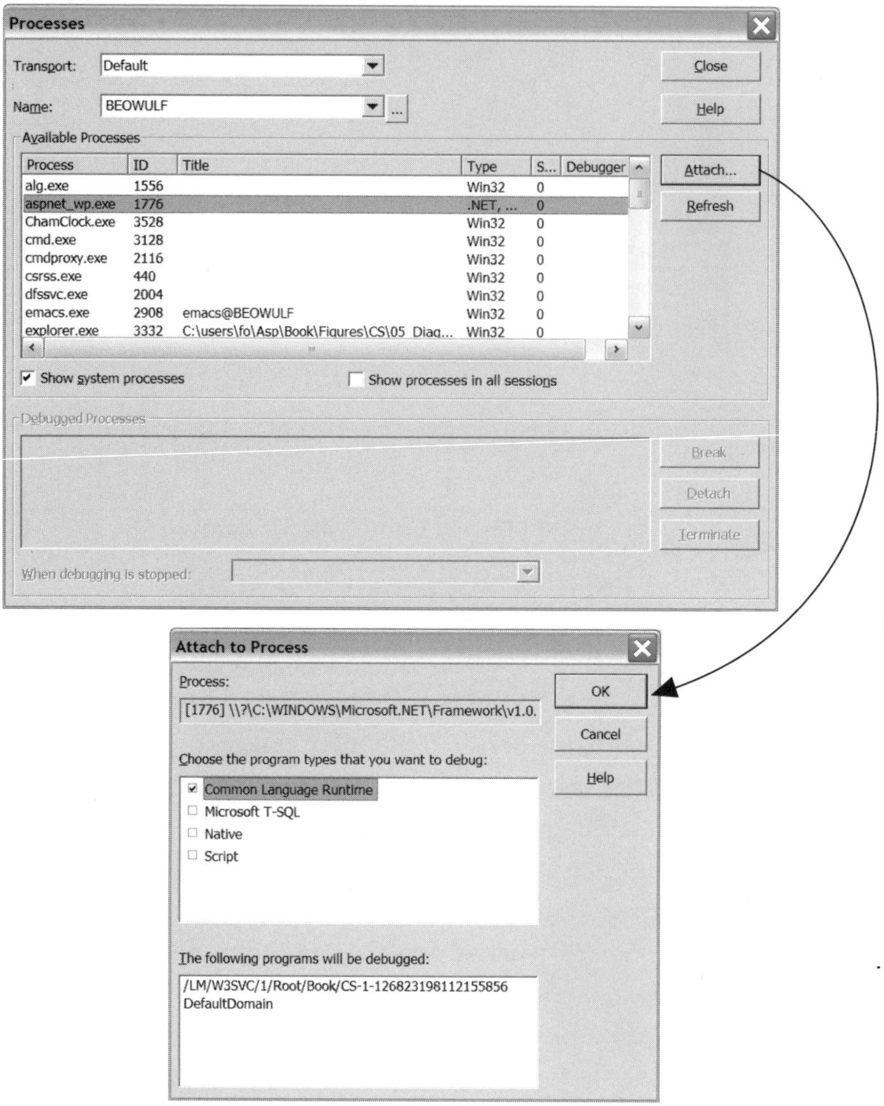

FIGURE 5-5: Attaching a Debugger to the ASP.NET Worker Process

5.3 Error Handling

By default, ASP.NET displays generic error pages for any server errors that occur, such as missing files or internal server errors. The default display for a 404 error is shown in Figure 5-6.

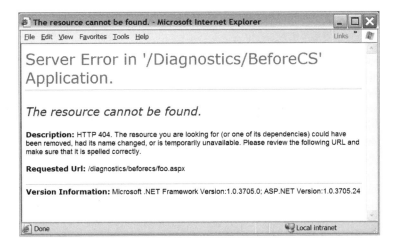

FIGURE 5-6: Default ASP.NET Display for HTTP 404 File-Not-Found Error

If you prefer, you can build specific error pages to display to users when an error occurs in your application. You can specify a particular page to be displayed when an error occurs on a page-by-page basis by using the ErrorPage attribute of the Page directive with the URL of the error page, as shown in Listing 5-3. It is more likely, however, that you will want to specify a general error page, or a collection of specific error pages, to be used for an entire application. Application-wide error pages can be specified in your web.config file by using the customErrors element, as shown in Listing 5-4.

LISTING 5-3: Specifying an Error Page

```
<%@ Page ErrorPage="MyErrorPage.aspx" %>
```

LISTING 5-4: Specifying Error Pages for an Application

```
<configuration>
  <system.web>
    <customErrors defaultredirect='ouch.aspx' mode='On'>
      <error statuscode='404' redirect='nofile.aspx'/>
    </customErrors>
  </system.web>
</configuration>
```

With the `customErrors` element, you can specify a unique error page (or URL) for each HTTP error code, and one top-level page that users will be redirected to if none of the specific error codes are encountered. The other attribute of the `customErrors` element, `mode`, controls when these custom error pages are displayed. By default, `mode` is set to `RemoteOnly`, which shows the custom error pages only when the pages are accessed by a remote machine (any machine but the server). This is useful because the ASP.NET error page that is displayed for an unhandled exception contains useful information, including source code and a stack trace. If you are developing on a test server machine, it is useful to see the full diagnostic information in the generated error page for unhandled exceptions. However, you probably don't want clients to see that level of detail, which is exactly what the `RemoteOnly` setting does for you—show the detailed error information when the page is accessed locally, and show whatever you have specified in the `customErrors` element when the page is accessed remotely. Table 5-4 shows the complete set of attributes associated with the `customErrors` element, with associated descriptions.

TABLE 5-4: customErrors Attributes

customErrors Attribute	Values	Description
Mode	On Off RemoteOnly	Specifying On forces display of custom errors locally as well as remotely. Specifying Off does not use custom errors, but always shows the default ASP.NET error pages. Specifying RemoteOnly (the default) shows the ASP.NET error pages locally, but the custom error pages remotely.
defaultRedirect	URL to redirect to	If there is no specific page designated to display when an error is encountered, the URL specified here is used.

5.3.1 **Unhandled Exceptions**

One of the most compelling aspects of working with the CLR is that even poorly written code is unlikely to cause your program to crash. Because all memory is accessed through references, array boundaries are maintained and checked on access, and direct pointers into memory are a thing of the past,[12] it is almost impossible to cause a program error by writing to the wrong block of memory. This is not to say, however, that programs are now guaranteed error-free, but that errors are recognized by the runtime and can be dealt with programmatically.

Whenever errors are detected by the runtime, such as a divide by zero or a failure to connect to a database, an exception is thrown. Ideally, your ASP.NET pages and components should trap any potential exceptions and decide what to do for recovery where the exception occurred. Often, however, programs do not check for all potential exceptions, so any unhandled exceptions propagate up the call stack to a top-level exception handler provided by ASP.NET. If you receive an unhandled exception when you are running on the server machine, ASP.NET will print a useful diagnostic message containing a stack trace and source code showing the location the error was generated. If your application is accessed remotely when an unhandled exception occurs, however, your clients will see an error page that looks like the one shown in Figure 5-7.

As a developer, you should be embarrassed if your clients ever see this page. Not only does it state that an unhandled error occurred on the server, but it gives advice on how to configure the application to avoid showing this page again. The second piece of advice given by this page is one you should always follow: Include a `customErrors` element in your configuration file that provides a redirection to your own internal error handling page so that clients never see this page. The only disadvantage to this solution is that you lose the exception information when ASP.NET redirects

---

12. Note that it is still possible to use pointers in C# with code that is marked as "unsafe," and managed C++ still works directly with pointers. Code written with pointers is known as unverifiable code and can be prevented from running at all by imposing the appropriate Code Access Security restriction. Most code written for ASP.NET applications will be verifiable C# or VB.NET code.

FIGURE 5-7: Default ASP.NET Display for Unhandled Exceptions

clients to the default error page you specify, so there is no way to log information about the error or to give clients information to pass along to you so that you can analyze what went wrong.

To deal with this lack of error information in your default redirection page, you can provide a handler for the Error event of the HttpApplication class. This event is issued whenever there is an unhandled exception, and it is called before the internal ASP.NET unhandled event code executes, giving you the chance to deal with the error yourself and perhaps not display an error page at all. To add a handler to this even, create a `global.asax` file, and define a function named `Application_Error`, as shown in Listing 5-5. By calling the `ClearError()` method of the `Http-Context` class, you can prevent ASP.NET's unhandled exception code from ever being executed. Be warned, however, that calling `ClearError()` also prevents any redirection to other error pages you may have defined for specific HTTP error codes.

LISTING 5-5: Dealing with Unhandled Exceptions

```
<!-- global.asax -->
<%@ Application Language='C#' %>
<script runat=server>
protected void Application_Error(object src, EventArgs e)
{
  Exception ex = Server.GetLastError();
  // do something with the error here, such as
  // writing to the event log
  // The following line writes the error message
  // to the event log with a source of "MyApp"
  // Note that the "MyApp" source must be preregistered
  EventLog.WriteEntry("MyApp", ex.Message,
                      EventLogEntryType.Error);

  // At this point you could call:
  // Context.ClearError();
  // to clear the error and continue execution.
  // In general, you don't want to do this, because it will
  // prevent ASP.NET from redirecting to your error pages
}
</script>
```

The one other possible approach, which gives you the best of both worlds, is to look at the error in your `Error` handler, and if it is an unhandled exception, perform a `Server.Transfer()` to a custom error page you have built that displays information to users about the unhandled exception, which they could then relay to you. If it is any other type of error, just let it pass through, and ASP.NET will take care of redirecting users to the appropriate error page. It is important to perform the `Server.Transfer()` to the error page to retain the exception information, because performing a `Server.Redirect()` cause a round-trip back to the client, and the error information will be lost. Listing 5-6 shows the technique for performing the test on the exception and executing a transfer to the error page, and Listing 5-7 shows the sample error page that then has access to the exception information. Note that the exception typically is passed through the `Inner-Exception` field of the `Exception` class.

LISTING 5-6: Retaining Exception Information

```
// in global.asax
protected void Application_Error(Object sender, EventArgs e) {
  if (Server.GetLastError() is HttpUnhandledException)
    Server.Transfer("MyErrorPage.aspx");

  // Otherwise, we fall through, and the normal ASP.NET
  // error handling takes over
}
```

LISTING 5-7: Accessing Exception Information in an Error Page

```
<!- MyErrorPage.aspx ->
<%@ Page Language='C#' %>
<html>
<h1>My error page</h1>
<%
Exception ex = Server.GetLastError();
    if (ex != null)
    {
        string err="";
        if (ex.InnerException != null)
        Response.Output.Write("The error was: {0}",
                    ex.InnerException.Message);
}
%>
</html>
```

SUMMARY

ASP.NET provides a welcome set of new diagnostic tools to Web application development. The shift from interpretation to compilation means that all the debugging facilities available for standard application development are now available for Web application development too. Page and application tracing provide comprehensive diagnostic output for any page in an application, and generating custom trace messages is a great way to track problems in an application. The installation of ASP.NET also includes a number of performance monitor counters that track virtually every aspect of an application. Finally, it is possible to specify custom error pages to display to users when things inadvertently go wrong.

6

Validation

IN ADDITION TO visual controls, discussed in Chapter 2, which render HTML based on their current state, ASP.NET provides a set of validation controls, which make it simple to add even sophisticated validation to any page. These controls enforce validation constraints on user-populated form data through both client-side and server-side techniques, and are easy to customize in their appearance and their behavior.

6.1 Form Validation

It is common and often critical for Web forms to validate user data entry. Forms are used to collect data from users to be stored in databases, and the types of information stored must match the types of the fields in the database used to store them. Furthermore, there are often dependencies on data entered by a user that should be validated as the data is entered, such as checking to be sure that a user entered a password identically in two separate fields. A good form should strive to make it easy to enter correct data and hard to enter bad data, through a combination of client-side scripting and server-side validation.

Figure 6-1 shows a sample Web form implementing validation. Client-side scripting is used to highlight the fields in which there are errors (the e-mail address is not formatted correctly, and the user neglected to fill in the day phone number). Finally, the form provides a summary of all the errors

Account information:

First name: Foo

Last name: Bar

E-mail address: foobar   ←oops!
(e.g. joe@foo.com)

Password: ●●●
(4 to 10 characters)

Re-enter password: ●●●●●●

Shipping Address

Company:

Address Line 1: nowhere

Address Line 2:

City: Wonderland

State/Province: NH

Zip/Postal Code: 88998

Country: United States

Day Phone: ←oops!

Submit

Please correct the following errors:

- E-mail must be of the form joe@develop.com.
- The two passwords you entered did not match, please reenter
- Day Phone must be filled in.

FIGURE 6-1: Sample Form with Validation Errors

in a bulleted list on the side, with a request to the user to correct the errors before resubmitting the form.

6.1.1 Client-Side Validation

Form validation can take place on the client side, on the server side, or ideally on both. Validation on the client side is useful because it reduces the number of round-trips necessary for a user to complete a form successfully and can provide immediate feedback to the user as she enters the data (such as highlighting fields that are incorrect in red).

Listing 6-1 shows one example of performing client-side validation with two fields that are validated using client-side scripting. If the user tries to submit the form without entering her name or e-mail address, red text will appear next to the invalid field, indicating that it must be filled in before submitting the form will work.

LISTING 6-1: Client-Side Script Validation Example

```
<!- ClientScriptValidate.htm ->
<html>
<head>
<script language=javascript>
function checkForm()
{
  var ret = false;
  if (document.all["cname"].value == "")
    document.all["err_cname"].style.visibility = "visible";
  else if (document.all["email"].value == "")
    document.all["err_email"].style.visibility = "visible";
  else
    ret = true;
  return ret;
}
</script>
</head>

<form name="SIGNUP" method="post"
      onSubmit="return checkForm()">
<table cellspacing=0 cellpadding=1 border=0>
<tr valign=top>
  <td align=right><b>Name:</b></td>
  <td><input id="cname" /></td>
  <td><span id="err_cname"
            style="visibility:hidden;color:red">
      Please enter a name here</span></td></tr>
<tr valign=top>
  <td align=right><b>E-mail address:</b></td>
  <td><input id="email" /></td>
  <td><span id="err_email"
            style="visibility:hidden;color:red">
      Please enter your email here</span></td></tr>
</table>
<input type=submit value="sign up!" />
</form>
</body>
</html>
```

It is important to note that client-side validation should never be used as the sole source of validation for two reasons. First, it requires that the client browser support scripting, which may not always be the case. And second, client-side scripting can be easily subverted by a malicious user to submit bad data, perhaps corrupting your database. This is why client-side validation is most often used in conjunction with server-side validation.

6.1.2 Server-Side Validation

Before saving data entered by a user, the server should always validate it. Whether that means verifying that an e-mail address has an "@" sign in it or ensuring that the phone number contains only digits, it guarantees that any data you are storing will be consistent. Where you do this validation depends on your server implementation, but it is important for the server to be able to redisplay the form to the user if it does encounter errors.

6.1.3 Validation Observations

Validation is performed in an ad hoc way in most Web applications today. The goal of the ASP.NET validation controls is to provide a generic way to perform validation without compromising flexibility. To that end, it is useful to summarize some of the fundamental elements of Web validation so that we can verify that they are incorporated in the ASP.NET validation control scheme.

Many validation schemes involve placing error messages next to the offending input element. This makes it obvious to the user which field is in error. For convenience, all the problems with the data a user has entered in a form are often summarized in a list or paragraph somewhere on the page. It is important that both client-side and server-side validation be incorporated when possible. For any particular form field, we may want to perform multiple types of validation and display a different error message depending on the particular validation that failed. For example, we might want to display a message such as "Please enter an e-mail address" if the user has neglected to enter an e-mail address, but we would want a message such as "The e-mail address is not formatted correctly" if the user has given us a badly formatted e-mail address. We also want to be able to validate interdependent fields. For example, we may want to verify that a password field and a password verification field contain the same value. Finally, it is convenient to use regular expressions when performing validation.

6.2 Validation Control Architecture

Validation controls provide a simple, yet flexible way of validating form data on both the client and the server. To use a validation control, you add it to your form where you would like an error indicator to be displayed, typically adjacent to the field it is validating. You then associate it with another control on the page to validate, and when the user interacts with the form, the validation control enforces its validation on the control, both on the client, using client-side JavaScript, and the server, all with just one control. As an example, Listing 6-2 shows the use of a `RequiredField-Validator` control to validate that a field contains a value. In this case, we are validating that the `TextBox` with an ID equal to _name is not left blank.

LISTING 6-2: Adding a RequiredFieldValidator Control to a Form

```
<asp:TextBox id="_name" runat=server/>
<asp:RequiredFieldValidator
    ControlToValidate="_name"
    Display="Static"
    InitialValue=""
    runat=server
    ErrorMessage="The name field must be completed.">
***
</asp:RequiredFieldValidator>
```

Note that the `ControlToValidate` property of the validation control associates it with the `TextBox` with the identifier _name in this case. The `ErrorMessage` property contains the string that is used in the summary of errors for a page. We will see how this is used when we discuss the `ValidationSummary` control. Finally, the HTML that you place within the validation control (in our case, just the text character "*") is what is displayed when the validation fails. It is your job to place the validation control at the location where this error HTML should appear—very often this will be in a table cell adjacent to the input control it is validating. If you neglect to place any HTML in the body of the validation control, it will display the `ErrorMessage` string both at the location of the control and in the `ValidationSummary` control, if there is one.

The `Display` property of a validation control indicates whether the value of this control should occupy space when it is not being shown. If this is set to `static`, the validation control renders as a span element whose visibility style attribute is toggled between `hidden` and `visible`. If it is set to `dynamic`, the control renders as a span element whose display style is toggled between `none` and `inline`. The difference between these two is that setting it to dynamic causes the span element to not occupy space on the form when it is not visible. You may want to specify dynamic if you have more than one validation control associated with a field, only one of which will ever display a message at a time (such as validating that a field is not empty and that it has a correctly formatted telephone number). You could also specify none for the Display property if the control never displayed any HTML error message (perhaps it displays only errors in the summary of errors for a page). Figure 6-2 shows the two renderings of a Required-FieldValidator control with different Display attribute values.

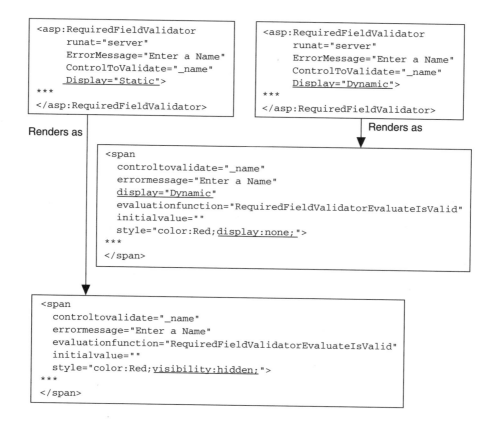

FIGURE 6-2: Validation Control Rendering

6.2.1 **Page Validation**

Adding a validation control to a form enables both client-side (for browsers that support it) and server-side validation. Server-side validation occurs once a page has been loaded and all the controls on the page have had their values restored. The Page class maintains a list of all the validation controls defined on that page in its Validators collection. Each validation control implements the IValidator interface, shown in Listing 6-3. This interface defines two properties, ErrorMessage and IsValid, and a method called Validate().

LISTING 6-3: The IValidator Interface

```
public interface IValidator
{
  string ErrorMessage {get; set;}
  bool IsValid {get; set;}
  void Validate();
}
```

Invoking the Validate() method on a validation control requests the control to execute its validation algorithm. The Page class also exposes a top-level Validate() method that can be used to collectively invoke all Validate() methods on all validation controls on that page. Similarly, the Page class exposes a Boolean property, IsValid, indicating whether or not all the validation controls succeeded their validation on that page. Figure 6-3 shows this validation control architecture.

As soon as you place a validation control on a page, it is imperative that you check the IsValid flag of the Page class before using any of the data posted by the client. It is a common misconception that if validation fails on a page, the code for that page will not execute. On the contrary, the only thing that happens when server-side validation fails is that the IsValid flag of the Page class is set to false, and each validation control that failed renders itself as a visible span so that the error indicator shows up when the page is redisplayed to the user.

It is also important to realize exactly when server-side validation occurs. The IsValid flag will be set properly after the validation controls have had

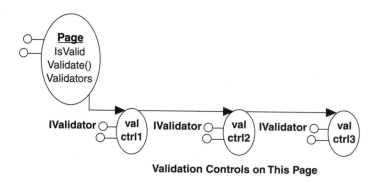

FIGURE 6-3: Validation Control Architecture

their `Validate()` routines invoked, which will happen implicitly in the `Page` class immediately after the `Load` event fires. This means that if you are looking at data submitted by the user in a handler for the `Load` event, there is no way for you to know whether it is valid yet or not. Instead, you should work with client-submitted data in server-side event handlers such as the `Click` event of a `Button`, at which point the `Page` will have performed validation, and you can safely check the `IsValid` property. (If you truly need to access client-submitted data in your `Load` handler, you can always explicitly invoke the `Validate()` method of your `Page` class.) Figure 6-4 shows the complete post-back sequence and where validation occurs in that sequence.

6.2.2 Client-Side Validation

If you try accessing a page with validation controls, you will notice that it performs validation within the browser and does not even submit the page until all the validated fields have acceptable data. ASP.NET performs client-side validation implicitly when you add validation controls to a page, as long as the client browser supports it.

As part of the HTML rendering of a `Page` with validation controls, ASP.NET generates a script reference to the file `WebUIValidation.js`, which contains a collection of validation routines. It also generates embedded client-side JavaScript in the rendered HTML page that interacts with

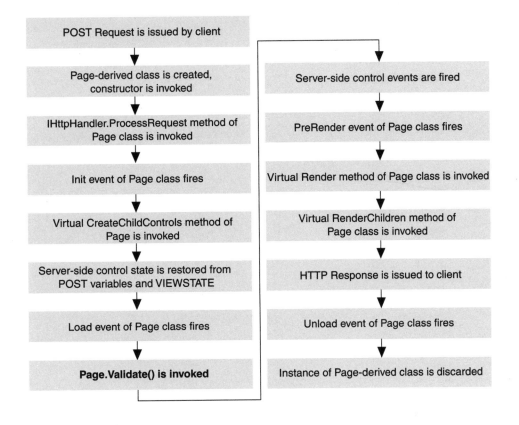

FIGURE 6-4: Server-Side Validation During Post-Back

the imported validation routines. Figure 6-5 shows the interaction of the various script elements involved with client-side validation.

One of the JavaScript elements that the Page class generates when it contains validation controls is a global array named Page_Validators. This array is initialized to contain references to all the span elements rendered by validation controls. Similarly, another global array, named Page_ValidationSummaries, contains all the ValidationSummary controls (usually just one) for that page. All the routines in the WebUIValidation.js file depend on these two arrays being populated when the page loads. The other thing a Page does when it renders with validation controls is to add an explicit call to Page_ClientValidate() in any controls that perform

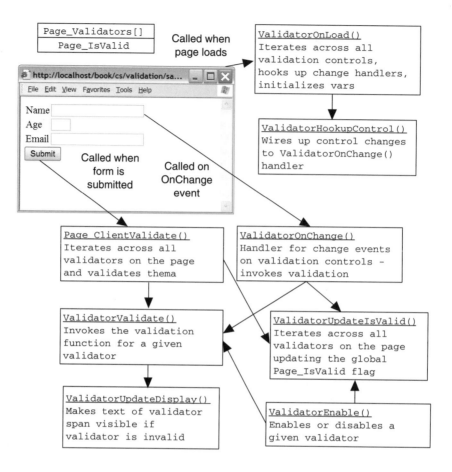

FIGURE 6-5: Script Elements of Client-Side Validation

post-backs (typically buttons). Finally, an explicit call to ValidatorOn-
Load() is injected into the rendered page that is called when the page
loads.

In the implementation of ValidatorOnLoad(), each of the span elements in the Page_Validators array is accessed, and the ControlToVal-
idate attribute is extracted. This control is then passed into a function called
ValidatorHookupControl, in which its onchange event is wired up to the
ValidatorOnChange() function. Now the actual validation can happen at
one of two times. First, it always happens when the user explicitly posts the

page back. When the entire page is submitted, the `Page_ClientVali-date()` routine is called, which iterates across all the validators, invoking their corresponding evaluation functions, and if any one of them fails, the submission of the form is aborted and the validation error messages are displayed. The other time validation can happen is when a control that has an associated validator loses focus and fires its `OnChange` event. This fires only the validator associated with that control. There is also logic in place to avoid enforcing `RequiredFieldValidator` controls until the page has been submitted (or has attempted to be submitted) at least once. This allows users to fill in fields in any order without being warned that a field is required.

6.3 Validation Controls

ASP.NET provides six built-in validation controls. These controls provide four types of validation, as well as a way to summarize errors and a way to construct your own validation algorithms.

The `BaseValidator` class is used as the base class for all the validation controls, providing a single generic implementation of many of the validation capabilities. Listing 6-4 shows a partial definition of the class. Note that it implements the `IValidator` interface and derives from `Label`. By deriving from the `Label` control, the `BaseValidator` class inherits the span-rendering capabilities of that class, which is convenient because all validation controls render as span elements. In addition, the `BaseValidator` class defines the `ErrorMessage` property used by the `ValidationSummary` control to display the collection of error messages for a form. It also defines the `ForeColor` property, which lets you change the color of the validation text (it defaults to red). The `Enabled` property of the `BaseValidator` class is a convenient way to disable individual validation controls.

LISTING 6-4: The BaseValidator Class

```
public abstract class BaseValidator : Label, IValidator
{
  protected BaseValidator();
      // Properties
```

continues

```
public static PropertyDescriptor
            GetValidationProperty(object component) {}
public ValidatorDisplay Display {get; set; }
public bool Enabled {override get; override set; }
public string ErrorMessage {get; set; }
public Color ForeColor {override get; override set; }
public bool IsValid {get; set; }
    // Methods
public void Validate();
protected void CheckControlValidationProperty(
            string name, string propertyName);
protected abstract bool EvaluateIsValid();
protected string GetControlRenderID(string name);
protected string GetControlValidationValue(string name);
protected void RegisterValidatorCommonScript();
protected void RegisterValidatorDeclaration();
//...
}
```

For a control to be validated with the validation controls, it must have the
`ValidationPropertyAttribute` attribute set to the field that is to be validated. Validation controls apply only to controls that can define a single
field that is to be validated, so controls such as grids cannot be used with validation controls. In addition, for the client-side validation to work for a control, its `value` attribute must evaluate to the field that is to be validated,
because the validation functions operate under this assumption. Figure 6-6
shows a list of all the controls that can be validated in ASP.NET.

Controls That Work With Validation

HTMLInputText

HTMLTextArea

HTMLSelect

HTMLInputFile

TextBox

DropDownList

ListBox

RadioButtonList

FIGURE 6-6: Controls That Can Be Used with Validation Controls

Six validation controls are available in ASP.NET. The `RequiredField-Validator`, as we have seen already, is used to verify that a field is not left empty. The `ValidationSummary` control is used to display a summary of all the error messages on a given form and optionally to display a client-side message box. The `CompareValidator` control is used for comparing the value of one field to the value of another field (or a constant). The `RangeValidator` control is used to verify that a field value falls within a given range. The `RegularExpressionValidator` control is used to verify the contents of a field against a regular expression, and finally the `Custom-Validator` control is used for executing your own validation algorithms.

It is important to note that for all these controls except the `Required-FieldValidator`, an empty field is considered valid. Thus, it is common to combine the `RequiredFieldValidator` control with other validation controls to enforce both population and some other form of validation. Table 6-1 shows the properties of each of the six validation controls and their associated values.

TABLE 6-1: Validation Controls and Their Properties

Validation Control	Properties	Values/Description
`RequiredFieldValidator`	-	-
`CompareValidator`	`Operator`	`Equal, NotEqual, GreaterThan, GreaterThanEqual, LessThan, LessThanEqual, DataTypeCheck`
	`Type`	`String, Currency, Date, Double, Integer`
	`ValueToCompare`	Constant value to compare to
	`ControlToCompare`	Other control to compare to

TABLE 6-1: Validation Controls and Their Properties (continued)

Validation Control	Properties	Values/Description
RangeValidator	MaximumValue	Constant value for upper bound
	MinimumValue	Constant value for lower bound
	Type	String, Currency, Date, Double, Integer
RegularExpression-Validator	Validation-Expression	Regular expression to validate against
CustomValidator	ServerValidate	Server-side validation routine
	ClientValidation-Function	Client-side validation routine
ValidationSummary	DisplayMode	BulletList, List, SingleParagraph
	HeaderText	Title text of summary
	ShowMessageBox	Display alert?
	ShowSummary	Display summary paragraph?

The ValidationSummary control culls all the ErrorMessages of each validation control on a page and displays them in a bullet list, a plain list, or a single paragraph format. Listing 6-5 shows the ValidationSummary control and its additional properties. The HeaderText property defines the title string for the summary of error messages. The ShowMessageBox property causes a message box with the summary of errors to appear when the user tries to submit a form that has validation errors. The ShowSummary property turns the summary on or off (you may want to turn it off if you elect to use the ShowMessageBox property). Finally, the DisplayMode property selects which of the three types of display you would like the summary to appear as. Listing 6-5 shows an example of using the `ValidationSum-mary` control, along with two `RequiredFieldValidator` controls to validate the text inputs.

LISTING 6-5: ValidationSummary Control Example

```
<!— File: ValidationSummary.aspx —>
<html><body>
<form runat=server>
<table cellspacing=0 cellpadding=2 border=0>
  <tr><td><table cellspacing=0 cellpadding=1 border=0>
    <tr><td align=right><b>Name:</b></td>
      <td><asp:TextBox id="cname" runat=server/></td>
        <td><asp:RequiredFieldValidator id="cnameValidator"
          ControlToValidate="cname"
          Display="Static"
          ErrorMessage="Name must be filled in."
          InitialValue="" runat=server>*
        </asp:RequiredFieldValidator>
      </td></tr>
    <tr><td align=right><b>Phone:</b></td>
      <td><asp:TextBox id="phone" runat=server/></td>
        <td><asp:RequiredFieldValidator id="phoneValidator"
          ControlToValidate="phone"
          Display="Static"
          ErrorMessage="Phone must be filled in."
          InitialValue="" runat=server>*
        </asp:RequiredFieldValidator>
      </td></tr>
    <tr><td></td>
      <td><input value="Enter" type=submit /></td>
    </tr></table><td>
      <asp:ValidationSummary id="valSum" runat=server
      HeaderText="Please correct the following errors:"
      ShowMessageBox="True"/></td></tr>
</table>
</form>
</body></html>
```

Listing 6-6 shows the `CompareValidator` control and its additional properties. The `Operator` property defines what comparison operation to perform, and the `Type` property specifies the type of the two values to compare. Either the `ValueToCompare` or the `ControlToCompare` property contains the value (or reference to a field containing the value) to compare with the target input. Listing 6-6 shows an example of using the `CompareValidator` control to verify that the user is over 21 years of age.

LISTING 6-6: CompareValidator Control Example

```
<!— File: CompareValidator.aspx —>
<%@ Page %>

<html>
<body>
<h1>Compare Validator Example</h1>
<form runat="server">
Age: <asp:TextBox id="_age" runat=server/>
<asp:CompareValidator id="ageValidator"
       ControlToValidate="_age"
       ValueToCompare="21"
       Type="Integer"
       Operator="GreaterThan" runat=server>
       You must be over 21!
</asp:CompareValidator>
<br/>
<input value="Enter" type=submit />
</form>
</body> </html>
```

Listing 6-7 shows the `RegularExpressionValidator` control with its one additional property: `ValidationExpression`. With this control, you can specify any JavaScript regular expression to validate a field. Listing 6-7 shows an example of validating a zip code to ensure that it is of the correct format. Table 6-2 shows some of the more common regular expression characters and their meaning.

LISTING 6-7: RegularExpressionValidator Control Example

```
<!— File: RegularExpressionValidator.aspx —>
<%@ Page %>

<html>
<body>
<h1>Regular Expression Validator Example</h1>
<form runat="server">
Zipcode:<asp:TextBox id="_zipcode"
runat=server/><asp:RegularExpressionValidator
     ControlToValidate="_zipcode"
     Display="static"
     ErrorMessage="Zip code must be of the form 11111-1111"
     InitialValue="" width="100%" runat=server
     ValidationExpression="\d{5}(-\d{4})?">**
</asp:RegularExpressionValidator>
<br/>
```

```
<input value="Enter" type=submit />
</form>
</body> </html>
```

TABLE 6-2: Some Regular Expression Characters and Their Meaning

Character	Meaning
[...]	Match any one character between brackets
[^...]	Match any one character not between brackets
\w	Match any word character [a–zA–Zo–9_]
\W	Match any whitespace character [^ \t\n\r\f\v]
\s	Match any non-whitespace character [^ \t\n\r\f\v]
\d	Match any digit [o–9]
\D	Match any nondigit character [^o–9]
[\b]	Match a literal backspace
{n,m}	Match the previous item ┈┈>= n times, <┈┈= m times
{n,}	Match the previous item ┈┈>= n times
{n}	Match the previous item exactly n times
?	Match zero or one occurrence of the previous item {o,1}
+	Match one or more occurrences of the previous item {1,}
*	Match zero or more occurrences of the previous item {o,}
|	Match the subexpression either on the left or the right
(...)	Group items together in a unit
^	Match the beginning of the string
$	Match the end of the string
\b	Match a word boundary
\B	Match a position that is not a word boundary

The `CustomValidator` control lets you define your own validation function to perform whatever arbitrary validation you would like on a field. In keeping with the other validation controls, you can provide both a client-side validation routine (in JavaScript) and a server-side validation routine. Listing 6-8 shows an example of using a `CustomValidator` control to verify that a number is divisible by three. Note that two script sections are defined—one client script and one server script—each containing a validation function that performs the same check on the incoming data. The client-side validation function is specified in the `ClientValidationFunction` property of the control, and the server-side validation function is specified as the event handler for the `ServerValidate` event by assigning the function name to the `OnServerValidate` property of the control. Note that the form of the validation function is always the same: `bool ValFunc(object source, object args);`. The `object` parameter is the validator element, and the `args` parameter is an object containing two properties, `Value` and `IsValid`.

LISTING 6-8: CustomValidator Control Example

```
<!- File: CustomValidator.aspx ->
<%@ Page Language="C#" %>
<script language=javascript>
<!-
function ValModThreeClient(source, args)
{
  if (args.value % 3)
    args.IsValid=false;
  else
    args.IsValid=true;
}
->
</script>

<script language="C#" runat=server>
void ValModThreeServer(object source,
                ServerValidateEventArgs e)
{
  e.IsValid = false;
  try
  {
    int num = Convert.ToInt32(e.Value);
    if (num % 3 == 0)
      e.IsValid = true;
```

```
  }
  catch (Exception)
  {}
}
</script>

<html>
<body>
<h1>Custom Validator Example</h1>
<form runat="server">
Number: <asp:TextBox id="_num" runat=server/>
<asp:CustomValidator id="numValidator"
       ControlToValidate="_num"
       Display="static"
       InitialValue=""
       ClientValidationFunction = "ValModThreeClient"
       OnServerValidate = "ValModThreeServer"
       width="100%"
       ErrorMessage="Please enter a value divisible by three"
runat=server/>
<br/>
<input value="Enter" type=submit />
</form>
</body> </html>
```

SUMMARY

Validation controls in ASP.NET relieve the tedium of enforcing validation on a page. Simply placing a validation control on a page and pointing it to another control to validate provides both client-side validation for clients that support it and server-side validation each time the page is posted back. Four validation controls are provided for performing standard validation tasks such as checking that required fields have been populated, comparing the value of one field with another, verifying that the contents of a field fall within a given range, and performing a regular expression check on the contents of a field. Another control is available to generate a list of errors encountered on a page, either in paragraph summary form, as an alert dialog box, or both. Finally, if none of these controls perform the validation you need, a custom validation control lets you specify whatever validation algorithms you want on both the client and the server.

■ 7 ■
Data Binding

T HIS CHAPTER COVERS the process of binding data to controls. ASP.NET introduces a new syntax for data binding that is convenient to use in conjunction with the ADO.NET `DataSet` and `DataReader` classes. While data can be bound to any control, several controls simplify the common case of data presentation, including the `DataGrid`, `Repeater`, and `DataList` controls. We look in detail at these three controls for data presentation, with particular focus on how to customize each control's appearance using templates.

This chapter focuses on the controls used in data binding and less on the details of ADO.NET. For a complete treatment of ADO.NET, see the book *Essential ADO.NET,* by Bob Beauchemin (Boston, Massachusets: Addison-Wesley, 2002).

7.1 Fundamentals

At its core, data binding is a very straightforward process. Controls that support data binding expose a property named `DataSource` and a method called `DataBind()`. When a page is loaded, the user of the control initializes the `DataSource` property to some collection of data, such as an array, a `DataReader`, or a `DataSet`. When the data source is ready to be read from, the user of the control calls the `DataBind()` method on the control, at which point the control reads in all the data from the data source, making a local copy of it. When the page is ultimately rendered, the control takes the cached data it retrieved from the data source and renders its contents into the response buffer in whatever format the control is built to provide. Figure 7-1 shows the data binding process for a control.

As we will see, it is possible to bind many different types of data sources, including simple collection classes and data readers connected to a database. The most common data source to bind is typically a data reader, however, because it is the most efficient means of transferring data from a database into a data-bound control. Several controls support data binding, including simple controls, such as the ListBox, and controls designed

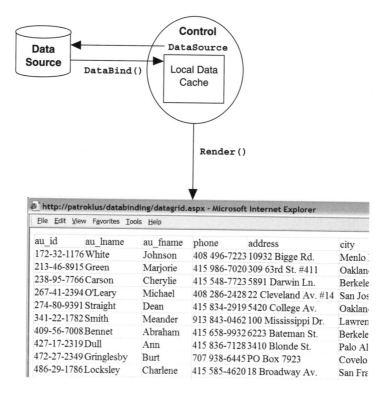

FIGURE 7-1: Data Binding Process

exclusively for data binding, such as the DataGrid and Repeater. As an example of a common use of data binding, Listing 7-1 shows a page that contains a DataGrid, which is data-bound to the "authors" table in the "pubs" database in SQL Server. This example uses the IDataReader interface to retrieve the data, and it takes care to invoke the DataBind() method immediately after the data reader is prepared and before it is closed.

LISTING 7-1: Binding a DataReader to a DataGrid

```
<!- File: DataGrid.aspx ->
<%@Page Language="C#" %>
<%@ Import Namespace="System.Data" %>
<%@ Import Namespace="System.Data.SqlClient" %>

<html>
<script language="C#" runat="server">
protected void Page_Load(Object src, EventArgs e)
{
  IDbConnection conn =
    new SqlConnection("server=.;uid=sa;pwd=;database=Pubs");

  IDbCommand cmd = conn.CreateCommand();
  cmd.CommandText = "SELECT * FROM Authors";

  try
  {
    conn.Open();
    IDataReader reader = cmd.ExecuteReader();
    gd1.DataSource = reader;
    gd1.DataBind();
  }
  finally
  {
    conn.Dispose();
  }
}
</script>

<body>
<form runat=server>
  <asp:DataGrid id="gd1" runat=server />
</form>
</body>
</html>
```

7.2 **Data Binding Controls**

Many server controls in ASP.NET support data binding for populating their contents. These controls expose a `DataSource` property to be initialized to any object that supports the `IEnumerable` interface, as well as `DataTables` and `DataSets`. When the control's `DataBind()` method is invoked, the collection is traversed, and the contents of the control are filled with whatever was in the collection. Like the `Render` method of controls, the `DataBind` method invokes `DataBind` on any of the control's child controls. So invoking the `Page`'s top-level `DataBind()` method implicitly invokes all the `Data-Bind()` methods for all controls on that page. Alternatively, you can elect to invoke each control's `DataBind()` method independently. Figure 7-2 shows a list of all the controls that support data binding, and some of the most common classes that support `IEnumerable` and are thus suitable for attaching to a data-bound control.

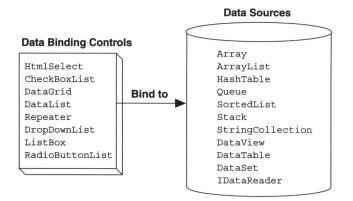

Data Sources

Data Binding Controls

```
HtmlSelect
CheckBoxList
DataGrid
DataList
Repeater
DropDownList
ListBox
RadioButtonList
```

Bind to →

```
Array
ArrayList
HashTable
Queue
SortedList
Stack
StringCollection
DataView
DataTable
DataSet
IDataReader
```

FIGURE 7-2: Controls Capable of Data Binding, and Some Common Collections to Bind To

Note that the list of data sources includes many collection classes in addition to the ADO.NET classes. This means that binding data to a control does not necessarily mean that you are retrieving data from a database; it could just as well mean that you have manually populated an array of values that you want displayed in a list box. Listing 7-2 shows a page that binds a hand-constructed `ArrayList` to a number of server controls, and Figure 7-3 shows an instance of this page running.

LISTING 7-2: Binding an ArrayList to Several Server Controls

```
<!- File: ArrayListBind.aspx ->
<%@ Page Language="C#" %>
<html>
<body>
<head>
<script runat=server>
  void Page_Load(Object sender, EventArgs e)
  {
    if (!Page.IsPostBack) {
      ArrayList vals = new ArrayList();
      vals.Add("v1");
      vals.Add("v2");
      vals.Add("v3");
      vals.Add("v4");
      s1.DataSource  = vals;
      cbl1.DataSource= vals;
      dd1.DataSource = vals;
      lb1.DataSource = vals;
      rbl1.DataSource= vals;
      DataBind();
    }  }
</script>
</head>
<form runat=server>
  <Select id="s1" runat=server /> <br/>
  <asp:CheckBoxList id="cbl1" runat=server /> <br/>
  <asp:DropDownList id="dd1" runat=server /> <br/>
  <asp:ListBox id="lb1" runat=server /> <br/>
  <asp:RadioButtonList id="rbl1" runat=server /> <br/>
</form>
</body>
</html>
```

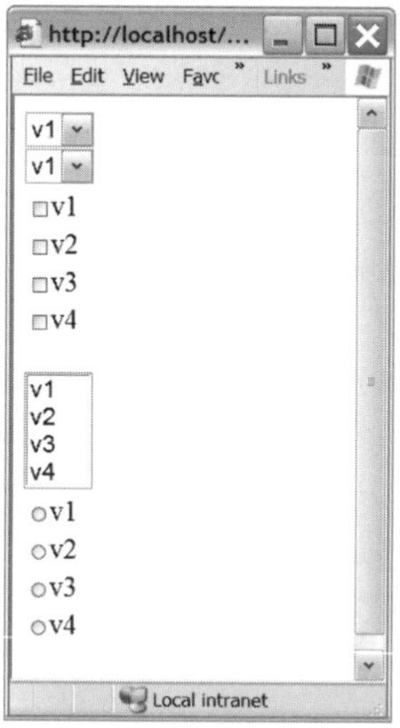

FIGURE 7-3: ArrayListBind.aspx Page Instance

7.3 Binding to Database Sources

As we have seen, it is possible to bind to many different types of collections in .NET. The most common type of binding by far, however, is to bind to a result set retrieved from a database query. ADO.NET provides two ways of retrieving result sets from a database: the streaming `IDataReader` interface and the disconnected `DataSet` class. We will look at each of these in turn.

7.3.1 IDataReader Binding

The most efficient way to retrieve data for binding from a database is to use the streaming `IDataReader` interface from ADO.NET. This interface provides access to the results of a query in a stream, in forward-only fashion, and makes no additional copy of the data. In all the existing ADO.NET data providers, the data reader implementation classes also support `IEnumerable` so that they are compatible with data binding, and in general, it should be safe to assume that any data reader implementation provides an `IEnumerable` interface implementation as well.

In our first example of using a data reader, shown in Listing 7-1, we bound to a `DataGrid`, which provides a tabular rendering of the data. If

you are trying to bind a data reader to a single column control such as a
`ListBox` or a `DropDownList`, however, it is ambiguous which fields of the
result set should be mapped to the strings and values of the control. To deal
with this, controls like the `DropDownList` define two additional fields:
`DataTextField` and `DataValueField`. These fields can be initialized to
the appropriate column names of the data reader to specify the column
from which the data should be drawn when the control populates itself
with data. Listing 7-3 shows an example of binding an `IDataReader` to a
drop-down list.

LISTING 7-3: Binding a Data Reader to a DropDownList

```
<!- File: DataReaderBind.aspx ->
<%@Page Language="C#" %>
<%@ Import Namespace="System.Data" %>
<%@ Import Namespace="System.Data.SqlClient" %>

<html>
<script language="C#" runat="server">
protected void Page_Load(Object src, EventArgs e)
{
  if (!IsPostBack)
  {
    IDbConnection conn =
    new SqlConnection("server=.;uid=sa;pwd=;database=Pubs");

    IDbCommand cmd = conn.CreateCommand();
    cmd.CommandText = "SELECT * FROM Authors";

    try
    {
      conn.Open();
      IDataReader reader = cmd.ExecuteReader();
      _authors.DataSource = reader;
      _authors.DataTextField = "au_lname";
      _authors.DataValueField = "au_id";
      _authors.DataBind();
    }
    finally
    {
      conn.Dispose();
    }
  }
  else
```

continues

```
      {
        _message.Text =
                  string.Format("You selected employee #{0}",
                                _authors.SelectedItem.Value);
      }
  }
  </script></head>

  <form runat=server>
    <asp:DropDownList id="_authors" runat=server />
    <br/>
    <asp:Label id="_message" runat=server/>
    <br/>
    <input type=submit value="Submit" />
  </form>
  </body>
  </html>
```

In this example, we are only populating the `DropDownList` control if the incoming request is the initial GET request to the page, not a subsequent POST back to the same page. By default, all the data-bound controls retain their state across post-backs, so it is not necessary to repopulate them on a post-back. Also note in this example that we are able to associate two data values with each item in the `DropDownList`. The `DataTextField` determines what string is displayed in the control, and the `DataValueField` determines what value is associated with that field. This is a convenient mechanism for retaining primary-key information for table values without resorting to additional data structures. Figure 7-4 shows a sample instance of this page running.

7.3.2 DataSet Binding

It is also common to bind `DataSets` to controls for display. Because a `DataSet` can represent the results of multiple database queries, however, you need to specify which portion of the `DataSet` should be used for binding. If you simply bind to the entire `DataSet`, the default view of the first table in the `DataSet` is used. If you want more control over which table within a `DataSet` to use during binding, data-bound controls support an additional field, `DataMember`, that indicates which "set" of data to bind to the control. For a `DataSet`, this means which table to bind. Alternatively, you can be explicit about it and bind to a table within a `DataSet`, in which

FIGURE 7-4: DataReaderBind.aspx Page Running

case the default view of that table is used. Or you can be even more explicit and use the `DataView` that provides a "view" into a data set and can be created with custom sorting and filtering rules.

Listing 7-4 shows an example of binding data from a `DataSet` to a pair of controls. Note that the first control is bound directly to the `DataSet`, which implicitly binds to the default view of the `DataSet`. The second control is bound to an explicitly created `DataView`, whose `Filter` property has been populated to show only authors with last names beginning with G and whose `Sort` property has been set to the `au_id` field of the table.

LISTING 7-4: Binding to a DataView

```
<!— File: DataViewBind.aspx —>
<%@ Page Language="C#" %>
<%@ Import Namespace="System.Data" %>
<%@ Import Namespace="System.Data.SqlClient" %>

<html>
<script language="C#" runat="server">
protected void Page_Load(Object src, EventArgs e)
{
  if (!IsPostBack)
  {
    SqlConnection conn =
```

continues

```
    new SqlConnection("server=.;uid=sa;pwd=;database=pubs");
    SqlDataAdapter da =
        new SqlDataAdapter("select * from Authors", conn);

    DataSet ds = new DataSet();
    da.Fill(ds, "Authors");

    _lb1.DataSource = ds;
    _lb1.DataTextField = "au_lname";
    _lb1.DataValueField = "au_id";

    DataView view = new DataView(ds.Tables["Authors"]);
    view.RowFilter = "au_lname like 'G%'";
    view.Sort = "au_lname";
    _lb2.DataSource = view;
    _lb2.DataTextField = "au_lname";
    _lb2.DataValueField = "au_id";

    DataBind();
  }
  else
  {
    _message.Text =
      string.Format("LB1 = {0}, LB2 = {1}",
                    _lb1.SelectedItem.Value,
                    _lb2.SelectedItem.Value);
  }
}
</script>

<body>
<form runat=server>
  <asp:ListBox id="_lb1" runat=server /> <br/>
  <asp:ListBox id="_lb2" runat=server /> <br/>
  <asp:Label id="_message" runat=server/> <br/>
  <input type=submit value="Submit"/>
</form>
</body>
</html>
```

The biggest difference between binding to a `DataSet` and binding to data readers is that the `DataSet` makes a local copy of the data, and the connection to the database is closed immediately after the call to the `Sql-DataAdapter.Fill()` method completes. Figure 7-5 shows the `DataView-Bind.aspx` page running.

FIGURE 7-5: DataViewBind.aspx Page Instance

7.3.3 **DataSet versus DataReader for Data Binding**

As we have seen, both the `DataSet` and the `DataReader` can be used to
bind data to a control, but when should you choose one over the other? A
good rule of thumb to answer this question is, if you are not taking advantage of the `DataSet`'s cache of the data, you should probably use a
`DataReader`. If you use a `DataSet` simply to retrieve data from a data
source and then immediately bind it to a control, subsequently discarding
the `DataSet`, you are creating an unnecessary duplicate copy of the data,
since all data-bound controls keep their own local copy of any data to
which they are bound.

   In addition, because data-bound controls guarantee that they will retain
any data you bind to them, even across post-backs, it is quite easy to generate three distinct copies of the data in-memory in the server, which can be
problematic for large rowsets. The first copy of the data is loaded into the
`DataSet`'s cache after it is filled from the data source. The second copy is
created when you perform a `DataBind` on the control, which takes the data
from the `DataSet` and make its own local copy using its own internal storage mechanism. The third, and final, copy exists in the `ViewState` state
bag, which the control populates with its data to ensure that it can be fully
restored on subsequent post-backs. Figure 7-6 shows this inefficient data
propagation scenario.

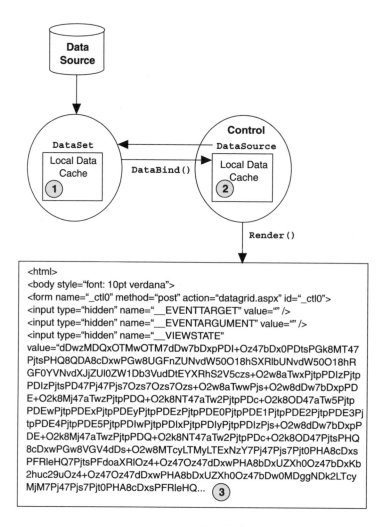

FIGURE 7-6: The Hazards of Naïve Data Binding

To avoid this duplication of data during data binding, you can take two steps. First, use a `DataReader` in place of a `DataSet` when you are doing nothing with the data but binding it to a control. Second, disable the view state of the data-bound control by setting the control's `EnableViewState` flag to `false` (although there are caveats to doing this, discussed later). Performing both of these steps removes the two extra copies of the data, leaving only the local copy managed by the control, as shown in Figure 7-7.

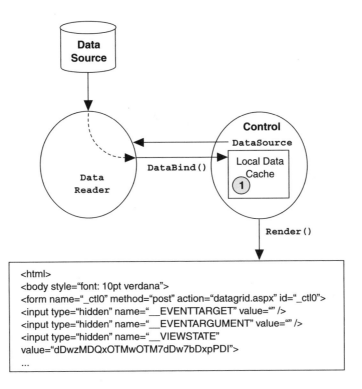

FIGURE 7-7: Efficient Data Binding

Unfortunately, you cannot always disable the view state of a control without impacting its behavior, which you may be relying on in your application. For example, server-side events rely on the EnableViewState flag being enabled for a control, so if you have added handlers for any server-side events issued by a data-bound control, you have no choice but to leave view state enabled. Also, by disabling view state, you must take care to explicitly repopulate the data-bound control on each request. It is no longer sufficient merely to populate it once on the initial GET request and assume that it will retain its state on subsequent POST requests to the same page. If you can live with these restrictions, however, you can save significant bandwidth space and server memory by disabling view state on your data-bound controls.

There are also occasions where using the `DataSet` makes more sense than using a `DataReader`. As mentioned earlier, if you are taking advantage of the fact that the `DataSet` creates a local cache of the data, by all means use it. One case in which to consider a `DataSet` is when you bind one set of data to multiple controls, especially by taking advantage of the `DataView` mechanism of the `DataSet` to provide filtering and ordering during the binding process. Another appealing application of the `DataSet` is to keep an instance of a `DataSet` in the cache (discussed in Chapter 9) for binding to controls without having to go back to the database over and over. This works especially well for small result sets, such as lookup tables.

7.4 DataGrid

Of all the controls provided by ASP.NET, the `DataGrid` is by far the most complex, with literally hundreds of properties, methods, and events. Understanding the full set of features of this control is a daunting prospect. Instead of enumerating all the various options available for the `DataGrid`, this section presents some of the more commonly used techniques for presenting tabular data with the `DataGrid`. For a full reference of all the available styles and features, refer to the MSDN documentation[13] for the `DataGrid` class.

To begin with, the `DataGrid` control displays tabular data from a data source. In its simplest usage, as shown earlier in Listing 7-1, you can use a `DataGrid` to quickly generate a table rendering of any data source. Its object model includes a collection of columns, a header, and a footer, all of which can be customized to create the appearance you need. `Columns` can be auto-generated from the underlying data source schema, where each column of the data source table generates a column in the grid. Alternatively, you can be explicit about which columns to display by disabling the `AutoGenerateColumns` property and adding `BoundColumns` to the `Columns` collection. Figure 7-8 demonstrates a `DataGrid` with `AutoGenerateColumns` set to `false` and with several other style attributes to alter the appearance.

---

13. MSDN documentation is available through Visual Studio .NET or at http://msdn.microsoft.com.

```
<asp:DataGrid id="gd1" runat=server
     GridLines=None
     AutoGenerateColumns=false
     CellSpacing=2
     HeaderStyle-BackColor=limegreen
     FooterStyle-BackColor=thistle
     ShowFooter=true
     HorizontalAlign=Center
     ItemStyle-BackColor=moccasin
     ItemStyle-HorizontalAlign=Center>
   <Columns>
     <asp:BoundColumn HeaderText="Employee Name" DataField="Name" />
     <asp:BoundColumn HeaderText="Age" DataField="Age" />
   </Columns>
</asp:DataGrid>
```

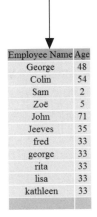

FIGURE 7-8: A DataGrid with Custom BoundColumns

7.4.1 **DataGrid Paging**

Paging of data is a common approach to giving clients control over how much data they want to view at a time. Instead of generating one giant table with all of the data, you can generate a table with a fixed number of rows and specify an interface to navigate forward and backward through the data source.

To enable paging on a `DataGrid`, you must set the `AllowPaging` property to `true`, and you must provide a handler for the `PageIndexChanged` event of the `DataGrid`. In the `PageIndexChanged` event handler, you need to set the `CurrentPageIndex` property of the `DataGrid` to the `New-PageIndex` passed in via the `DataGridPageChangedEventArgs` parameter to the handler. Without doing anything else, you will have a paged grid with a default page size of 10. However, for this default paging mechanism to work, you must supply the `DataGrid` with the complete set of records each time its `DataBind` method is called, because this is how it calculates how many pages to display. Unfortunately, although this gives the appearance of paging, it loses the main benefit of paging, which is to avoid retrieving all of the data with each access to the page. And even worse, this technique implicitly sends all of the data associated with the `DataGrid` through the `__VIEWSTATE` field across each post-back.

A more compelling alternative is to add a little more logic to your `Data-Grid` and use its custom paging capabilities. You enable custom paging by setting the `AllowCustomPaging` property to `true`. It is then left up to you to manage the page count and page navigation by setting the `Virtual-ItemCount` property of the `DataGrid` to the total number if items it should display, and then when performing data binding, by determining what subset of the underlying data source to retrieve based on the current page index. Figure 7-9 shows a sample custom paging data grid in action.

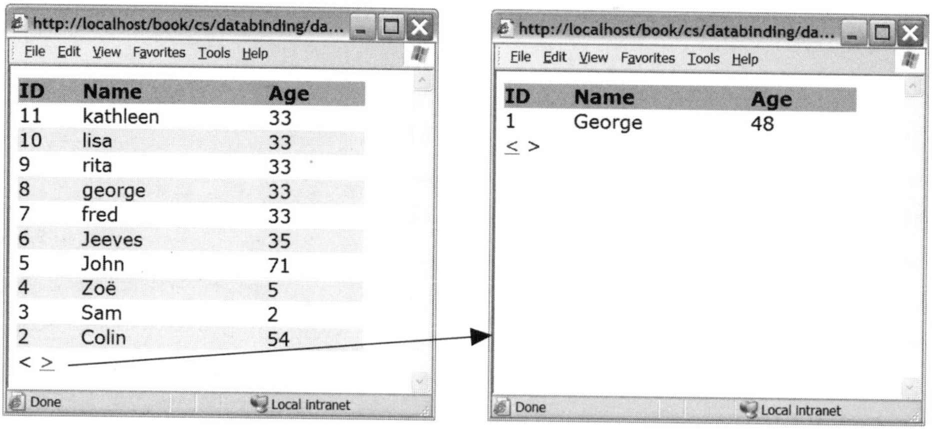

FIGURE 7-9: Custom Paging DataGrid in Action

Listing 7-5 shows the page with the `DataGrid` declaration supporting custom paging (additional style attributes are not shown). Note that `AllowCustomPaging` has been set to `true`, and the `PageSize` has been explicitly specified, in addition to `AllowPaging` and the `PageIndex-Changed` handler necessary for standard paging.

LISTING 7-5: Page with a DataGrid Implementing Custom Paging

```
<!- File: DataGridPage.aspx ->
<%@ Page language="C#" Debug="True"
     Src="DataGridPage.aspx.cs" Inherits="DataGridPage" %>
<html>
<body>
<form runat="server">

  <asp:DataGrid id=_gd1
         Width="90%"
         Runat="server"
         AllowCustomPaging='true'
         AllowPaging='true'
         OnPageIndexChanged="Grid_Change"
         PageSize=10
    />
</form>
</body>
</html>
```

Listing 7-6 shows the code-behind class that implements the logic behind the custom paging `DataGrid`. When this page is loaded for the first time, it queries the data source to discover how many items are in the collection to be displayed by the paged `DataGrid`. This number is assigned to the `VirtualItemCount` of the `DataGrid` so that it knows how many pages of data there are and can change the page navigation indicators appropriately. The total count of items is obtained via a private method called `GetItemCount` that issues a "SELECT COUNT(*)..." query to discover the number of rows in the underlying table. The logic for the `GetItemCount` function varies from application to application depending on the underlying data source, but this is one common approach.

Perhaps the most important piece of logic in this class is provided by the `BindGrid()` method, used to populate the `DataGrid` whenever necessary.

This function issues a query against the data source for precisely the number of rows necessary to display the current page. Again, the logic in this function varies from application to application. In this particular application, the ID field of the Employees table is a linear indexer, so to retrieve records 11 through 20, you can query the table for records whose IDs range from 11 through 20.

Finally, the Grid_Change method is our handler for the PageIndex-Changed event of the DataGrid. In it, we assign the CurrentPageIndex property of the DataGrid to the incoming NewPageIndex of the Data-GridPageChangedEventArgs parameter. We also calculate the beginning index of the underlying data source to be retrieved by taking the current page index (plus 1), multiplying it by the page size, and subtracting the result from the total VirtualItemCount. This starting index is saved in a field of our class called _startIndex, used during the BindGrid method to retrieve the correct rows from the underlying table.

LISTING 7-6: Code-Behind Class Implementing Custom Paging Logic

```
// File: DataGridPage.aspx.cs
public class DataGridPage : Page
{
  private    int       _startIndex = 0;
  protected DataGrid _gd1;

  protected void Page_Load(object Src, EventArgs e)
  {
    if (!IsPostBack)
    {
      _gd1.VirtualItemCount = GetItemCount();
      _startIndex = _gd1.VirtualItemCount-_gd1.PageSize;
      BindGrid();
    }
  }

  private int GetItemCount()
  {
    int count = 0;

    SqlConnection conn =
```

```
    new SqlConnection("server=.;uid=sa;pwd=;database=Test");

  SqlCommand cmd =
    new SqlCommand("SELECT COUNT(*) FROM Employees", conn);

  try
  {
    conn.Open();
    count = (int)cmd.ExecuteScalar();
  }
  finally { conn.Dispose(); }

  return count;
}

private void BindGrid()
{
  string select = "SELECT * FROM Employees WHERE ID > " +
                  _startIndex + " AND ID <= " +
                  (_startIndex + _gd1.PageSize) +
                  " ORDER BY ID DESC";
  SqlConnection conn =
  new SqlConnection("server=.;uid=sa;pwd=;database=Test");

  SqlCommand cmd = new SqlCommand(select, conn);

  try
  {
    conn.Open();
    IDataReader reader = cmd.ExecuteReader();
    _gd1.DataSource = reader;
    _gd1.DataBind();
  }
  finally { conn.Dispose(); }
}

protected void Grid_Change(object sender,
                           DataGridPageChangedEventArgs e)
{
  _gd1.CurrentPageIndex = e.NewPageIndex;
  _startIndex = _gd1.VirtualItemCount -
     ((_gd1.CurrentPageIndex+1) * _gd1.PageSize);
  BindGrid();
}
}
```

7.4.2 DataGrid Sorting

When most users see a grid with column headers on a Web page, they expect to be able to click the headers to sort the grid based on that column. If they click the header and nothing happens, they become frustrated and are less likely to visit that page again. To avoid this kind of disappointment, the `DataGrid` class supports sorting through the `AllowSorting` property and the `SortCommand` event. As with paging, the details of sorting are left up to you, but the `DataGrid` takes care of turning the column headers into hyperlinks and issuing the `SortCommand` event whenever one of the links is pressed. Figure 7-10 shows an example of a `DataGrid` that supports sorting in action.

To add support for sorting to a `DataGrid`, you need to enable the `AllowSorting` property of the grid, and you need to associate a handler with the `SortCommand`. Enabling `AllowSorting` turns all your `DataGrid` headers into hyperlinks, which when clicked perform a post-back and fire the `SortCommand` event, passing in the sort expression associated with the clicked column. The sort expression of a column defaults to the column name, but you can change it by explicitly describing the column in your `DataGrid` declaration and assigning a string to the `SortExpression` property of the column. Listing 7-7 shows a sample page with a `DataGrid` that has sorting enabled.

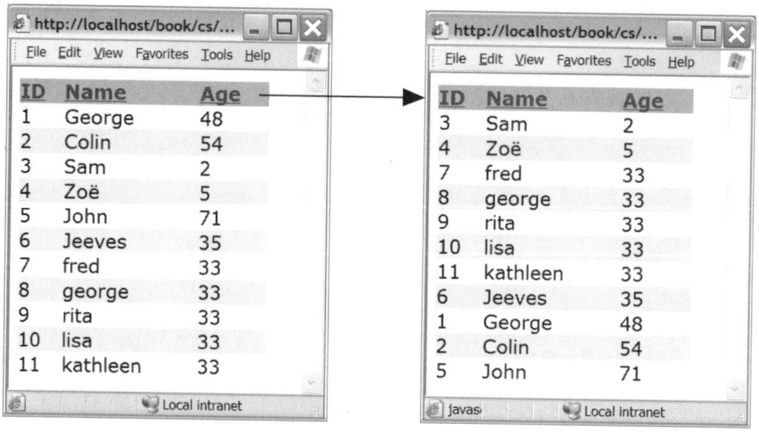

FIGURE 7-10: DataGrid Supporting Sorting in Action

LISTING 7-7: Page with a DataGrid Supporting Sorting

```
<!— File: DataGridSort.aspx —>
<%@ Page language="C#" Src="DataGridSort.aspx.cs"
    Inherits="DataGridSort" %>
<html>
<body>
<form runat="server">

  <asp:datagrid id=_gd1
                Width="90%"
                Runat="server"
                AllowSorting="True"
                OnSortCommand="gd1_Sort"
  />

</form>
</body>
</html>
```

The logic behind a sortable grid involves repopulating the grid with whatever the current sort expression selected by the user is. Listing 7-8 shows the code-behind page for a grid with sorting enabled. In this implementation, a local field named _sortExpression is maintained to determine what to pass into the ORDER BY clause of our query. The sort expression is set in the gd1_Sort method, our handler for the SortCommand event. The details of how the sorting of the data is performed may vary from application to application, but the core methods and sort expression management should stay the same.

LISTING 7-8: Code-Behind Class Implementing DataGrid Sorting Logic

```
// File: DataGridSort.aspx.cs
public class DataGridSort : Page
{
  private   string   _sortExpression;
  protected DataGrid _gd1;

  protected void Page_Load(object Src, EventArgs e)
  {
    if (!IsPostBack)
      BindGrid();
  }
```

continues

```
protected void gd1_Sort(object src,
                           DataGridSortCommandEventArgs e)
{
   _sortExpression = e.SortExpression;
   BindGrid();
}

public void BindGrid()
{
   string select = "SELECT * FROM Employees";
   if (_sortExpression != null)
      select +=  " ORDER BY " + _sortExpression;

   SqlConnection conn =
   new SqlConnection("server=.;uid=sa;pwd=;database=Test");

   SqlCommand cmd = new SqlCommand(select, conn);

   try
   {
     conn.Open();
     IDataReader reader = cmd.ExecuteReader();
     _gd1.DataSource=reader;
     _gd1.DataBind();
   }
   finally { conn.Dispose(); }
  }
 }
```

(handwritten annotation: → BY ID DESC ;)

7.4.3 DataGrid Editing

In addition to paging and sorting, the DataGrid class supports editing of individual rows. Editing is supported through a property of the DataGrid named EditItemIndex. When this property is set to a non-negative integer, the row associated with that number is redisplayed using text input controls instead of just table cells, giving the user a chance to edit the values in the fields. This property is used in conjunction with the EditCommandColumn, which you place in the Columns collection of your DataGrid, where it renders an additional column in your table containing hyperlinks for the user to click to perform editing. This column also issues three server-side events for you to handle, the EditCommand, the CancelCommand, and the UpdateCommand, corresponding to the three hyperlinks that the user

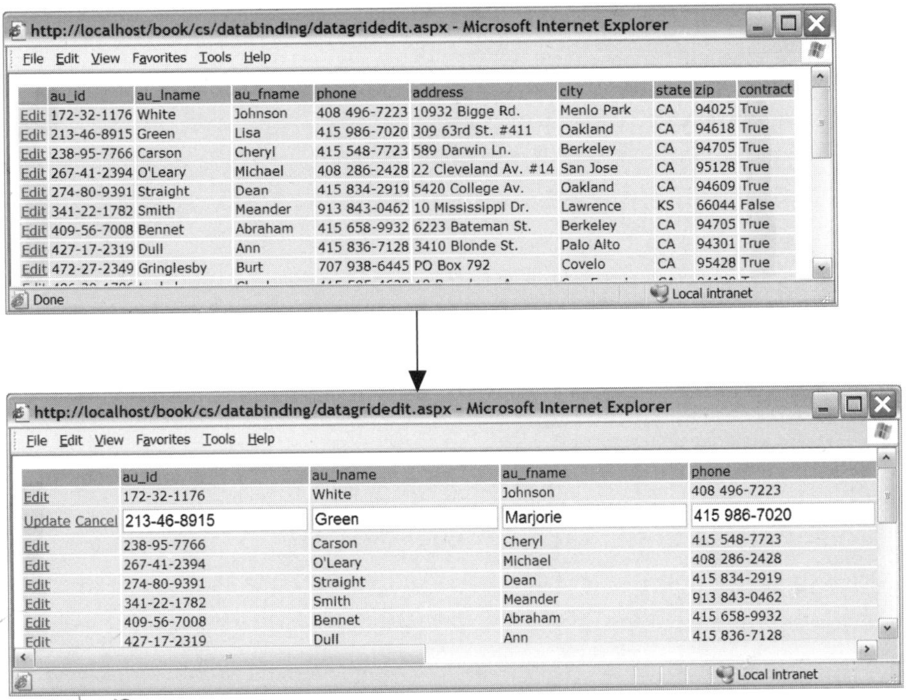

FIGURE 7-11: A DataGrid with Editing Support in Action

might press when working with your grid. Figure 7-11 shows a sample DataGrid page with editing support in action.

As with both paging and sorting, the DataGrid merely provides the shell for performing row updating. It is up to you to implement the internal details of responding to events and propagating the information back to your data source. To enable editing on a DataGrid, you first need to add to your grid's Columns collection the EditCommandColumn, which describes the appearance and behavior of the supplemental column that is added, indicating that individual rows can be edited. Next, you need to add server-side event handlers for the EditCommand, CancelCommand, and Update-Command events the grid issues when the corresponding hyperlinks are pressed. Listing 7-9 shows a sample page with a DataGrid that supports editing.

LISTING 7-9: Page with a DataGrid Supporting Editing

```
<!- File: DataGridEdit.aspx ->
<%@ Page language="C#" Src="DataGridEdit.aspx.cs"
         Inherits="DataGridEdit" %>
<html>
<body>
<form runat="server">

<asp:datagrid id="_gd1" runat=server
  GridLines=None
  OnEditCommand="gd1_Edit"
  OnCancelCommand="gd1_Cancel"
  OnUpdateCommand="gd1_Update">
  <Columns>
    <asp:EditCommandColumn EditText="Edit"
                           CancelText="Cancel"
                           UpdateText="Update"
                           ItemStyle-Wrap="false"
    />
  </Columns>
</asp:datagrid>

</form>
</body>
</html>
```

Adding EditCommandColumn to grid's column's Collection.

Once the `DataGrid` is declared with editing support, you have to build pieces of logic to make the grid truly editable. First, in your handler for the `EditCommand` event, you need to set the `EditItemIndex` property of your `DataGrid` class equal to the incoming `ItemIndex` property of the `Item` property on the `DataGridCommandEventArgs` parameter. When the grid renders back to the client after setting this property, it renders the columns for the selected row as text boxes instead of plain table cells, indicating that the user can edit the values. It also changes the `EditCommandColumn` to display two hyperlinks for that row: `Update` and `Cancel`. Second, in your handler for the `CancelCommand` event, you need to reset the `EditItemIndex` to -1, indicating that none of the rows are currently being edited. This makes no row selected when the grid renders back to the client. Third, and most importantly, in your handler for the `UpdateCommand` event, you need to query the contents of the text boxes for the selected row and propagate back to your data source any changes made. The `DataGridCommandEventArgs` parameter passed into your `UpdateCommand` handler exposes the current row through its Item property, which in turn has an array of controls called Cells, which you can index to obtain the control in the column you need. An example of a page implementing this logic is shown in Listing 7-10.

LISTING 7-10: Code-Behind Class Implementing DataGrid Editing Logic

```
// File: DataGridEdit.aspx.cs

public class DataGridEdit : Page
{
  protected DataGrid _gd1;

  protected void Page_Load(object Src, EventArgs e)
  {
    if (!IsPostBack)
      BindGrid();
  }

  public void gd1_Edit(object sender,
                    DataGridCommandEventArgs e)
  {
    _gd1.EditItemIndex = e.Item.ItemIndex;
    BindGrid();
  }

  public void gd1_Cancel(object sender,
                    DataGridCommandEventArgs e)
  {
    _gd1.EditItemIndex = -1;
    BindGrid();
  }

  public void BindGrid()
  {
    SqlConnection conn =
    new SqlConnection("server=.;uid=sa;pwd=;database=Pubs");

    SqlDataAdapter da =
        new SqlDataAdapter("select * from Authors", conn);

    DataSet ds = new DataSet();
    da.Fill(ds, "Authors");

    _gd1.DataSource=ds;
    _gd1.DataBind();
  }
```

continues

```
public void gd1_Update(object sender,
                        DataGridCommandEventArgs e)
{
  string updateCmd = "UPDATE Authors SET au_lname = "+
    "@vLname, au_fname = @vFname, phone = @vPhone, "+
    "address = @vAddress, city = @vCity, state = " +
    "@vState, zip = @vZip, contract = @vContract " +
    "where au_id=@vId";

  SqlConnection conn =
  new SqlConnection("server=.;uid=sa;pwd=;database=pubs");

  SqlCommand cmd = new SqlCommand(updateCmd, conn);

  cmd.Parameters.Add("@vId",
        ((TextBox)e.Item.Cells[1].Controls[0]).Text);
  cmd.Parameters.Add("@vLname",
        ((TextBox)e.Item.Cells[2].Controls[0]).Text);
  cmd.Parameters.Add("@vFname",
        ((TextBox)e.Item.Cells[3].Controls[0]).Text);
  cmd.Parameters.Add("@vPhone",
        ((TextBox)e.Item.Cells[4].Controls[0]).Text);
  cmd.Parameters.Add("@vAddress",
        ((TextBox)e.Item.Cells[5].Controls[0]).Text);
  cmd.Parameters.Add("@vCity",
        ((TextBox)e.Item.Cells[6].Controls[0]).Text);
  cmd.Parameters.Add("@vState",
        ((TextBox)e.Item.Cells[7].Controls[0]).Text);
  cmd.Parameters.Add("@vZip",
        ((TextBox)e.Item.Cells[8].Controls[0]).Text);

  // The bool is stored in a textbox too, so parse it
  // into a bool before passing in as a parameter
  bool contract =
  bool.Parse(((TextBox)e.Item.Cells[9].Controls[0]).Text);

  cmd.Parameters.Add("@vContract", contract);
  try
  {
    conn.Open();
    cmd.ExecuteNonQuery();
    _gd1.EditItemIndex = -1;
  }
  finally { conn.Dispose(); }

  BindGrid();
}
}
```

7.5 **Templates**

Templates provide a mechanism for separating the appearance of a control from the core data binding functionality of the control. A templated control manages the data and (typically) the layout of that data, but it leaves the rendering of the data to a user-provided template, giving you much more flexibility in how a data-bound control displays its contents. Conceptually, you can think of templated controls as providing a place for you to "plug in" whatever output you want displayed for each row in the data source during data binding. Figure 7-12 shows this conceptual model. Note that the templated data-bound control manages the data source and the process of data binding, but leaves the rendering of each row to a "user-defined template." Inside the user-defined template, the user of the control specifies what should be output for each row that is bound.

ASP.NET provides three templated data-bound controls: the `Repeater`, the `DataList`, and the `DataGrid`. Each of these controls provides varying degrees of flexibility in layout, and support for different sets of templates, as we will see.

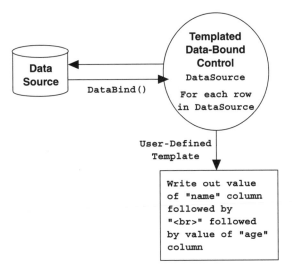

FIGURE 7-12: Conceptual Model of Templated Controls

7.5.1 Data Binding Evaluation Syntax

To be able to define the rendering portion of a data-bound control, we need a mechanism to access the currently bound row. ASP.NET defines a special syntax using the "<%# %>" notation for template-based data binding. It looks somewhat similar to traditional ASP evaluation syntax but is evaluated differently. Instead of being evaluated during page rendering, data binding evaluation expressions are evaluated during data binding. And typically, if the expression occurs within the item template of a data-bound control, it is evaluated once per row of the data source during binding.

As a concrete example of using this syntax, Listing 7-11 shows a sample use of the Repeater template control, the most generic of the templated controls. In this example, the Repeater control consists of an ItemTemplate containing two data binding expressions and some static HTML. The data binding expressions are evaluated once per row of the underlying data source—in this case, an SqlDataReader. Figure 7-13 shows the rendering of this page.

LISTING 7-11: Sample Use of Data Binding Evaluation Syntax

```
<!— File: SimpleRepeater.aspx—>
<%@ Page language=C# %>
<%@ Import Namespace="System.Data" %>
<%@ Import Namespace="System.Data.SqlClient" %>

<html>
<script language="C#" runat="server">
protected void Page_Load(Object src, EventArgs e)
{
  if (!IsPostBack)
  {
    SqlConnection conn =
    new SqlConnection("server=.;uid=sa;pwd=;database=Test");
    SqlCommand cmd =
      new SqlCommand("SELECT Name, Age FROM Employees",
                     conn);

    try
    {
      conn.Open();
      SqlDataReader reader = cmd.ExecuteReader();
      rp1.DataSource = reader;
      DataBind();
    }
    finally
```

```
      { conn.Dispose(); }
    }
}
</script>

<body>
<form runat=server>
<asp:Repeater id="rp1" runat=server>
  <ItemTemplate>
    <%# ((IDataRecord)Container.DataItem)["Name"] %><br>
    <%# ((IDataRecord)Container.DataItem)["Age"] %><br>
  </ItemTemplate>
</asp:Repeater>
</form>
</body>
</html>
```

FIGURE 7-13: Simple Repeater Page Rendering

To understand what types of expressions can go into a data binding expression within a templated control, we must understand where the expression is going to end up in the generated `Page`-derived class definition for this .aspx file. Typically, each data binding expression that occurs within a template turns into an instance of the `DataBoundLiteralControl` class and is added as a child control to the templated control (the `Repeater` in our example). In addition, the page parser generates a handler function that is wired up to the `DataBinding` event of the `DataBoundLiteralControl` class. It is within this handler function that the contents of the data binding expression are inserted, as shown in Figure 7-14.

The `DataBinding` event of the `DataBoundLiteralControl` class is triggered once for each row of the data source during the `DataBind()` call to the `Repeater` control. The generated code for this handler also prepares a local variable named `Container`, which is set to the `BindingContainer`

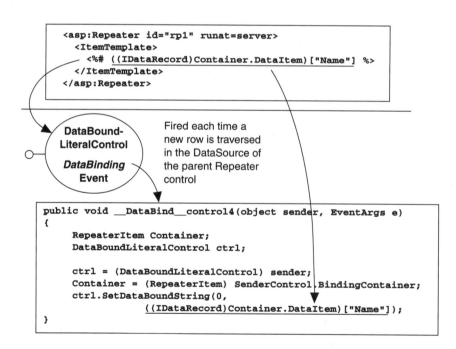

FIGURE 7-14: Code Generation for Data Binding Expression within a Template

property of the control that issued the event. In our example, the control that issues the event is our `DataBoundLiteralControl`, and the `BindingContainer` property returns a reference to the current template, the `ItemTemplate`, which for the `Repeater` class is an instance of the `RepeaterItem` class. Finally, to access the current row in the underlying data source, the `RepeaterItem` class exposes a `DataItem` property. Because we chose to bind our `Repeater` control to an `SqlDataReader`, the underlying data source exposes the `IDataRecord` interface, which we can then use to access the current value of the "Name" column.

If, instead of adding data binding expressions to the top-level of an `ItemTemplate`, you assign the property of a server-side control to a data binding expression, the code generation changes slightly. Listing 7-12 shows a `Repeater` control that sets the `Text` property of a server-side `TextBox` control to a data binding expression.

LISTING 7-12: Data Binding Expressions as Property Values

```
<asp:Repeater id="rp1" runat=server>
  <ItemTemplate>
    <asp:TextBox id=_name
      Text='<%# ((IDataRecord)Container.DataItem)["Name"] %>'
    />
  </ItemTemplate>
</asp:Repeater>
```

In this case, instead of turning the data binding expression into an instance of the `DataBoundLiteralControl` class, it generates a handler for the `DataBinding` event of the `TextBox` control and places the contents of the data binding expression on the right-hand side of an assignment to the `Text` property of the `TextBox` control. The end result is the same, but the creation of the `DataBoundLiteralControl` control is unnecessary.

7.5.2 DataBinder

In the previous example of using the data binding evaluation syntax within a template, the `DataItem` property of the implicit `Container` variable was cast to an `IDataRecord` and then indexed to retrieve the value of a named column for the current row. If, instead of using an `SqlDataReader` as a data source, we had used a `DataSet`, this cast would have failed, because rows of a `DataSet` are not exposed with the `IDataRecord` interface. We would instead have to cast the `Container.DataItem` to a `DataRowView`, which we could then index with our desired column name or index. This means that changing the data source to which your templated controls are bound would involve changing the data binding expressions as well.

Fortunately, another solution works regardless of the type of data source—it is called the `DataBinder` class. This class defines a static method called `Eval()` that evaluates a generic `DataItem` by first using reflection to determine what type of data source it is and then dynamically constructing a call to its default indexer to retrieve the desired value. This method supports two overloads, the second of which includes a format string that should be applied when retrieving the data. Although this mechanism incurs slightly more overhead, it ensures that any future changes to the type of data source used for binding will work with the existing data binding expressions. Listing 7-13 shows our earlier `Repeater` example rewritten to use the `DataBinder` class instead of direct casting. Note that in the second usage, a format string of "`{0:2d}`" is applied to the requested string, indicating that the resulting value should be displayed as a two-digit decimal value.

LISTING 7-13: Using DataBinder.Eval to Create Data-Source-Independent Expressions

```
<asp:Repeater id="rp1" runat=server>
  <ItemTemplate>
  <%# DataBinder.Eval(Container.DataItem, "Name") %><br>
  <%# DataBinder.Eval(Container.DataItem, "Age","{0:2d}") %>
  <br>
  </ItemTemplate>
</asp:Repeater>
```

7.5.3 Templated Controls

Now that we have covered the mechanism of data binding in templates, it is time to turn to the templated controls provided by ASP.NET. The three templated controls available are the `Repeater`, `DataList`, and `DataGrid`. Each of these controls supports a different set of templates, beginning with the most common `ItemTemplate`. Table 7-1 shows the various templates that are available in each of the three classes.

TABLE 7-1: Available Templates and the Controls That Support Them

Template	Description	DataGrid	DataList	Repeater
ItemTemplate	Generates appearance of items	Yes	Yes	Yes
Alternating-ItemTemplate	Generates appearance of every other row item	No	Yes	Yes
Header-Template	Generates appearance of header for columns	Yes	Yes	Yes
Footer-Template	Generates appearance of footer for columns	Yes	Yes	Yes
Separator-Template	Generates appearance between items	No	Yes	Yes
EditItem-Template	Generates appearance of item currently being edited	Yes	Yes	No

For an example of applying templates, consider the editable `DataGrid` presented in the last section. The last column shown in the `DataGrid` was a `Boolean` field called `Contract`, which when displayed in the grid, showed up as the string "true" or "false". Instead of displaying a string in that column, it makes more sense to show a `CheckBox` that is either checked or not based on the value of the underlying column in the data table. Figure 7-15 shows a new version of our `DataGrid`, running with a `CheckBox` instead of a string.

FIGURE 7-15: Use of a DataGrid Control with a Template Column

To place a `CheckBox` in a column of a `DataGrid`, first we need to turn off `AutoGenerateColumns` so that we control the column creation completely. Then, in place of the `Contract` column, we define a `TemplateColumn` consisting of an `ItemTemplate`, the content of which is a `CheckBox` control. We then use the declarative data binding syntax described earlier to extract the `Boolean` value from the `Contract` column in the underlying data row. Listing 7-14 shows the modified `DataGrid` declaration (excluding styles) that generates the page shown in Figure 7-15.

LISTING 7-14: DataGrid declaration with template column

```
<!— File: DataGridEditTemplate.aspx —>
<asp:datagrid id="_gd1" runat=server
  AutoGenerateColumns="false"
  OnEditCommand="gd1_Edit"
  OnCancelCommand="gd1_Cancel"
  OnUpdateCommand="gd1_Update">
  <Columns>
    <asp:EditCommandColumn EditText="Edit"
                           CancelText="Cancel"
                           UpdateText="Update"
                           ItemStyle-Wrap="false"/>
    <asp:BoundColumn HeaderText="Id"
                     ReadOnly="true" DataField="au_id"/>
    <asp:BoundColumn HeaderText="LastName"
                     DataField="au_lname"/>
    <asp:BoundColumn HeaderText="FirstName"
                     DataField="au_fname"/>
    <asp:BoundColumn HeaderText="Phone" DataField="phone"/>
```

```
    <asp:BoundColumn HeaderText="Address"
                     DataField="address"/>
    <asp:BoundColumn HeaderText="City" DataField="city"/>
    <asp:BoundColumn HeaderText="State" DataField="state"/>
    <asp:BoundColumn HeaderText="Zip" DataField="zip"/>
    <asp:TemplateColumn HeaderText="Contract">
      <ItemTemplate>
        <asp:CheckBox id="contract" runat=server
                      Checked=
    '<%# DataBinder.Eval(Container.DataItem, "Contract") %>'
        />
      </ItemTemplate>
    </asp:TemplateColumn>
    </Columns>
</asp:datagrid>
```

In addition to the `DataGrid` declaration change, we have to change the `UpdateCommand` event handler to extract the `Boolean` value from the embedded `CheckBox` control. The easiest way to do this is to call the `Find-Control` method of the cell with the ID of the `CheckBox`, as shown in Listing 7-15.

LISTING 7-15: Extracting the Value of a Nested Control in a DataGrid

```
// File: DataGridEditTemplate.aspx.cs
public void gd1_Update(object sender,
                       DataGridCommandEventArgs e)
{
  // other control extraction values not shown

  // Change au_id field access because it is read-only
  cmd.Parameters.Add("@vId",    e.Item.Cells[1].Text);

  // Find the checkbox control in column 9
  CheckBox cb =
        (CheckBox)e.Item.Cells[9].FindControl("contract");
  cmd.Parameters.Add("@vContract", cb.Checked);
  //...
}
```

7.5.4 **Repeater**
The `Repeater` control is a very generic shell that gives you complete control over how data is rendered. It requires that you provide all the HTML

layout, formatting, and style tags within the templates of the control. You may want to consider using a DataGrid or DataList before using a Repeater because they will do much more of the work on your behalf. If, however, you have a complex data layout that cannot be represented as a list or a grid, the Repeater will accommodate any formatting you can imagine. Figure 7-16 shows a sample use of the Repeater control.

7.5.5 DataList

The DataList control provides a simple way to display data from a data source in a repeating list. While similar functionality can be achieved using the DataGrid control, the DataList is simpler to work with and is designed

```
<asp:Repeater id="rp1" runat=server>
  <ItemTemplate>
    <%# DataBinder.Eval(Container.DataItem, "Name") %> is a
    <%# DataBinder.Eval(Container.DataItem, "Breed") %>
    and looks like this:
    <asp:Image runat=server
       ImageUrl=<%# DataBinder.Eval(Container.DataItem, "Image") %> />
  </ItemTemplate>
  <SeparatorTemplate><hr/></SeparatorTemplate>
</asp:Repeater>
```

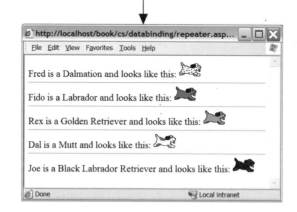

FIGURE 7-16: A Repeater Control in Use

to make displaying lists trivial. At the very least, you must define an
`ItemTemplate` to describe how each item appears. Styles are provided for
each of the templates, which make it easy to modify the appearance of any
templated item. For example, the `HeaderStyle` property gives you control
over the appearance of items in the header, including border, background
color, width, and so on. Another set of properties affects how the list flows
on the page. Setting the `RepeatLayout` to `Flow`, for example, generates `div`
and `span` elements instead of a table (which is the default). Setting the
`RepeatDirection` lets you control whether elements flow horizontally or
vertically. Setting `RepeatColumns` gives you control over how many
columns are displayed before another row is generated. Figure 7-17 shows
an example use of the `DataList` control.

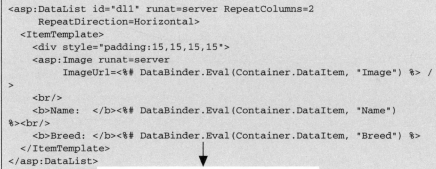

```
<asp:DataList id="dl1" runat=server RepeatColumns=2
    RepeatDirection=Horizontal>
  <ItemTemplate>
    <div style="padding:15,15,15,15">
    <asp:Image runat=server
        ImageUrl=<%# DataBinder.Eval(Container.DataItem, "Image") %> /
>
    <br/>
    <b>Name:  </b><%# DataBinder.Eval(Container.DataItem, "Name")
%><br/>
    <b>Breed: </b><%# DataBinder.Eval(Container.DataItem, "Breed") %>
  </ItemTemplate>
</asp:DataList>
```

Name: Fred   **Name:** Fido
Breed: Dalmation   **Breed:** Labrador

Name: Rex   **Name:** Dal
Breed: Golden Retriever   **Breed:** Mutt

Name: Joe
Breed: Black Labrador Retriever

FIGURE 7-17: DataList Control Example

SUMMARY

One of the most common tasks encountered in building Web applications is retrieving data from a data source and rendering that data to the client browser. ASP.NET provides an architecture for binding data to controls that greatly simplifies and modularizes this task. Instead of manually walking through result sets, you can initialize the data source, point one or more server-side controls to it, and ask them to bind themselves to the data. The source of data can be most any collection, whether it is a result set from a database query or a programmatically populated `ArrayList`. The controls are equally diverse, beginning with simple list controls such as `SELECT` elements and `ListBoxes`, and going all the way up to the more complex data-bound controls such as the `DataGrid`, `DataList`, and `Repeater`.

Templates give you even more control over the data binding process by letting you specify exactly how each row of the data source should be rendered in the context of the data-bound control. For the `DataGrid`, this means that you can provide a shell, or template, of HTML sprinkled with data binding syntax to indicate where the data should be inserted for each column in the rendered grid. The `DataList` gives you a similar tabular layout with precise control over each cell rendered in the table, and the `Repeater` gives you complete control over how the data should be rendered, without even generating the containing table for you.

■ 8 ■
Custom Controls

A T ITS CORE, ASP.NET is a control-based architecture, defined in the following way:

- A Page is a control.
- Any control may contain child controls.
- A control is rendered by rendering its contents and then iteratively rendering its children.

This architecture is analogous to the window architecture in the Win32 API. The desktop itself is a window (like the Page), and any window may contain child windows. Each window is rendered by first rendering its contents and then rendering the contents of its children. The rendering of a window on the desktop involves drawing pixels to a display, whereas the rendering of an ASP.NET control involves generating HTML to populate a portion of the response to an HTTP request. ASP.NET's control architecture is a completely extensible framework, and in this chapter, we look at techniques for building custom controls to create truly reusable Web components that encapsulate details of presentation and server interaction.

8.1 Fundamentals

Before we delve into the details of control creation, it is important to understand what a control is and how the existing controls in the framework function. When an .aspx page is parsed, an instance of the System.Web.UI.Page-derived class is constructed. This instance in turn contains controls that render the contents of the page. It may contain members of the HtmlControls hierarchy, which mirror their respective HTML elements. It may also contain WebControls, which are higher-level controls with a more uniform interface than native HTML elements, but which render HTML when the page is rendered as well. It is also likely to contain instances of the LiteralControl class, which simply renders the literal HTML it stores when requested. For example, consider the .aspx page shown in Listing 8-1.

LISTING 8-1: A Simple .aspx Page

```
<!– File: SimplePage.aspx –>
<%@ Page language='C#' trace='true' %>
<html>
<head>
<script runat='server'>
protected void OnEnterName(object src, EventArgs e)
{
  _message.Text =
string.Format("Hi, {0}, how are you?", _name.Text);
}
</script>
</head>
<body>
<form runat='server'>
<h2>Enter your name:
    <asp:TextBox id='_name' runat='server'/>
</h2>
<asp:Button Text='Enter'
            OnClick='OnEnterName' runat='server'/>
<br/>
<asp:Label id='_message' runat='server'/>
</form>
</body>
</html>
```

When this page is accessed, it is compiled into a `Page`-derived class with a collection of child controls. The literal HTML is placed into instances of the `LiteralControl` class, which when asked to render, simply regurgitates whatever text it was assigned. Any controls marked with `runat=server` are turned into server-side controls and then added to the controls collection of their immediate parent control. The `Page` class serves as the root control, and it has three immediate child controls: two literal controls to generate the beginning and end of the page text, and a server-side `HtmlForm` control. Because all the remaining server-side controls are within the server-side form, they are added as child controls to the `HtmlForm` control. Note that the order in which controls are added to their parent's `Controls` collection is important because it determines the rendering order of the controls. Figure 8-1 shows the control hierarchy that is generated for this page.

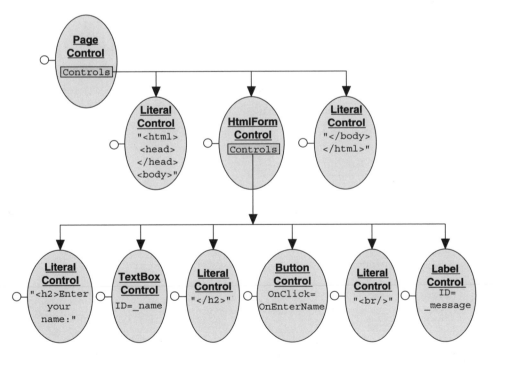

FIGURE 8-1: Control Hierarchy for a Parsed .aspx Page

Once this hierarchy is constructed, the page can be rendered by invoking the top-level `Render` method (this happens implicitly when the `IHttpHandler.ProcessRequest` method of the `Page` class is invoked). The effect of calling `Render` on the `Page` class is to perform a depth-first traversal of the control tree, asking each control to add its contribution to the `Response` buffer in turn. As the user interacts with the page, controls take on new state and render themselves differently. For example, when the user performs a post-back in our sample page by pressing the `Enter` button, the value of the `Label` control is a string greeting the user with his name.

8.1.1 Writing Custom Controls

All the ASP.NET controls, including the `Page` class, derive from the common base class `System.Web.UI.Control`, which provides the necessary methods, events, and fields to define a control's behavior. To create your own custom control, you must create a new class that derives from `System.Web.UI.Control`, and typically you override the virtual `Render()` method to generate whatever HTML is necessary to display the contents of your control. Any public methods, properties, or events added to your `Control`-derived class become part of the interface to the control as well. Listing 8-2 shows a simple control called `NameControl` that renders its string `Name` property as either an `h1` or `h2` tag, depending on the public `IsImportant` property.

LISTING 8-2: The Name Control

```
// File: name.cs
using System;
using System.Web;
using System.Web.UI;

namespace EssentialAspDotNet.CustomControls
{
  public class NameControl : Control
  {
    private string _name;
    private bool   _isImportant;

    public string Name
    {
      get { return _name;  }
```

```
      set { _name = value; }
   }

   public bool IsImportant
   {
      get { return _isImportant;  }
      set { _isImportant = value; }
   }

   protected override void Render(HtmlTextWriter writer)
   {
      string txt;
      if (_isImportant)
         txt = string.Format("<h1>{0}</h1>", _name);
      else
         txt = string.Format("<h2>{0}</h2>", _name);
      writer.Write(txt);
   }
  }
 }
```

To deploy this control, we would first compile it into an assembly and then deploy that assembly into the /bin directory of the ASP.NET application in which it was to be used. Alternatively, we could sign the compiled assembly with a public/private key pair and deploy it in the global assembly cache so that it could easily be accessed on a machine-wide basis. A sample showing how to compile and deploy this from the command prompt is shown in Listing 8-3.

LISTING 8-3: Command-Line Compilation of NameControl

```
csc /t:library /out:bin\Name.dll Name.cs
```

8.1.2 Using Custom Controls

One of the most appealing features of custom controls is that their usage is syntactically identical to the intrinsic controls built into ASP.NET. Once you include a Register directive at the top of your .aspx file to reference the custom control, you can then use the TagPrefix string assigned in the Register directive to refer to any controls in the referenced namespace. For example, Listing 8-4 shows a sample .aspx client file to our NameControl described earlier, with two instances of the custom control.

LISTING 8-4: Client Page Using NameControl

```
<%@ Page Language='C#' %>
<%@ Register Namespace='EssentialAspDotNet.CustomControls'
             TagPrefix='eadn' Assembly='name' %>
<html>
<body>
<eadn:NameControl runat='server' Name='Fred'
             IsImportant='false'/>
<eadn:NameControl runat='server' Name='George'
                  IsImportant='true' />
</body>
</html>
```

Notice that the tag attributes of your control are implicitly mapped to the public properties in the target control. Also note that the system implicitly converts the text-based attributes of your custom control tag into the type expected by the control's property. In our case, the IsImportant attribute must be converted from a string to a Boolean, and the Name property requires no conversion. This implicit conversion works for all standard built-in types and can be customized by providing your own converter, as we discuss in the section Designer Integration later in this chapter.

It is a testament to the simplicity and elegance of the custom control model that we have covered the details of both control creation and usage in only a few pages. The remainder of this chapter covers individual pieces of the control architecture in more detail, but the core architecture has been presented in its entirety.

8.1.3 System.Web.UI.Control

Every custom control that you create derives either directly or indirectly from System.Web.UI.Control, so it is important to understand the features provided by this class in detail. We have so far looked only at the virtual Render method, but there are several other methods, properties, and events you should be familiar with as you start building controls. Listing 8-5 shows the core methods, properties, and events of this class.

LISTING 8-5: Core Methods, Properties, and Events of System.Web.UI.Control

```
public class Control : IComponent,
                       IDisposable,
                       IParserAccessor,
```

```
                        IDataBindingsAccessor
{
  // Rendering
  protected virtual void Render(HtmlTextWriter);
  public            void RenderControl(HtmlTextWriter);
  protected virtual void RenderChildren(HtmlTextWriter);
  public    virtual bool Visible {get; set;}

  // Child control management
  protected virtual void    CreateChildControls();
  protected virtual void    EnsureChildControls();
  public    virtual Control FindControl(string);
  public    virtual bool    HasControls();
  public    virtual ControlCollection Controls {get;}
  public    virtual Control NamingContainer   {get;}
  protected         bool  ChildControlsCreated {get; set;}

  // Identification
  public virtual string  ClientID           {get;}
  public virtual string  ID                 {get; set;}
  public virtual string  UniqueID           {get;}

  // Accessors
  public    virtual Page       Page      {get; set;}
  public    virtual Control    Parent    {get;}
  protected virtual HttpContext Context   {get;}

  // State management
  public    virtual bool        EnableViewState {get; set;}
  protected virtual StateBag     ViewState            {get;}
  protected         bool       HasChildViewState   {get;}
  protected         bool       IsTrackingViewState {get;}

  // Events
  public event EventHandler DataBinding;
  public event EventHandler Init;
  public event EventHandler Load;
  public event EventHandler PreRender;
  public event EventHandler Unload;

  // Misc
  public virtual void   DataBind();
  public         string ResolveUrl(string);
}
```

The first function you typically override in classes derived from this class is the Render method. Render is called whenever a control is asked to render its content into the response buffer. It takes as a parameter a reference to an `HtmlTextWriter` object, which contains helper methods for writing HTML tags to the response buffer. Notice that the `Render` method is a protected method and cannot be called outside the `Control` class. To explicitly ask a control to render its contents, you call the `RenderControl` function, which internally invokes the `Render` method. This gives the base class an opportunity to pre- and postprocess render requests if needed (currently it is used to generate additional trace information when tracing is enabled).

The other method related to rendering is the `RenderChildren` method, whose default implementation iterates across the `Controls` collection, invoking `RenderControl` on each child control. The base class implementation of `Render` calls `RenderChildren` as a default behavior that is useful for composite controls, as we will see later. Keep in mind that if you override the `Render` method, the base class version is not called unless you explicitly call `base.Render()`. Thus, if your control contains other controls as child controls, you should decide whether it makes sense to render those child controls in your `Render` implementation and call `base.Render()` as appropriate.

Finally, note that if you set the `Visible` property of your control to `false`, the base class implementation of `RenderControl` does not dispatch the call to your `Render` method at all.

Control authors should understand how controls are identified, both internally and when they are rendered to the client. Three identifiers are associated with a control: `ClientID`, `ID`, and `UniqueID`. Most of the time, these identifiers will be the same. If your control is labeled with an `ID` attribute when it is used, the value of that attribute will be your control's `ID`, and if not, ASP.NET synthesizes an `ID` for your control when it is rendered. If, however, your control is a child control of another control that is a naming container (such as a `Repeater`), these three values will be different. In this scenario, the `ID` will still be whatever string was placed in the `ID` attribute for your control, but the `UniqueID` will be that `ID` prefixed with the `ID` of the containing control (such as `_ctrl0:myid`), and the `ClientID` will be the same as the `UniqueID` but with the ":" character replaced with the "_" character (such as `_ctrl0_my_id`). This ensures that repeated instances of a control marked with the same ID are scoped by its container control, avoiding `ID` clashes in the client. When rendering your control, if you need a unique ID in your generated HTML, you should use the ClientID, because it will always be an HTML-compatible ID. The convention used by the WebControls and HtmlControls is to use the UniqueID for the name attribute of rendered HTML controls, and ClientID for the ID attribute.

Finally, it is useful to know what accessors are available when you are authoring controls. You have direct access to your containing Page class through the Page property and to the current HttpContext through the Context property. The Parent property can be used to query your immediate parent control. The remaining elements of the Control class are discussed as we explore control implementation techniques in more detail next.

8.1.4 HtmlTextWriter

Although you can completely render your control by using only the Write method of the HtmlTextWriter class, many other methods are available that can both simplify rendering and make the output more browser generic. Internally, all the Web controls defined in the System.Web.UI hierarchy use the HTML-rendering methods of the HtmlTextWriter class to generate their output. This class can be used in three ways to generate HTML output. First, you can use the overridden versions of Write and WriteLine to generate whatever text you need into the response buffer. Second, you can use the non-stack-based convenience methods, such as WriteBeginTag and WriteEndTag, to generate each HTML element programmatically instead of generating string literals. The third, and most appealing, way is to use the stack-based methods, such as RenderBeginTag and RenderEndTag, for easily constructing blocks of nested HTML elements. Listing 8-6 shows the core methods of the HtmlTextWriter class, grouped into methods you would use for each of the three rendering techniques supported by the class.

LISTING 8-6: Core Methods of HtmlTextWriter

```
public class HtmlTextWriter : TextWriter
{
  // Convenience, stack-based methods
  public virtual void
        AddAttribute(HtmlTextWriterAttribute, string);
```

continues

```
public virtual void
        AddStyleAttribute(HtmlTextWriterStyle, string);
public virtual void RenderBeginTag(HtmlTextWriterTag);
public virtual void RenderEndTag();

// Convenience, non-stack-based methods
public virtual void WriteAttribute(string, string);
public virtual void WriteBeginTag(string);
public virtual void WriteEndTag(string);
public virtual void WriteFullBeginTag(string);
public virtual void WriteStyleAttribute(string, string);

// Do-it-yourself methods
public override void Write(string);
public override void WriteLine(string);

// Indent controls level of indentation in output
public int Indent { get; set; }
// Newline character
public override string NewLine {get; set;}

// Note - many of these methods have overloads to
// support alternate types not shown here
}
```

The stack-based methods for rendering keep track of tags written using the RenderBeginTag method, and when a corresponding call to the RenderEndTag method is made, the appropriate terminating tag is generated into the output stream. The AddAttribute and AddStyleAttribute methods are a way of decorating the next call to RenderBeginTag with standard or style attributes, and once the call to RenderBeginTag has been made, the attributes are flushed. The indentation of the rendered HTML is also performed implicitly when you use the stack-based method of rendering. For example, consider the Render method of a control, shown in Listing 8-7, that generates a table using only the Write method, and manually adjusts the indentation level.

LISTING 8-7: Sample Control Render Method Using Write/WriteLine

```
protected override void Render(HtmlTextWriter output)
{
  output.WriteLine("<table width='50%' border='1'>");
  output.Indent++;
  output.WriteLine("<tr>");
  output.Indent++;
```

```
    output.Write("<td align='left'");
    output.Write(" style='font-size:medium;color:blue;'>");
    output.WriteLine("This is row 0 column 0");
    output.WriteLine("</td>");
    output.Write("<td align='right' ");
    output.WriteLine("style='color:green;'>");
    output.WriteLine("This is row 0 column 1");
    output.WriteLine("</td>");
    output.Indent—;
    output.WriteLine("</tr>");
    output.Indent—;
    output.WriteLine("</table>");
}
```

There are two problems with rendering a control this way. First, it is very difficult to reuse portions of this rendering, because each piece must be placed specifically in order in the output string. Second, because we are writing out literal strings, there is no opportunity for ASP.NET classes to alter the output based on the capabilities of the current browser. For example, in our generated table definition, we are using the `style` attribute to alter the appearance of the column text. If this were rendered for Netscape 4.0, this style attribute would have no effect, because it is not supported in that browser type. The alternative to generating raw text is to use the stack-based HTML-rendering methods of the `HtmlTextWriter` class, as shown in Listing 8-8.

LISTING 8-8: Sample Control Render Method Using Stack-Based Methods

```
protected override void Render(HtmlTextWriter output)
{
  output.AddAttribute(HtmlTextWriterAttribute.Width,
                      "50%");
  output.AddAttribute(HtmlTextWriterAttribute.Border, "1");
  output.RenderBeginTag(HtmlTextWriterTag.Table); //<table>
  output.RenderBeginTag(HtmlTextWriterTag.Tr); // <tr>
  output.AddAttribute(HtmlTextWriterAttribute.Align,
                      "left");
  output.AddStyleAttribute(HtmlTextWriterStyle.FontSize,
                           "medium");
  output.AddStyleAttribute(HtmlTextWriterStyle.Color,
                           "blue");
  output.RenderBeginTag(HtmlTextWriterTag.Td); // <td>
  output.Write("This is row 0 column 0");
```

continues

```
    output.RenderEndTag(); // </td>
    output.AddAttribute(HtmlTextWriterAttribute.Align,
                        "right");
    output.AddStyleAttribute(HtmlTextWriterStyle.Color,
                        "green");
    output.RenderBeginTag(HtmlTextWriterTag.Td); // <td>
    output.Write("This is row 0 column 1");
    output.RenderEndTag(); // </td>
    output.RenderEndTag(); // </tr>
    output.RenderEndTag(); // </table>
}
```

Although a bit longer-winded, this version of our table rendering is easier to modify without breaking the syntax in the rendered HTML. Most importantly, it will render the table differently based on the client's browser capabilities. If accessed by a browser that can render only HTML 3.2 (instead of the more current HTML 4.0), this rendering method, instead of passing a reference to `HtmlTextWriter`, will pass a reference to an `Html32TextWriter` object, and it will render HTML 3.2–compliant tags. For example, it converts HTML 4.0–style attributes into the equivalent tags and attributes in HTML 3.2. `Html32TextWriter` will also standardize the propagation of attributes such as colors and fonts, which tend to vary in behavior in earlier browsers, by using HTML tables.

Adding an attribute to any element is simply a matter of adding an `AddAttribute` call before the `RenderBeginTag` that generates that element. Tables 8-1, 8-2, and 8-3 show all the possible values for the `HtmlText-WriterAttribute`, `HtmlTextWriterStyle`, and `HtmlTextWriterTag` enumerations, for use with these stack-based rendering functions.

TABLE 8-1: HtmlTextWriterAttribute Enumeration Values

Values		
Accesskey	Align	Alt
Background	Bgcolor	Border
Bordercolor	Cellpadding	Cellspacing

TABLE 8-1: HtmlTextWriterAttribute Enumeration Values (continued)

Values		
Checked	Class	Cols
Colspan	Disabled	For
Height	Href	Id
Maxlength	Multiple	Name
Nowrap	Onchange	Onclick
ReadOnly	Rows	Rowspan
Rules	Selected	Size
Src	Style	Tabindex
Target	Title	Type
Valign	Value	Width
Wrap		

TABLE 8-2: HtmlTextWriterStyle Enumeration Values

Values		
BackgroundColor	BackgroundImage	BorderCollapse
BorderColor	BorderStyle	BorderWidth
Color	FontFamily	FontSize
FontStyle	FontWeight	Height
TextDecoration	Width	

TABLE 8-3: HtmlTextWriterTag Enumeration Values

Values		
A	Acronym	Address
Area	B	Base
Basefont	Bdo	Bgsound
Big	Blockquote	Body
Br	Button	Caption
Center	Cite	Code
Col	Colgroup	Dd
Del	Dfn	Dir
Div	Dl	Dt
Em	Embed	Fieldset
Font	Form	Frame
Frameset	H1	H2
H3	H4	H5
H6	Head	Hr
Html	I	Iframe
Img	Input	Ins
Isindex	Kbd	Label
Legend	Li	Link
Map	Marquee	Menu
Meta	Nobr	Noframes
Noscript	Object	Ol
Option	P	Param

TABLE 8-3: HtmlTextWriterTag Enumeration Values (continued)

Values		
Pre	Q	Rt
Ruby	S	Samp
Script	Select	Small
Span	Strike	Strong
Style	Sub	Sup
Table	Tbody	Td
Textarea	Tfoot	Th
Thead	Title	Tr
Tt	U	Ul
Unknown	Var	Wbr
Xml		

The final technique for implementing the `Render` method of a custom control is to use the non-stack-based helper methods to generate the output. This involves using the `Write` methods of `HtmlTextWriter` class, such as `WriteBeginTag` and `WriteEndTag`. While the stack-based rendering with the `HtmlTextWriter` class should be the technique of choice in most circumstances, these `Write` methods can be used where you want more precise control over the rendered HTML, but you don't want to resort to writing string literals. These methods can also be used when you are writing out nonstandard HTML elements or even, perhaps, generic XML elements, with specific formatting requirements that must be met. These methods are not stack based, so you must take responsibility for rendering each begin and end tag separately. Also, these methods do not take into consideration the current indentation level, so you must explicitly add tab or space characters to indent your output. Listing 8-9 shows the same table we have been rendering, using the non-stack-based methods for rendering. In this example, several literal characters are used in `Write` method invocations. The complete list of the literal characters defined in the `HtmlTextWriter` class is shown in Table 8-4.

LISTING 8-9: Sample Control Render Method Using Non-Stack-Based Methods

```
protected override void Render(HtmlTextWriter output)
{
  output.WriteBeginTag("table");
  output.WriteAttribute("width", "50%");
  output.WriteAttribute("border", "1");
  output.Write(HtmlTextWriter.TagRightChar);
  output.Write(output.NewLine);
  output.WriteFullBeginTag("tr");
  output.Write(output.NewLine);
  output.WriteBeginTag("td");
  output.WriteAttribute("align", "left");
  output.Write(HtmlTextWriter.SpaceChar);
  output.Write("style");
  output.Write(HtmlTextWriter.EqualsDoubleQuoteString);
  output.WriteStyleAttribute("font-size", "medium");
  output.WriteStyleAttribute("color", "blue");
  output.Write(HtmlTextWriter.DoubleQuoteChar);
  output.Write(HtmlTextWriter.TagRightChar);
  output.Write("This is row 0 column 0");
  output.WriteEndTag("td");
  output.Write(output.NewLine);
  output.WriteBeginTag("td");
  output.WriteAttribute("align", "right");
  output.Write(HtmlTextWriter.SpaceChar);
  output.Write("style");
  output.Write(HtmlTextWriter.EqualsDoubleQuoteString);
  output.WriteStyleAttribute("color", "green");
  output.Write(HtmlTextWriter.DoubleQuoteChar);
  output.Write(HtmlTextWriter.TagRightChar);
  output.Write("This is row 0 column 1");
  output.WriteEndTag("td");
  output.Write(output.NewLine);
  output.WriteEndTag("tr");
  output.Write(output.NewLine);
  output.WriteEndTag("table");
}
```

TABLE 8-4: HtmlTextWriter Static Character Properties

Property	Value
DefaultTabString	\<tab character\>
DoubleQuoteChar	"
EndTagLeftChars	\</
EqualsChar	=
EqualsDoubleQuoteString	="
SelfClosingChars	/
SelfClosingTagEnd	/>
SemicolonChar	;
SingleQuoteChar	'
SlashChar	/
SpaceChar	\<space character\>
StyleEqualsChar	:
TagLeftChar	<
TagRightChar	>

8.1.5 Browser Independence

One of the most appealing features of server-side controls is the potential for browser-independent, reusable Web components. Several of the controls that ship with ASP.NET generate different HTML based on the client browser. For example, several of the IE Web controls use HTML Components (HTCs) to define DHTML behaviors if the client browser supports them (IE5 or higher), and if not, the controls render the appropriate JavaScript to provide equivalent behavior.

You can build controls that conditionally generate different HTML as well by querying the client browser capabilities through the `Browser` property of the `Request` object of the `Page`. The `Browser` is an instance of the `HttpBrowserCapabilities` class, which contains information about the capabilities of the client browser. Listing 8-10 shows the properties of the `HttpBrowserCapabilities` class, and Listing 8-11 shows a simple control that changes its rendering based on whether the client browser supports JavaScript or not.

LISTING 8-10: The HttpBrowserCapabilities Class

```
class HttpBrowserCapabilities : HttpCapabilitiesBase
{
  public bool            ActiveXControls       {get;}
  public bool            AOL                   {get;}
  public bool            BackgroundSounds      {get;}
  public bool            Beta                  {get;}
  public bool            Browser               {get;}
  public bool            CDF                   {get;}
  public Version         ClrVersion            {get;}
  public bool            Cookies               {get;}
  public bool            Crawler               {get;}
  public Version         EcmaScriptVersion     {get;}
  public bool            Frames                {get;}
  public bool            JavaApplets           {get;}
  public bool            JavaScript            {get;}
  public int             MajorVersion          {get;}
  public double          MinorVersion          {get;}
  public Version         MSDomVersion          {get;}
  public string          Platform              {get;}
  public bool            Tables                {get;}
  public string          Type                  {get;}
  public bool            VBScript              {get;}
  public string          Version               {get;}
  public Version         W3CDomVersion         {get;}
  public bool            Win16                 {get;}
  public bool            Win32                 {get;}
  //...
}
```

LISTING 8-11: Example of a Control That Changes Its Rendering Based on Browser Capabilities

```
public class BrowserIndependentControl : Control
{
  protected override void Render(HtmlTextWriter output)
```

```
    {
        if (Page.Request.Browser.JavaScript)
    output.Write(
            "<h3 onclick=\"alert('Hi there')\">click me!</h3>");
        else
            output.Write("<h3>Don't bother</h3>");
    }
    }
```

The information used to populate the HttpBrowserCapabilities class for any given request is drawn from the <browserCaps> element of the systemwide machine.config file. This element contains regular expression matches for browser headers and assigns the values in the HttpBrowserCapabilities class based on the current capabilities of that browser and version. This section may be augmented if browsers that are not handled may be used to access your pages. In the machine.config file there is a note that this section can be updated by retrieving the latest browser capabilities information from http://www.cyscape.com/browser-caps. As of this writing, however, this site has no such update.

It can be useful, for testing, to change the browser type, even if you are using the same browser for testing. You can do this by using the Client-Target attribute of the Page directive in your .aspx file. There are four pre-defined client targets—ie4, ie5, uplevel, and downlevel—and you can define additional targets by using the clientTarget element in your web.config file. By setting the ClientTarget to downlevel, as shown in Listing 8-12, you can easily test to see how your page will behave when accessed by an unknown browser type.

LISTING 8-12: Setting the ClientTarget for a Page

```
<%@ Page Language='C#' ClientTarget='downlevel' %>
```

This ClientTarget value is accessible through the Page class as a read/write property. You should be aware, however, that the value is set only if you explicitly set it yourself either programmatically in your Page-derived class or as an attribute in your Page directive. You should never use the ClientTarget property to test for browser capabilities. Instead, you should always use the HttpBrowserCapabilities class, which will be filled in properly based either on the headers of the HTTP request or on the value of the `ClientTarget` attribute (which takes precedence). To add your own browser alias for testing to the `ClientTarget` attribute list, add a `clientTarget` element to your `web.config` file with an embedded `add` element containing the alias string you want to use and the `userAgent` string that would be submitted by the browser you want to test against. Listing 8-13 shows an example of defining an additional `ClientTarget` type in a `web.config` file for testing to see how a page will render in Netscape 6.0.

LISTING 8-13: Adding a ClientTarget Alias to web.config

```
<!- web.config file ->
<configuration>
  <system.web>
  <clientTarget>
    <add alias='nn6'
         userAgent='Mozilla/5.0 (en-US;) Netscape6/6.0' />
  </clientTarget>
  </system.web>
</configuration>
```

8.1.6 Subproperties

In addition to exposing properties on a custom control, it is also possible to expose subproperties. Subproperties are a convenient way of gathering a set of common properties under a single, top-level property, with the potential for reuse in other controls as well. The syntax for setting subproperties is identical to the syntax used in traditional HTML, which means that it will be familiar to users of your control. For example, suppose we wanted to expose font properties used by our control for rendering text as subproperties, so that a client could set font attributes, such as `Color` and `Size`, through our single `Font` property, as shown in Listing 8-14.

LISTING 8-14: Client Syntax for Setting Subproperties on a Custom Control

```
<%@ Page Language='C#' %>
<%@ Register Namespace='EssentialAspDotNet.CustomControls'
             TagPrefix='eadn' Assembly='SubProperties' %>
```

```
<html>
<body>
<eadn:SubPropertyControl runat='server' Name='Test'
                         Font-Color='red' Font-Size='24'/>
</body>
</html>
```

The mechanism for exposing subproperties in a custom control is to
define a helper class that exposes all the properties you want to include as
subproperties on your control, and then to add an instance of that class to
your control class and expose it as a read-only property. Listing 8-15 shows
a sample subproperty class that exposes two properties for controlling font
rendering: Size and Color.

LISTING 8-15: Sample Subproperty Class Exposing Font Properties

```
public class FontFormat
{
  private int   m_size;
  private Color m_color;

  public FontFormat(int size, Color clr)
  {
    m_size  = size;
    m_color = clr;
  }

  public int Size
  {
    get { return m_size;  }
    set { m_size = value; }
  }

  public Color Color
  {
    get { return m_color;  }
    set { m_color = value; }
  }
}
```

Listing 8-16 shows how this class could be used to expose the properties of the FontFormat class as subproperties of a control, achieving the
subproperty access syntax shown initially in Listing 8-14.

LISTING 8-16: Exposing Subproperties in a Custom Control

```
public class SubPropertyControl : Control
{
  private string m_Name;
  private FontFormat m_Font =
                    new FontFormat(3, Color.Black);

  public string Name
  {
    get { return m_Name;  }
    set { m_Name = value; }
  }

  public FontFormat Font
  {
    get { return m_Font; }
  }

  protected override void Render(HtmlTextWriter writer)
  {
    writer.AddStyleAttribute(
      HtmlTextWriterStyle.FontSize, m_Font.Size.ToString());
    writer.AddStyleAttribute(HtmlTextWriterStyle.Color,
                             m_Font.Color.Name);
    writer.RenderBeginTag(HtmlTextWriterTag.Span);
    writer.Write(m_Name);
    writer.RenderEndTag();
  }
}
```

8.1.7 Inner Content

Although properties can be used to initialize all of the state in a control, it sometimes makes more syntactic sense to have the user specify control state through the contents of a control tag, as shown in Listing 8-17.

LISTING 8-17: Specifying Control State through Using Inner Content

```
<%@ Page Language='C#' %>
<%@ Register Namespace='EssentialAspDotNet.CustomControls'
             TagPrefix='eadn' Assembly='InnerContent' %>
<html>
<body>
  <eadn:InnerContentControl runat='server'>
```

```
      Inner content goes here
   </eadn:InnerContentControl>
 </body>
 </html>
```

To retrieve this inner content from within a custom control class, you need to understand what the ASP.NET page parser does when it encounters content inside the tag of a control. Looking back at Figure 8-1, you can see that the parser turns the contents of any control tag into child controls and adds them to the Controls collection for that control. If the contents of the tag are simple text or client-side HTML tags, an instance of a LiteralControl class is created to represent it on the server. Thus, in our case of building a custom control that wants to use its inner content as part of its rendering, we need to access the LiteralControl class in our Controls array and extract its text content.

An example of a control that uses its inner content as part of its rendering is shown in Listing 8-18. Note that it is important to determine whether there actually is any inner content before trying to access it. The HasControls() method returns true only if one or more controls are in your Controls collection. Furthermore, note that we check to see that the first control in the Controls array is in fact a LiteralControl before accessing its Text field.

LISTING 8-18: Custom Control That Accesses Inner Content

```
public class InnerContentControl : Control
{
  protected override void Render(HtmlTextWriter output)
  {
    if (HasControls())
    {
      output.RenderBeginTag(HtmlTextWriterTag.H1);
      LiteralControl lc = Controls[0] as LiteralControl;
      if (lc != null)
        output.Write(lc.Text);
      output.RenderEndTag();
    }
  }
}
```

8.1.8 Generating Client-Side Script

Often a control may want to generate client-side script in addition to static HTML as part of its rendering process. If the client browser supports DHTML, it is often possible to shift some of the behavior of a control to the client and thus avoid unnecessary round-trips. For example, suppose we wanted to build a control that rendered a tic-tac-toe game board, which allows the user to click in a square to add an X or an O in alternating fashion, as shown in Figure 8-2.

A naïve approach to building a control that would render this board might be to add a client script block with a handler function to toggle the Xs and Os for the Onclick event, followed by the HTML table and cells that would generate the client-side events. This approach is shown in Listing 8-19.

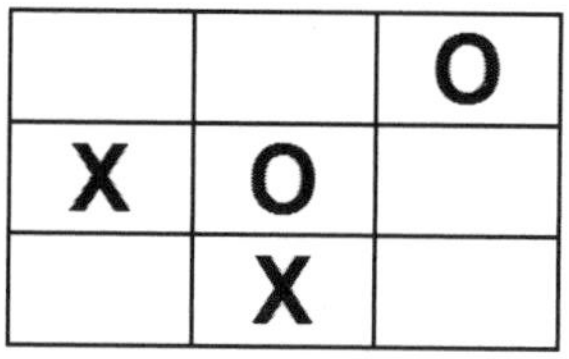

FIGURE 8-2: Tic-tac-toe Board Rendered with DHTML

LISTING 8-19: Naïve Client Script Generation

```
public class TicTacToe : Control
{
  protected override void Render(HtmlTextWriter output)
  {
    output.WriteLine("<script language=javascript>   ");
    output.WriteLine("var g_bXWentLast;                ");
    output.WriteLine("function OnClickCell(cell) {    ");
    output.WriteLine("  if (cell.innerText == ' ') {  ");
    output.WriteLine("    if (g_bXWentLast)            ");
    output.WriteLine("      cell.innerText = 'O';      ");
    output.WriteLine("    else                         ");
    output.WriteLine("      cell.innerText = 'X';      ");
    output.WriteLine("    g_bXWentLast = !g_bXWentLast;");
    output.WriteLine("  }                              ");
```

```
output.WriteLine("  else                                ");
output.WriteLine("    cell.innerText = ' ';             ");
output.WriteLine("  } </script>                         ");

/* additional style attributes not shown */
output.RenderBeginTag(HtmlTextWriterTag.Table);
for (int row=0; row<3; row++)
{
    output.RenderBeginTag(HtmlTextWriterTag.Tr);
    for (int col=0; col<3; col++)
    {
        output.AddAttribute(
                    HtmlTextWriterAttribute.Onclick,
                    "OnClickCell(this)");
        output.RenderBeginTag(HtmlTextWriterTag.Td);
        output.Write(" ");
        output.RenderEndTag();
    }
    output.RenderEndTag();
}
output.RenderEndTag();
}
}
```

This control will work well as long as it is never used more than once on a single page. Placing multiple instances of this control on a page, however, causes two problems. The first problem is that the script block will be rendered twice to the page, which can cause undetermined behavior, especially since we are declaring a global script variable to keep track of whether an X or an O should be placed in the next square. The second problem is that our single global script variable, g_bXWentLast, will not have the correct value if a user clicks in one instance of our control and then another (it is easy to generate two Xs in a row on one board, for example). These two problems are indicative of problems that most controls encounter when they try to add client-side script as part of their rendering.

The first problem can easily be solved by using the helper function RegisterClientScriptBlock in the Page class. This function takes a pair of strings as parameters; the first string is a name for the script block, so that if a script block is ever registered multiple times on a given page, it will still be rendered only once. The second string is the actual script block you want included in the page. The best place to call this function is in a handler for the Init event of your control, as shown in Listing 8-20.

LISTING 8-20: Calling RegisterClientScriptBlock

```
protected override void OnInit(EventArgs e)
{
  Page.RegisterClientScriptBlock("MyScriptBlock",
    "<script language=javascript>/*code here*/</script>");
}
```

The second problem is maintaining client-side state on behalf of each instance of our control. This is a common problem for controls rendering client-side script and relying on a single set of functions to perform some client-side logic. It is important to plan for the scenario that someone places multiple instances of your control on a page, and not have the behavior become undefined. Fortunately, as covered earlier in this chapter, there is a unique identifier associated with each control that will always be a valid JavaScript identifier: ClientID. Thus, the solution to our tic-tac-toe control problem is to keep an associative array of Booleans, indexed by the ClientID of our control, thereby guaranteeing unique state for each instance of our control. The complete and correct implementation of our tic-tac-toe control is shown in Listing 8-21.

LISTING 8-21: Correct Client-Side Script Generation

```
public class TicTacToe : Control
{
  protected override void OnInit(EventArgs e)
  {
    string sCode = @"<script language=javascript>
      var g_rgbXWentLast = new Object();
      function OnClickCell(cell, idx) {
        if (cell.innerText == \"" \"") {
          if (g_rgbXWentLast[idx])
            cell.innerText = 'O';
          else
            cell.innerText = 'X';
          g_rgbXWentLast[idx] = !g_rgbXWentLast[idx];
        }
        else
          cell.innerText = ' ';
      }";
    Page.RegisterClientScriptBlock("CellCode", sCode);
  }

  protected override void Render(HtmlTextWriter output)
```

```
  {
    output.RenderBeginTag(HtmlTextWriterTag.Table);
    for (int row=0; row<3; row++)
    {
      output.RenderBeginTag(HtmlTextWriterTag.Tr);
      for (int col=0; col<3; col++)
      {
        string clk = string.Format(
                  "OnClickCell(this, '{0}')", ClientID);
        output.AddAttribute(
                  HtmlTextWriterAttribute.Onclick, clk);
        output.RenderBeginTag(HtmlTextWriterTag.Td);
        output.Write(" ");
        output.RenderEndTag();
      }
      output.RenderEndTag();
    }
    output.RenderEndTag();
  }
}
```

8.1.9 System.Web.UI.WebControls.WebControl

Another class that derives from `Control` can be used as the base class for custom controls: `WebControl`. The `WebControl` class contains several additional fields, properties, and methods that are used commonly by all the controls in the `WebControls` namespace (such as `Button` and `ListBox`). The most significant difference between deriving from `Control` and `WebControl` is that `WebControl` adds several properties to your class. Listing 8-22 shows the additional properties you will inherit if you use `WebControl` as your base class.

LISTING 8-22: Additional Properties Defined in the WebControl Class

```
public class WebControl : Control
{
  public virtual string      AccessKey    {get; set;}
  public virtual Color       BackColor    {get; set;}
  public virtual Color       BorderColor  {get; set;}
  public virtual BorderStyle BorderStyle  {get; set;}
  public virtual Unit        BorderWidth  {get; set;}
  public virtual string      CssClass     {get; set;}
```

continues

```
public virtual bool        Enabled    {get; set;}
public virtual FontInfo    Font       {get;     }
public virtual Color       ForeColor  {get; set;}
public virtual Unit        Height     {get; set;}
public virtual short       TabIndex   {get; set;}
public virtual string      ToolTip    {get; set;}
public virtual Unit        Width      {get; set;}
//...
}
```

On the other hand, most controls will probably support only a subset of the additional properties defined by `WebControl` and may be better off defining the common properties explicitly rather than deriving from `Web-Control`. If you are using Visual Studio.NET to build your custom control, it automatically derives your control from `WebControl` instead of `Control`. You should be aware of this, and either change the base class to `Control` if you do not plan on supporting most of the additional properties, or make sure you do support these additional properties (or explicitly disable them in your class).

For an example of a control that derives from `WebControl` and implements all the additional properties, consider the `NameWebControl` class shown in Listing 8-23. This class has a single custom property, `Text`, used to store a string to be rendered as a `<span>` element. This control is very similar to the `Label` control defined in the `WebControls` namespace.

LISTING 8-23: Sample Control Deriving from WebControl

```
public class NameWebControl : WebControl
{
  private string m_Text;
  public string Text
  {
    get { return m_Text;   }
    set { m_Text = value; }
  }

  protected override void Render(HtmlTextWriter writer)
  {
    writer.AddStyleAttribute(
      HtmlTextWriterStyle.BorderColor, BorderColor.Name);
    writer.AddStyleAttribute(
      HtmlTextWriterStyle.BackgroundColor, BackColor.Name);
    writer.AddStyleAttribute(
      HtmlTextWriterStyle.BorderStyle,
```

```
        BorderStyle.ToString());
    writer.AddStyleAttribute(
      HtmlTextWriterStyle.BorderWidth,
      BorderWidth.ToString());
    writer.AddStyleAttribute(
      HtmlTextWriterStyle.FontFamily, Font.Name);
    writer.AddStyleAttribute(HtmlTextWriterStyle.FontSize,
      Font.Size.ToString());
    if (Font.Bold)
      writer.AddStyleAttribute(
        HtmlTextWriterStyle.FontWeight, "bold");
    if (Font.Italic)
      writer.AddStyleAttribute(
        HtmlTextWriterStyle.FontStyle, "italic");
    string decoration = "";
    if (Font.Underline)
      decoration += "underline";
    if (Font.Overline)
      decoration += " overline";
    if (Font.Strikeout)
      decoration += " line-through";
    if (decoration.Length > 0)
      writer.AddStyleAttribute(
        HtmlTextWriterStyle.TextDecoration, decoration);
    writer.AddStyleAttribute(HtmlTextWriterStyle.Color,
      ForeColor.Name);
    writer.AddStyleAttribute(HtmlTextWriterStyle.Height,
      Height.ToString());
    writer.AddStyleAttribute(HtmlTextWriterStyle.Width,
      Width.ToString());
    writer.AddAttribute(HtmlTextWriterAttribute.Class,
      CssClass);
    writer.AddAttribute(HtmlTextWriterAttribute.Title,
      ToolTip);
    if (!Enabled)
      writer.AddAttribute(HtmlTextWriterAttribute.Disabled,
                          "true");
    writer.RenderBeginTag(HtmlTextWriterTag.Span);
    writer.Write(m_Text);
    writer.RenderEndTag();
  }
}
```

Because the WebControl class defines all these additional properties, using it as a base class for your control means that your control should respond if a client changes one of these properties. For our simple text control that rendered as a span, this was pretty straightforward because the

`<span>` element supports all these properties natively. Applying all these properties to a more complex control (like our tic-tac-toe control) would require more thought, and in all likelihood, several of the properties would not make sense for our control. This is important to keep in mind, because when someone uses your control within Visual Studio .NET, they will be presented with a complete list of your properties and will probably expect them to have some effect on the appearance of your control. An example of this property list for our `NameWebControl` is shown in Figure 8-3.

If it does not make sense for your control to implement all the additional properties defined by `WebControl`, you have two options. First, you can

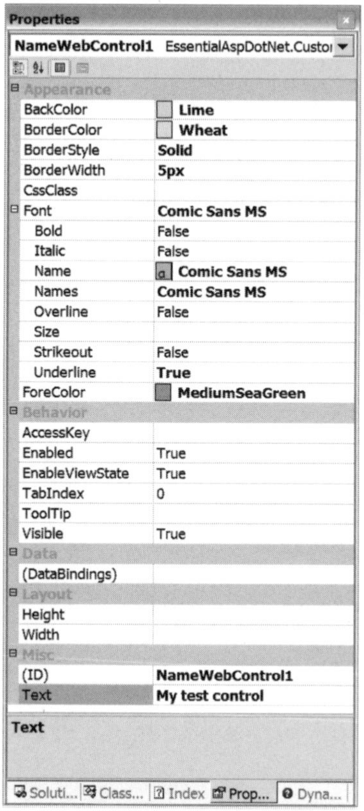

Properties	
NameWebControl1	EssentialAspDotNet.Custo▼

Appearance	
BackColor	☐ Lime
BorderColor	☐ Wheat
BorderStyle	**Solid**
BorderWidth	**5px**
CssClass	
Font	**Comic Sans MS**
Bold	False
Italic	False
Name	a **Comic Sans MS**
Names	**Comic Sans MS**
Overline	False
Size	
Strikeout	False
Underline	**True**
ForeColor	■ **MediumSeaGreen**
Behavior	
AccessKey	
Enabled	True
EnableViewState	True
TabIndex	0
ToolTip	
Visible	True
Data	
(DataBindings)	
Layout	
Height	
Width	
Misc	
(ID)	**NameWebControl1**
Text	**My test control**

Text	

Soluti... | Class... | Index | Prop... | Dyna...

FIGURE 8-3: Property Page for Web Control

choose to derive your control from the `Control` base class instead of `Web-Control`, and define your own properties as needed. Alternatively, you can choose the subset of properties inherited from `WebControl` that make sense for your control to implement, and for the remainder of the properties, provide a virtual override that sets the `Browsable` attribute to false to hide them in the designer. We will discuss designer integration in more detail later in this chapter, but for now, Listing 8-24 shows an example of a control that derives from `WebControl` but has set the `Browsable` attribute to `false` for several of the inherited properties.

LISTING 8-24: WebControl-Derived Class Disabling Some Inherited Properties

```
public class PartialWebControl : WebControl
{
  [Browsable(false)]
  public override Color BorderColor
  { get {return base.BorderColor;} }

  [Browsable(false)]
  public override BorderStyle BorderStyle
  { get {return base.BorderStyle;} }

  [Browsable(false)]
  public override Unit BorderWidth
  { get {return base.BorderWidth;} }

  // ...
}
```

8.2 State Management

As with most aspects of Web application development, building custom controls involves thinking carefully about state management. In this section, we explore two mechanisms for maintaining state in custom controls: using view state and explicitly handling post-back data.

8.2.1 ViewState

All the Web controls in the base class libraries retain their state across post-backs, and thus users will expect all controls they use to work this way. This means that any controls you develop should support state retention. Fortunately, ASP.NET helps you by providing a collection of name/value pairs accessible by any control through its `ViewState` property that is an instance of `System.Web.UI.StateBag`. Any name/value pair placed in this collection before the rendering of a page is stored in the hidden __VIEWSTATE input field, and when the page is next accessed via a POST request, the contents of the hidden __VIEWSTATE input field are parsed and used to reconstitute the `ViewState` collection.

As an example of retaining state using the `ViewState` collection, Listing 8-25 shows the `Name` control shown earlier rewritten to save and restore its two properties from the `ViewState` collection. This version of the control no longer maintains local fields to store the property values but relies instead on the `ViewState` collection to always have the current values for all its properties.

This technique of using the `ViewState` collection as the state repository for properties works well for any simple property. More complex properties (such as lists or arrays of data) need to be saved to and restored from `ViewState` more carefully, as we will see shortly. It is important to note that you should always initialize any elements your control depends on in your control's constructor to guarantee that they will be initialized to some default values if they are accessed before they are set. Alternatively, you could implement the `get` method of each property to conditionally check that there is a valid entry in the `ViewState` collection before returning that value, and if there is none, initialize it with some default value.

LISTING 8-25: Name Control Rewritten to Use ViewState

```
public class NameControl : Control
{
  public NameControl()
  {
    ViewState["IsImportant"] = true;
    ViewState["Name"] = "";
  }

  public string Name
  {
    get { return (string)ViewState["Name"]; }
    set { ViewState["Name"] = value; }
```

```
  }

  public bool IsImportant
  {
    get { return (bool)ViewState["IsImportant"]; }
    set { ViewState["IsImportant"] = value; }
  }

  protected override void Render(HtmlTextWriter writer)
  {
    if (IsImportant)
      writer.RenderBeginTag(HtmlTextWriterTag.H1);
    else
      writer.RenderBeginTag(HtmlTextWriterTag.H2);

    writer.Write(Name);
    writer.RenderEndTag();
  }
}
```

The effect of retaining our state across post-backs is that clients can now rely on our control retaining its state like all the other controls. Keep in mind that if the client explicitly disables ViewState at either the control or the Page level, the ViewState collection will be empty at the beginning of each request, and your control properties will always have their default values.

For an example of a client that depends on our control retaining its state across post-backs, consider the page shown in Listing 8-26. Notice that when the page is first accessed (when IsPostBack is false), the Name and IsImportant properties of the Name controls are initialized, but on subsequent post-backs to the same page (when IsPostBack is true), the control properties are not touched. Because our control is now saving its properties in the ViewState collection, the values of these properties will be properly restored.

LISTING 8-26: Name Control Client Page Relying on Post-Back State Retention

```
<%@ Page Language='C#' %>
<%@ Register Namespace='EssentialAspDotNet.CustomControls'
            TagPrefix='eadn' Assembly='name' %>
<script runat='server'>
    protected void DoSubmit(object src, EventArgs e)
    { /* do something */    }
```

continues

```
      protected void Page_Load(object src, EventArgs e)
      {
        if (!IsPostBack) // populate custom controls
        {
          m_nc1.Name = "Foo";
          m_nc1.IsImportant = true;
          m_nc2.Name = "Bar";
          m_nc2.IsImportant = false;
        }

        // if not IsPostBack, no need to repopulate
        // controls because their state will have been
        // retained
      }
</script>

<html><body>
<form runat='server'>
<eadn:NameControl id='m_nc1' runat='server' />
<eadn:NameControl id='m_nc2' runat='server' />
<br/>
<asp:Button runat='server' text='submit'
            Onclick='DoSubmit'/>
</form>
</body></html>
```

Using the ViewState collection works well for primitive types and for state that maps directly to properties. If you have more complex state in your control that can reasonably be represented only by using local data structures, it will be cumbersome to figure out how to use the ViewState to cache all your data structure state. Instead, you can override a pair of virtual methods defined in the Control base class, and manually populate and retrieve state from the ViewState stream. Any object that is serializable can be persisted to the ViewState stream, which includes all the standard collection classes in the base class libraries (and any of your own classes that are marked with the Serializable attribute).

For an example of a control that performs more sophisticated view state management, consider the BarGraph control shown in Listing 8-27. This control maintains three pieces of data internally: a list of strings, a list of doubles, and a single double instance. Its rendering involves showing a table consisting of color-filled span elements displaying the current values of the two lists, as shown in Figure 8-4. The values that populate these two

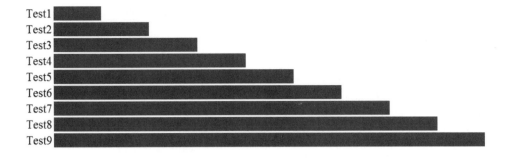

FIGURE 8-4: BarGraph Control Rendering

lists are added when a client programmatically invokes the AddValue() method of the control, so there is no simple mapping between the state of this control and the ViewState property inherited from the Control class. Instead, the BarGraphControl class overrides the SaveViewState and LoadViewState functions to manually populate the object array to be serialized into the __VIEWSTATE field. The SaveViewState function is called when a control is asked to add what it wants to into the outgoing __VIEW-STATE field, and should return an array of objects to be serialized into the __VIEWSTATE field. In almost all cases, you will want to invoke the base class's version of SaveViewState and add the result into your locally constructed object array, as shown in the BarGraphControl's implementation. This will ensure that any state managed by the base class will also be saved. In the BarGraphControl's function, the three other pieces of state in the class are added to a locally constructed object array, and because each of the types added to the array is serializable, they will be successfully added to the view state stream. The LoadViewState function does the opposite—it is called just before the Load event is fired, and it receives an object array as input used to rehydrate any local control state from the view state stream. Again, most implementations will want to call the base class version of LoadViewState with the first element of the array. In our Bar-GraphControl example, once the base class has been called, we load the state from each element of the array into our local fields.

LISTING 8-27: BarGraph Control Performing Manual View State Management

```
public class BarGraphControl : Control
{
  private ArrayList _dataDescriptions;
  private ArrayList _dataValues;
  private double    _max = 0;

  protected override void LoadViewState(object savedState)
  {
    if (savedState != null)
    {
      // Load State from the array of objects that
       // was saved in SaveViewState
      object[] vState = (object[])savedState;
      if (vState[0] != null)
        base.LoadViewState(vState[0]);
      if (vState[1] != null)
        _dataDescriptions = (ArrayList)vState[1];
      if (vState[2] != null)
        _dataValues = (ArrayList)vState[2];
      if (vState[3] != null)
        _max = (double)vState[3];
    }
  }

  protected override object SaveViewState()
  {
    object[] vState = new object[4];
    vState[0] = base.SaveViewState();
    vState[1] = _dataDescriptions;
    vState[2] = _dataValues;
    vState[3] = _max;

    return vState;
  }

  public BarGraphControl()
  {
    _dataDescriptions = new ArrayList();
    _dataValues = new ArrayList();
  }

  public void AddValue(string name, double val)
  {
    _dataDescriptions.Add(name);
    _dataValues.Add(val);
```

```
      if (val > _max)
        _max = val;
  }

  protected override void Render(HtmlTextWriter output)
  {
    output.RenderBeginTag(HtmlTextWriterTag.Table);
    foreach (object elem in _dataValues)
    {
     // rendering details omitted (see sample)
    }
    output.RenderEndTag(); //</table>
  }
}
```

8.2.2 Explicit Post-Back Data Handling

Using view state to retain control state across post-backs is necessary for controls that render themselves as HTML elements whose contents are not sent as part of a POST request (such as tables and spans). If you are building a control that renders itself using HTML elements whose contents *are* sent through a POST request, you can load the state of the control directly from the POST variable collection instead of further burdening the hidden __VIEWSTATE field.

For example, suppose you were building a control that rendered itself as an INPUT tag in HTML. The contents of INPUT tags within a FORM element are always sent back as part of a POST request, so instead of saving and loading your control's state to and from view state, you could tap directly into the POST body for its latest value. To do this, your control must implement the IPostBackDataHandler interface, shown in Listing 8-28.

LISTING 8-28: IPostBackDataHandler Interface Definition

```
public interface IPostBackDataHandler
{
  bool LoadPostData(string postDataKey,
                    NameValueCollection postCollection);
  void RaisePostDataChangedEvent();
}
```

For controls that implement this interface, the `LoadPostData` method will be invoked just before the `Load` event fires, and will contain the entire contents of the `POST` body in the `NameValueCollection`. The post-DataKey string passed in will contain the unique identifier associated with your control, which can be used to index the `postCollection` to find the current value of your control within the `POST` variable collection. The result of this method should be `true` if you change the value of the control's state, false otherwise.

If your control wants to propagate change notifications through server-side events, you can use a method of `IPostBackDataHandler` called `RaisePostDataChangedEvent` that is called whenever you return `true` from your implementation of `LoadPostData`. To fire this event when your control's data has changed, you need to keep track of the last value of your control in addition to the current value. The easiest way to do this is by using view state to store the current value of your control, and then checking the value stored in view state against the value sent back as part of the `POST` request. If they are different, you know that the control was changed between the last request and the current request, and you should return `true` from `LoadPostData` to indicate so.

Listing 8-29 shows a custom control called `CustomTextBox` that implements `IPostBackDataHandler`. It renders itself as an `INPUT` tag and can therefore extract its value from the `POST` body whenever a request is processed. It also exposes a public event called `TextChanged` that is fired whenever the `RaisePostDataChangedEvent` is invoked. To ensure that this event is fired only when the contents of the `INPUT` control have changed, it stores its `Text` property in `ViewState`, and when it loads a new value in from the `POST` body, it checks to see whether it has changed and returns `true` or `false` accordingly.

LISTING 8-29: A Control That Performs Explicit Post-Back Data Handling

```
public class CustomTextBox: Control, IPostBackDataHandler
{
  public string Text
  {
    get { return (string) ViewState["Text"]; }
    set { ViewState["Text"] = value;        }
```

```
    }

    public event EventHandler TextChanged;

    public virtual bool LoadPostData(string postDataKey,
                         NameValueCollection postCollection)
    {
        string presentValue = Text;
        string postedValue = postCollection[postDataKey];

        if (presentValue == null ||
            !presentValue.Equals(postedValue))
        {
          Text = postedValue;
          return true;
        }

        return false;
    }

    public virtual void RaisePostDataChangedEvent()
    {
        if (TextChanged != null)
          TextChanged(this,e);
    }

    protected override void Render(HtmlTextWriter output)
    {
        output.AddAttribute(HtmlTextWriterAttribute.Name,
                           UniqueID);
        output.AddAttribute(HtmlTextWriterAttribute.Value,
                           Text);
        output.RenderBeginTag(HtmlTextWriterTag.Input);
        output.RenderEndTag();
    }
  }
```

Many controls in the base class libraries implement IPostBackData-Handler, including TextBox, HtmlInputText, CheckBox, HtmlSelect, DropDownList, and so on. Because all the primitive HTML elements whose contents are propagated back within the body of a POST request already have control classes defined, it is unlikely that you will want to create your own control classes that implement IPostBackDataHandler very often. If you want to customize the behavior of one of these primitive control classes, it is often more convenient to create a new class that derives from the base class control implementation. The one other case where you may consider implementing this interface is for a composite control that contains several HTML controls in its rendering (such as a collection of INPUT controls). Controls that contain other controls, however, can usually be more conveniently implemented as composite controls, which are server controls that contain other server controls and which we discuss next.

8.3 Composite Controls

Many controls contain other controls as part of their definition—these are termed composite controls. By embedding other controls within them, custom controls can be used to define "chunks" of forms that can potentially be reused from many different pages, complete with their own properties, events, and methods. Composite controls are built by creating child controls and adding them to the Controls collection of the parent control. All creation of child controls should take place in an override of the virtual function CreateChildControls. This function is inherited from the Control base class and is called at the correct time to create child controls (after the Load event, just before rendering).

8.3.1 Creating Child Controls

Listing 8-30 shows a simple composite control that implements a calculator by using three TextBox controls, a Button control, and some Literal-Controls intermingled. A LiteralControl is a simple control that renders its Text property and is especially useful when building composite controls for properly laying out the child controls. This control also shows an example of hooking up an event handler to a child control.

LISTING 8-30: Composite Control Example

```
public class CalcComposite : Control, INamingContainer
{
  TextBox _operand1;
  TextBox _operand2;
  TextBox _result;

  private void OnCalculate(Object sender, EventArgs e)
  {
    int res = Convert.ToInt32(_operand1.Text) +
```

```
                    Convert.ToInt32(_operand2.Text);
    _result.Text = res.ToString();
  }

  public int Result
  { get { return Convert.ToInt32(_result.Text); }  }

  protected override void CreateChildControls()
  {
    _operand1 = new TextBox();
    _operand2 = new TextBox();
    _result   = new TextBox();

    Controls.Add(_operand1);
    Controls.Add(new LiteralControl(" + "));
    Controls.Add(_operand2);
    Controls.Add(new LiteralControl(" = "));
    Controls.Add(_result);
    Controls.Add(new LiteralControl("<br/>"));

    Button calculate = new Button();
    calculate.Text = "Calculate";
    calculate.Click += new EventHandler(this.OnCalculate);
    Controls.Add(calculate);
  }
}
```

Notice also that the control shown in Listing 8-30 implements the INam-ingContainer interface. This is a marker interface (one with no methods) that indicates to the containing page that this control has child controls that may need to be in a separate namespace. If there is more than one instance of a composite control on a given page, it is important that the child controls of each composite control not have ID clashes. Anytime you have child controls in a custom control, you should be sure to add support for INaming-Container to avoid ID clashes in the rendered HTML.

You may find that in your composite control, you would like to manipulate some of your child controls during the Load event of your control. The CreateChildControls method is not called until after the Load event has fired, however, so if you attempt to access any child controls within a Load handler, you will find none. To guarantee that your child controls have been created, you can always call EnsureChildControls(). This function checks to see if the CreateChildControls function has been called yet (by checking the ChildControlsCreated Boolean), and if not, calls it for you.

For example, the composite control shown in Listing 8-31 explicitly calls `EnsureChildControls` from within its `Load` handler before it tries to set one of the children's values.

LISTING 8-31: Calling EnsureChildControls

```
public class CalcComposite : Control, INamingContainer
{
  TextBox _operand1;
  TextBox _operand2;
  TextBox _result;

  protected void Page_Load(object src, EventArgs e)
  {
    EnsureChildControls();
    _operand1.Text = "42";
  }

  protected override void CreateChildControls()
  {
    _operand1 = new TextBox();
    _operand2 = new TextBox();
    _result   = new TextBox();
    //...
  }
}
```

With a composite control, it may also be useful to retrieve a child control dynamically. This is easily done with the `FindControl` method, which takes the string identifier of the control and returns a reference to the control.

8.3.2 Custom Events

For a custom control to truly provide all the attributes of standard Web controls, it must be able to define and propagate events. You define events in a custom control by adding a public event data member of delegate type `EventHandler`. A client then attaches a method to the event handler, and it is up to the control to invoke that method whenever the event logically occurs. Listing 8-32 shows a modified version of our `CalcComposite` control with a custom event added. Note that it declares a public `EventHandler` member called `MagicNumber` to which clients can hook delegates. In our example, the `EventHandler` is invoked whenever the user calculates the value 42 with the calculator. Listing 8-33 shows a sample .aspx page that traps the `MagicNumber` event and populates a label in response.

LISTING 8-32: Control with Custom Event Example

```csharp
public class CalcComposite : Control, INamingContainer
{
    // other members not shown

  public event EventHandler MagicNumber; // public event

  private void OnCalculate(Object sender, EventArgs e)
  {
    int res = Convert.ToInt32(_operand1.Text) +
              Convert.ToInt32(_operand2.Text);
    _result.Text = res.ToString();
    if ((res == 42) && (MagicNumber != null))
      MagicNumber(this, EventArgs.Empty); // Trigger event!
  }

  protected override void CreateChildControls()
  {
    // Other control creation not shown...
    Button calculate = new Button();
    calculate.Text = "Calculate";
    calculate.Click += new EventHandler(this.OnCalculate);
    this.Controls.Add(calculate);
  }
}
```

LISTING 8-33: Sample Custom Event Client

```aspx
<%@ Page Language="C#" %>
<%@ Register TagPrefix="eadn"
             Namespace="EssentialAspDotNet.CustomControls"
             Assembly="CalcComposite" %>

<html>
<script language="C#" runat=server>
private void MyCtrl_OnMagicNumber(Object src, EventArgs e)
{
  MagicNumberLabel.Text = "Magic number calculated!!";
}
</script>
```

continues

```
<body>
  <form runat=server>
    <asp:Label id=MagicNumberLabel runat=server />
    <eadn:SimpleComposite id="MyCtrl"
        OnMagicNumber="MyCtrl_OnMagicNumber" runat=server />
  </form>
</body>
</html>
```

8.4 User Controls

Like pages in ASP.NET, controls can also be defined mostly in code, mostly as tags on a page, or somewhere in between. So far, we have looked at defining controls entirely in code, but you can define something called a "user control" by using tags on a page as well. This is very convenient for composite controls, because it allows you to lay out your control's HTML tags on a page rather than programmatically.

To define a user control, you create a page with an .ascx extension and use the @Control directive where you would normally use an @Page directive in a standard .aspx page. The @Control directive takes the same attributes as the @Page directive. You then lay out the controls you want to appear in your user control, making sure not to include html, body, or form tags, because these will be supplied by the client. You can also add properties and events in a server-side script block. Listing 8-34 shows our calculator control rewritten as a user control. Notice that properties and methods are declared within the server-side script block as if we were inside our control class definition. This .ascx page will be compiled into a distinct control class when referenced by a client .aspx page.

LISTING 8-34: A User Control

```
<%@ Control Description="A simple calculator" %>

<asp:TextBox ID="Op1" runat=server/> +
<asp:TextBox ID="Op2" runat=server/> =
<asp:TextBox ID="Res" runat=server/>
<br/>
<asp:Button Text="Calculate"
            OnClick="OnCalculate" runat=server/>
```

```
<script language="C#" runat=server>
  private void OnCalculate(Object sender, EventArgs e)
  {
    int res = Convert.ToInt32(Op1.Text) +
              Convert.ToInt32(Op2.Text);
    Res.Text = res.ToString();
  }

  public int Result
  {
    get { return Convert.ToInt32(Res.Text); }
  }
</script>
```

User controls can be accessed from any .aspx page much like other custom controls. The one major difference is that the .ascx file must be accessible by the client page, and it must be referenced using the `Src` attribute of the `@Register` directive. If you need to load a user control dynamically, you can use the `LoadControl` method of the `Page` class, which takes the file name of the user control. When a user control is loaded programmatically, the name of the new control class is the name of the file containing the user control, replacing the "." with an underscore (_). For example, a user control written in file `Foo.ascx` would generate a new control class of type `Foo_ascx` when loaded with `LoadControl`. Listing 8-35 shows an example of an .aspx page that references two user controls. The first one, `user1`, is loaded using the `@Register` directive. The second, `user2`, is loaded programmatically using the `LoadControl` method of the `Page` class.

LISTING 8-35: A Sample Client to a User Control

```
<%@ Page Language="C#" %>
<%@ Register TagPrefix="uc1" TagName="UserControl1"
    Src="UserControl1.ascx" %>

<html>
  <script runat=server>
  void Page_Load(Object sender, EventArgs e)
  {
    Control uc2 = LoadControl("UserControl2.ascx");
    Page.Controls.Add(uc2);
  }
```

continues

```
    </script>
<body>

<form runat=server>
  <uc1:UserControl1 id="UC1" runat=server/>
</form>

</body>
  </html>
```

8.5 Validation and Data Binding

Depending on the features of your custom controls, it may make sense to add support for either validation or data binding. This section describes how to build controls that support these two capabilities.

8.5.1 Supporting Validation

You can add validation support for custom controls that collect information from the user. For a control to support validation, it must be annotated with the ValidationProperty attribute, indicating which of its public properties should be tested with the validation algorithm, and when rendered in HTML, the value attribute of the rendered HTML must equate to the value that is to be validated (for client-side validation). Listing 8-36 shows a sample control to which validation controls could be applied, and Listing 8-37 shows a sample client page applying a validation control to our Custom-TextBox control.

LISTING 8-36: A Control That Supports Validation

```
[ValidationProperty("Text")]
public class CustomTextBox : Control
{
  public CustomTextBox()
  { ViewState["Text"] = ""; }

  public string Text
  {
    get { return (string) ViewState["Text"]; }
    set { ViewState["Text"] = value;        }
  }
```

```
     protected override void Render(HtmlTextWriter output)
   {
      output.AddAttribute(HtmlTextWriterAttribute.Name,
                          UniqueID);
      output.AddAttribute(HtmlTextWriterAttribute.Value,
                          Text);
      output.RenderBeginTag(HtmlTextWriterTag.Input);
      output.RenderEndTag();
   }
 }
```

LISTING 8-37: Client to Custom Control Supporting Validation

```
<%@ Page Language='C#' %>
<%@ Register TagPrefix='eadn'
    Namespace='EssentialAspDotNet.CustomControls'
    Assembly='Validation' %>
<html>
<body>
<form runat=server>
  <eadn:ValidatableControl id='ctb' runat='server' />
  <asp:RequiredFieldValidator runat='server'
      ControlToValidate='ctb'>*
  </asp:RequiredFieldValidator>

  <input type='submit' value='submit' />
</form>
</body>
</html>
```

8.5.2 Data-Bound Controls

Many controls in the `WebControls` hierarchy support the concept of data binding. You can add data binding support to your custom controls as well by exposing a `DataSource` property. When your control renders itself, it pulls data from the data source and uses it as part of its rendering.

To begin with, it is important to understand how clients expect data-bound controls to work. Typically, a client prepares a connection to a data source in the `Load` event of a `Page` class and connects that data source to the `DataSource` property that all data-bound controls provide. The data source could be a simple collection, such as an `ArrayList`; a forward-only data reader, such as an `IDataReader`; or a fully cached data source, such as a `DataSet`, `DataView`, or `DataTable`. As an author of data-bound controls, you need to accommodate all these possibilities. Because all the data-bound controls in the base class hierarchy retain their state across post-backs, clients expect any data-bound control you write to do the same, so that a control need be populated only the first time a page is accessed. Once the client has attached a data source to the control, she may need to set the `DataTextField` and `DataValueField` properties of the control to indicate which field from a tabular data source should be used. Note that if your control can render tabular data (rows with multiple columns), there is no need to support these properties. Finally, once the data source, `DataTextField`, and `DataValueField` properties have been correctly populated, the client calls `DataBind()`, at which point your control's `OnDataBinding` method is called. Your control should iterate over the attached data source, saving the data locally within itself so that when your `Render()` method is called, you have the data to display. This interaction between a client page and a data-bound control is shown in Figure 8-5.

8.5.3 Implementing a Data-Bound Control

The first step in creating a data-bound control is to define a `DataSource` property. This involves adding a public property called `DataSource` to your class of type `object`. Next you need to override the virtual function `OnDataBinding`, inherited from the `Control` base class. Your implementation of `OnDataBinding` should iterate across the data source that was assigned through your control's property, saving the data to a local data structure for future rendering. Note that it is not safe to assume that the data source will be around during your `Render` method, so you must take this step to ensure that you save the data that your control needs to be able to render itself during the `OnDataBinding` method call.

If your control expects only a list of items, not a tabular set of data, to be bound to it, you should expose another property, called `DataTextField`. This field will contain the index into a rowset that the client expects you to dereference when you perform the data binding. If you have the capability of associating values with the data items, you can also expose a property called `DataValueField` (most of the data-bound list controls in the base

client.aspx   Data-Bound Control Class

```
<%@Page language='C#' %>
<%@ Register TagPrefix='eadn' ...%>
<script runat='server'>
protected void
  Page_Load(object src, EventArgs e)
{
  if (!IsPostBack)
  {(1)
    dbc.DataTextField =...
    dbc.DataValueField =...  (2)
    dbc.DataSource =...  (3)
    DataBind();  (4)
  }
}
</script>
<form runat=server>
<eadn:DataBoundControl
      id='dbc' runat='server' />
</form>
```

```
public class DataBoundControl
               : Control
{
(2) public string DataTextField {...}
    public string DataValueField {...}
(3) public object DataSource {...}

    protected override void
(5)       OnDataBinding(EventArgs e)
    {...}

    protected override void
(6)       Render(HtmlTextWriter htw)
    {...}
}
```

(1) Client prepares a data source (IDataReader, DataSet, IList, IEnumerable, DataView, DataTable, and so on.)

(2) Client assigns DataTextField/DataValueField properties if necessary.

(3) Client assigns DataSource field to point to prepared data source.

(4) Client calls DataBind to populate control with data from data source.

(5) Control's OnDataBinding method is invoked where the control must cache the data from the data source.

(6) Control's Render method is called where the control renders itself based on the cached data.

FIGURE 8-5: Interaction between a Page and a Data-Bound Control

class hierarchy expose both of these fields). You should also be as accommodating as possible in what your control supports for data sources. All the data binding controls in the base class hierarchy support binding to any class that supports the IEnumerable or IList interface, plus they support binding directly to DataSets or DataTables by locating the default Data-Table within a DataSet and the default DataView within a DataTable.

Clients of data-bound controls expect the controls to retain their state across post-backs. This lets page authors populate a control once if IsPost-Back is false, and avoid additional round-trips to the database if the page is posted to again. As the author of a data bound control, you are responsible for making sure that your control's state is retained across a post-back. Typically, you do this by using the ViewState mechanism described earlier in this chapter. Because data-bound controls usually need to persist collections of data into view state, it is typically most efficient to override the LoadViewState and SaveViewState methods in your control to explicitly populate and retrieve collections of data from view state. Keep in mind that clients can always disable view state on your control, so even if you suspect it will be inefficient for clients to rely on state retention for your control, you should leave that decision to the client and support it nonetheless for consistency.

Listing 8-38 shows a sample control that supports data binding to all the different data source types with state retention. It renders itself as an item list and caches the contents of the data source in an ArrayList. This control defines two helper functions that should be useful for any implementer of data-bound controls. The first is GetResolvedDataSource, which takes the data source as an object and returns a reference to an IEnumerable interface. This function accounts for the fact that the data source may be a collection class, an IDataReader, a DataView, a DataTable, or a DataSet, and returns the enumeration interface on the correct element of the data source. The second helper function is GetDataItem, which takes an item pointed to by an enumerator and indexes it with the m_DataTextField value if is a rowset, or simply returns the object as a string if not. This is necessary to accommodate items stored in simple collections and items stored in tabular data sets.

LISTING 8-38: A Data-Bound Control

```
public class DataBoundControl : Control
{
  private ArrayList _cachedData = new ArrayList();

  private object _dataSource;
  private string _dataTextField;
  private string _dataValueField;

  public string DataTextField
  {
    get { return _dataTextField;  }
    set { _dataTextField = value; }
```

```
}

public string DataValueField
{
  get { return _dataValueField;  }
  set { _dataValueField = value; }
}

public override object DataSource
{
  get {return _dataSource;}
  set {_dataSource = value;}
}

public IEnumerable GetResolvedDataSource(object ds)
{
  if (ds is IEnumerable)
    return (IEnumerable)ds;
  else if (ds is DataTable)
    return (IEnumerable)(((DataTable)ds).DefaultView);
  else if (ds is DataSet)
  {
    DataView dv = ((DataSet)ds).Tables[0].DefaultView;
    return (IEnumerable)dv;
  }
  else if (ds is IList)
    return (IEnumerable)((IList)ds);
  else
    return null;
}

protected string GetDataItem(object item)
{
  string ret;
  if (item is DataRowView)
  {
    DataRowView drv = (DataRowView)item;
    ret = drv[_dataValueField].ToString();
  }
  else if (item is DbDataRecord)
  {
    DbDataRecord ddr = (DbDataRecord)item;
    ret = ddr[_dataValueField].ToString();
  }
  else
    ret = item.ToString();

  return ret;
```

continues

```
    }

    protected override void OnDataBinding(EventArgs e)
    {
      base.OnDataBinding(e);

      if (DataSource != null)
      {
        IEnumerable ds = GetResolvedDataSource(_dataSource);
        IEnumerator dataEnum = ds.GetEnumerator();
        while (dataEnum.MoveNext())
          _cachedData.Add(GetDataItem(dataEnum.Current));
      }
    }

    protected override void Render(HtmlTextWriter htw)
    {
      htw.RenderBeginTag(HtmlTextWriterTag.Ul); // <ul>
      foreach (string s in _cachedData)
      {
        htw.RenderBeginTag(HtmlTextWriterTag.Li); // <li>
        htw.Write(s);
        htw.RenderEndTag(); // </li>
      }
      htw.RenderEndTag(); // </ul>
    }
    protected override void LoadViewState(object savedState)
    {
      if (savedState != null)
      {
        // Load State from the array of objects that
        // was saved in SaveViewState
        object[] vState = (object[])savedState;
        if (vState[0] != null)
          base.LoadViewState(vState[0]);
        if (vState[1] != null)
          _cachedData = (ArrayList)vState[1];
      }
    }

    protected override object SaveViewState()
    {
      object[] vState = new object[2];
      vState[0] = base.SaveViewState();
      vState[1] = _cachedData;

      return vState;
    }
  }
```

8.6 Designer Integration

Many controls are created with reuse in mind, whether it is across multiple applications within one company or perhaps for sale and distribution. Reusable controls should take advantage of **designer integration** so that they integrate into the Visual Studio .NET design environment. With designer integration you can control

- How your control appears in the Toolbox
- The appearance of the control's tag on the page
- The appearance of the control's @Register directive on the page
- How properties are categorized in the designer
- Editable string formats for any complex property types
- Custom GUIs for editing properties, if necessary
- The designer view of your control

Adding designer integration to your control is the final, critical step in making your control accessible to developers who want to use it.

8.6.1 Properties and Appearance

When a control you build is used in Visual Studio .NET, the first thing users of your control will see is the cool 16-by-16 graphic that represents your control in the Toolbox—or the lack thereof. To associate a Toolbox image with your control, you must create a bitmap that is 16 by 16 pixels. The lower left pixel of the bitmap is used as the transparent color when the control is rendered in the Toolbox. The file name of the bitmap must be the full class name of the control class with which it is associated. For example, if you have defined a control class named Control1 in the MyControls namespace, the bitmap file for that control must be named MyControls.Control1.bmp. Finally, the bitmap needs to be compiled into the control assembly as an embedded resource. You can do this in a Visual Studio .NET project by setting the Build Action of the bitmap file to Embedded Resource. Be aware that Visual Studio .NET prepends the default namespace associated with your project to any embedded resources, so you must either take that into consideration when naming your bitmap file to ensure that it matches the control class name, or remove the default namespace from your project altogether (accessible through the project properties dialog). In a command-line compilation, you can embed a bitmap as a resource by using the /resource switch referencing the bitmap file. The entire process of associating a Toolbox bitmap with your control is shown in Figure 8-6.

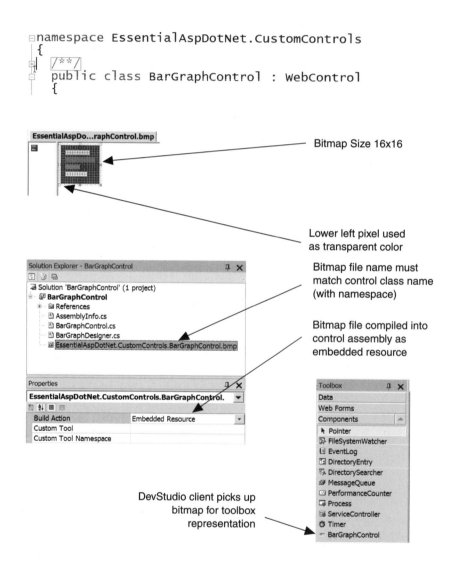

FIGURE 8-6: Setting the Toolbox Bitmap for Your Control

The second thing users of your control will notice is the tag that is placed into the .aspx page. You can control what this tag looks like through the class-level attribute `ToolboxData`. This attribute takes a string as a parameter that is the tag you would like rendered for your control, using the placeholder `{0}` wherever a tag prefix is used (which is also controllable through an assembly-level attribute). Listing 8-39 shows a custom control that specifies the tag that should be used through the `TooboxData` attribute. Note that you can specify any initial attributes or content you would like the tags for your control to have when they are first placed on a form.

LISTING 8-39: Specifying a Client Tag for a Custom Control

```
[ToolboxData("<{0}:BarGraphControl runat='server'/>")]
public class BarGraphControl : WebControl
{ /*...*/ }
```

In addition to the tag for your control, you can specify how the `@Register` directive should appear for your control when users place an instance of your control on their form for the first time. To do this, you specify an assembly-level attribute called `TagPrefix`, which takes two strings as parameters: the namespace of your control and the tag prefix to use when placing tags for your control on a form. Listing 8-40 shows an example of using the `TagPrefix` attribute to customize the `@Register` directive generated by Visual Studio .NET for a custom control.

LISTING 8-40: Customizing the @Register Directive for a Custom Control

```
[assembly: TagPrefix("EssentialAspDotNet.CustomControls",
                     "eadn")]
```

A number of attributes can be applied to properties of a control to influence their appearance and usage from within a designer. Table 8-5 shows a complete list of the attributes that apply to control properties. The two that should most often be applied are the `Category` and `Browsable` attributes, which control under which category a property should appear and whether it should appear at all.

TABLE 8-5: Control Property Attributes

Attribute	Values	Description
Bindable	BindableSupport. [Yes, No, Default]	Should this property be displayed in the DataBindings dialog?
Category	Any string	Property category this property should appear under in the designer (Appearance, Behavior, ...)
DefaultValue	Any value	The default value this property should take when the control is first created
PersistenceMode	PersistenceMode. [Attribute, Default, EncodedInner- DefaultProperty, InnerDefault- Property]	Whether changes made to the value of this property are persisted (and how)
Browsable	true, false	Whether this property is displayed in the designer
TypeConverter	Type of a class that derives from Type- Converter	Class to use to convert the string in the designer to the type required by this property
Editor	Type of a class that derives from UITypeEditor	Class to provide a custom interface for editing this property

8.6.2 Type Converters

You can also define custom type converters if your control has complex properties that may need special UI support in the designer. Because properties for controls can be specified as attributes (by default) within a control tag on a form, all property types need a way to be converted to and from a string representation. For many properties, this happens automatically because there are several built-in converter classes, as shown in Table 8-6.

TABLE 8-6: Built-in Type Converters

Converter Class
ArrayConverter
BooleanConverter
ByteConverter
CharConverter
CollectionConverter
ComponentConverter
CultureInfoConverter
DateTimeConverter
DecimalConverter
DoubleConverter
EnumConverter
Int16Converter
Int32Converter
Int64Converter
ReferenceConverter
UInt16Converter
UInt32Converter
UInt64Converter
ColorConverter
WebColorConverter
FontConverter

For other property types, however, you need to provide a custom converter to allow clients to specify property values within a control tag. To provide a custom converter for a property in your control, you must create a new class deriving from System.ComponentModel.TypeConverter to perform the conversions, and you must associate that type converter class with your property by using the TypeConverter attribute. For example, suppose we built a control that exposed a composite property to set the attributes of a Dog, including its name, age, and breed. These attributes could be encapsulated into a structure and exposed as subproperties, as shown in Listing 8-41.

LISTING 8-41: The Dog Structure

```
public enum eBreed
{
  Dalmation, Labrador, GoldenRetriever,
  Mutt, BlackLabradorRetriever
}

public struct Dog
{
  private string _name;
  private eBreed _breed;
  private int    _age;

  public Dog(string name, eBreed breed, int age)
  {
    _name = name;
    _breed = breed;
    _age = age;
  }

  public string Name {
    get { return _name; }
    set { _name = value; }
  }
  public eBreed Breed {
    get { return _breed; }
    set { _breed = value; }
  }
  public int Age {
    get { return _age; }
    set { _age = value; }
  }
}
```

If a custom control exposed the Dog structure as a property without adding a TypeConverter, users of this control would only be able to set the value of the dog property programmatically. For users to be able to manipulate the subproperties of the Dog structure through the designer, we must provide a way to convert the structure to and from a string representation. Listing 8-42 shows the implementation of DogConverter, a class that provides conversion between the Dog data type and its equivalent string representation (which, in this case, we have chosen to be "name, breed, age").

LISTING 8-42: A Custom Type Converter for Dog

```
public class DogConverter : TypeConverter
{
  public override bool CanConvertFrom(
                           ITypeDescriptorContext context,
                           Type destType)
  {
    if (destType == typeof(string))
      return true;
    else
      return base.CanConvertFrom(context, destType);
  }

  public override bool CanConvertTo(
                           ITypeDescriptorContext context,
                           Type destType)
  {
    if (destType == typeof(InstanceDescriptor) ||
        destType == typeof(string))
      return true;
    else
      return base.CanConvertTo(context, destType);
  }

  public override object ConvertFrom(
                           ITypeDescriptorContext context,
                           CultureInfo culture,
                           object value)
  {
    // Parse the string format, which is: name,breed,age
    string sValue = value as string;
    if (sValue != null)
    {
      string[] v = sValue.Split(new char[] {','});
```

continues

```
            return new Dog(v[0],
                    (eBreed)Enum.Parse(typeof(eBreed), v[1]),
                    Int32.Parse(v[2]));
    }
    else
        return base.ConvertFrom(context, culture, value);
}

public override object ConvertTo(
                    ITypeDescriptorContext context,
                    CultureInfo culture,
                    object value,
                    Type destinationType)
{
    Dog dg = (Dog)value;
    if (destinationType == typeof(InstanceDescriptor))
    {
        Type[] parms = new Type[]{typeof(string),
                          typeof(eBreed),
                          typeof(int)};
        object[] vals = new object[]
                          {dg.Name, dg.Breed, dg.Age};
        return new InstanceDescriptor(
                typeof(Dog).GetConstructor(parms), vals);
    }
    else if (destinationType == typeof(string))
    {
        return string.Format("{0},{1},{2}",
                          dg.Name, dg.Breed, dg.Age);
    }

    return base.ConvertTo(context, culture,
                          value, destinationType);
    }
}
```

Note that four core methods must be overridden in a type converter. First, the CanConvertFrom and CanConvertTo methods indicate what types this class can convert from and to. In our case, the purpose of providing this class is to convert from a Dog to a string and back again. Second, the ConvertFrom method requests that the class perform a conversion from a given type to the real type, which in our case will always be from a string to a Dog. Finally, the ConvertTo method involves taking a reference to the real type and returning a conversion of it into the target type, which in our case will always be a string. The one additional requirement of the designer is that it be able to generate code to create an instance of your type. To provide this information, we must also support conversion to an `InstanceDescriptor`, which is a class that stores information on how to create an instance of a particular class so that the designer can correctly rehydrate your class from its persistent store. In our case, we need to provide an `InstanceDescriptor` that describes how to invoke the three-parameter constructor of our `Dog` structure, shown in our implementation of `ConvertTo`.

The last step is to apply this custom type converter to our `Dog` structure, which we do by using the `TypeConverter` attribute, as shown in Listing 8-43.

LISTING 8-43: Applying a Type Converter to a Type

```
[TypeConverter(typeof(DogConverter))]
public struct Dog
{
  //...
}
```

Once a property has a valid converter associated with it, the designer lets the user modify the property value through the property window, taking whatever string is passed in, running it through the converter, and assigning it to the control's property. If you would like the user to be able to edit the subproperties of your type individually, you can derive your type converter from a special derivative of `TypeConverter` called `Expand-ableObjectTypeConverter`. Figure 8-7 shows what the property editor looks like when the `DogConverter` class is derived from `Expandable-ObjectTypeConverter`.

8.6.3 Property Editors

Some control authors may want to take this one step further and provide their own custom editors for users to edit properties with. Instead of having users type a formatted string in the property editor, they can associate an editor with a property that can launch a form or dialog to edit the property. Several built-in editors are available, as shown in Table 8-7.

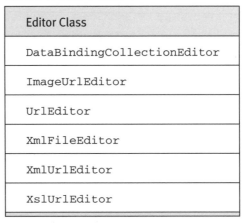

FIGURE 8-7: Expandable Properties

TABLE 8-7: Built-in Editors

Editor Class
DataBindingCollectionEditor
ImageUrlEditor
UrlEditor
XmlFileEditor
XmlUrlEditor
XslUrlEditor

For an example of using a custom editor, consider a class that maintains a URL property. If would be nice if instead of having users type in any random string for this property, there were a selection dialog that helped them construct a proper URL. By using the `Editor` attribute on the string property used to access and set the URL, the control builder can associate the built-in `UrlEditor` class to do just this, as shown in Figure 8-8. Note that the `Editor` takes two parameters, the type of the editor class and the base class from which it inherits, which currently should always be `System.Drawing.Design.UITypeEditor`.

To create your own custom editor for a property, you derive a new class from `System.Drawing.Design.UITypeEditor` and override the `EditValue` and `GetEditStyle` methods. The `GetEditStyle` returns an enumeration indicating what type of user interface the editor is going to use:

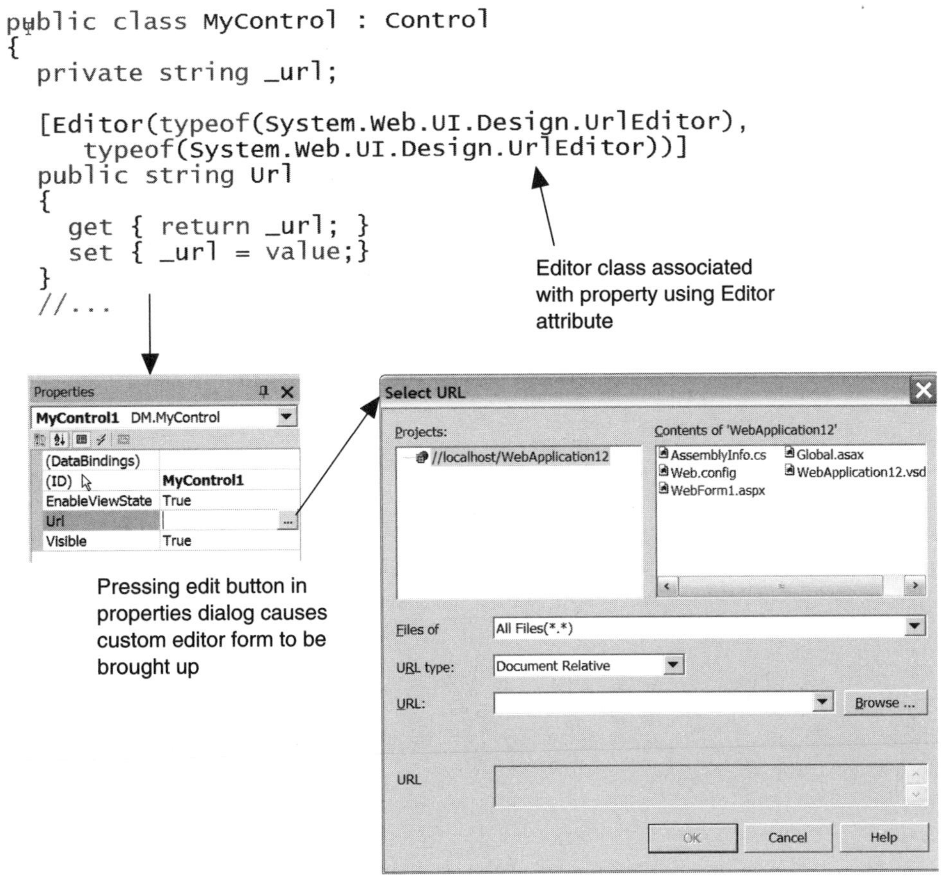

```
public class MyControl : Control
{
    private string _url;

    [Editor(typeof(System.Web.UI.Design.UrlEditor),
        typeof(System.Web.UI.Design.UrlEditor))]
    public string Url
    {
        get { return _url; }
        set { _url = value;}
    }
    //...
```

Editor class associated with property using Editor attribute

Pressing edit button in properties dialog causes custom editor form to be brought up

FIGURE 8-8: Associating a Custom Editor with a Control Property

modal dialog, drop-down box from within the property list, or none. Edit-Value takes a reference to the object it is editing and returns a new object with new values. What happens inside EditValue is completely up to you, but most often it invokes a modal dialog box with controls on it to edit the values for the object. Listing 8-44 shows an example of a custom editor for editing the Dog structure shown earlier and how to hook it up to the Dog structure using the Editor attribute.

LISTING 8-44: A Custom Editor Example

```
public class DogEditor : UITypeEditor
{
  public override object EditValue(
                    ITypeDescriptorContext tdc,
                    IServiceProvider sp, object obj)
  {
    Dog dg = (Dog)obj;
    // DogEditorDlg class now shown...

    DogEditorDlg dlg = new DogEditorDlg();
    dlg.DogName.Text = dg.Name;
    dlg.DogAge.Text  = dg.Age.ToString();
    dlg.DogBreed.SelectedIndex =
        dlg.DogBreed.Items.IndexOf(dg.Breed.ToString());

    if (dlg.ShowDialog() == DialogResult.OK)
    {
      return new Dog(dlg.DogName.Text,
                    (eBreed)Enum.Parse(typeof(eBreed),
                    dlg.DogBreed.SelectedItem.ToString()),
                    Int32.Parse(dlg.DogAge.Text));
    }
    else
      return obj; // no change
  }

  public override UITypeEditorEditStyle
                    GetEditStyle(ITypeDescriptorContext tdc)
  {
    return UITypeEditorEditStyle.Modal;
  }
}

// To hook up this editor to the Dog structure:
[Editor(typeof(DogEditor), typeof(UITypeEditor))]
public struct Dog
{ /*...*/ }
```

8.6.4 Designers

For each control you create, you can create an accompanying designer class that determines how that control appears and behaves within the designer. For many controls, this is unnecessary because the Visual Studio .NET designer creates an instance of your control when it is placed on a form and asks it to render itself. For controls whose rendering depends on runtime data population or that have no visual presence on a form, however, it makes sense to have something show up when such controls are dropped on a form in the designer. Whether this means artificially populating a control with initial data or providing a "stub" rendering indicating that it is a placeholder depends on the type of control.

Creating a designer involves creating a new class derived from `System.Web.UI.Design.ControlDesigner` and overriding its `GetDesignTimeHtml` method. This method should return the HTML you want to represent your control at design time. The last step is to associate the designer with your control class by using the `Designer` attribute. Listing 8-45 shows a custom control class with an associated designer. This listing also demonstrates the common practice of placing the designer in a new namespace called `Design` within the control class's namespace.

LISTING 8-45: A Custom Control with an Associated Designer Class

```
namespace Design
{
  public class MyControlDesigner : ControlDesigner
  {
    public override string GetDesignTimeHtml()
    {
      return "<h3>MyControl in design mode!</h3>";
    }
  }
}

[Designer(typeof(Design.MyControlDesigner))]
public class MyControl : Control
{ /*...*/ }
```

Providing a designer for a control does not change the fact that an instance of your control is created in design mode; it merely changes how that control renders itself in a designer. For controls that want to use the standard control rendering in their designer, it is possible to reference the control instance from within the designer via the `Component` property of the `ControlDesigner` class. A good example of when this would be appropriate is in the `BarGraph` control presented earlier in this chapter. This control renders a bar graph with data populated at runtime, so at design time there is nothing to render. To give it a visual presence in the designer, we can access the allocated instance of the control, populate it with some artificial data, and return the result of invoking the control's render function (by calling the base class implementation of `GetDesignTimeHtml`). This technique is shown in Listing 8-46.

LISTING 8-46: Using a Designer to Artificially Populate the BarGraph Control

```
public class BarGraphDesigner : ControlDesigner
{
  bool bGetDesignTimeHtmlCalled = false;

  public override string GetDesignTimeHtml()
  {
    // populate with data the first time only
    if (!bGetDesignTimeHtmlCalled)
    {
      BarGraphControl ctrl = (BarGraphControl)Component;
      // add some artifical data
      ctrl.AddValue("Value 1", 10.0);
      ctrl.AddValue("Value 2", 20.0);
      ctrl.AddValue("Value 3", 30.0);
      ctrl.AddValue("Value 4", 40.0);
      bGetDesignTimeHtmlCalled = true;
    }
    return base.GetDesignTimeHtml();
  }
}
```

The other type of controls that require designers are those that have no runtime rendering or whose rendering depends on too many runtime elements, making rendering in design mode impossible. For these controls, a helper function called `CreatePlaceHolderDesignTimeHtml` creates a standard placeholder for a control. This method takes a string and renders a gray box with the string displayed at design time, and is used by controls such as the Xml control and the Repeater control in the base class libraries. Listing 8-47 shows a sample designer that renders a placeholder.

LISTING 8-47: Rendering a Placeholder with a Designer

```
public class MyControlDesigner : ControlDesigner
{
  public override string GetDesignTimeHtml()
  {
    return CreatePlaceHolderDesignTimeHtml("see me later");
  }
}
```

SUMMARY

ASP.NET defines an architecture for extending its existing controls with custom controls. You can write controls to encapsulate portions of your Web applications into truly reusable components by deriving from System.Web.UI.Control and overriding the virtual Render method. An instance of the HtmlTextWriter class is passed into Render and provides a collection of helper routines for generating HTML to the response buffer. Inside your control's Render implementation, you are free to query the capabilities of the current client and render your control's state differently for different browsers. You can also render client-side JavaScript to clients that support it as part of your control's rendering, shifting some work to the client where possible.

Developers of custom controls must be very aware of how the state of their control is managed. Control users expect controls to retain their state across post-backs, which typically means that a control must use the ViewState mechanism to save and restore its state. It is also possible to manually parse the contents of the POST body if your control's state is propagated that way.

Composite controls are controls that contain other controls as children and are often used to build pieces of a form. You create composite controls by overriding the virtual CreateChildControls method and implementing the tagging interface `INamingContainer`. Even more useful are user controls, which create composite control definitions from .ascx files, letting you lay out your composite control with a designer.

The last step in building a user-friendly control is to ensure that it integrates cleanly with the Visual Studio .NET designer. Controls can specify what their Toolbox bitmap should look like, how their tags should appear when placed on a page, how to edit their properties, and what the control should look like in design mode.

■ 9 ■
Caching

T HE DISTRIBUTED NATURE of the Web provides many opportunities
for performance improvement through caching. In general, caching is
the temporary storage of state for faster retrieval. Caching for Web applications can occur on the client (browser caching), on a server between the
client and the Web server (proxy caching), and on the Web server itself
(page caching or data caching). Both browser caching and proxy caching
reduce Web server traffic by serving content either directly from the client's
machine or from an intermediate proxy server, and are thus not directly
managed by ASP.NET (although your ASP.NET pages can specify browser
and proxy caching options by adding the appropriate metatags, `Cache-`
`Control` headers, and `Expires` headers). Page caching and data caching,
however are directly applicable to ASP.NET and should be used, at least to
some extent, in any Web application built with ASP.NET.

9.1 Caching Opportunities in ASP.NET

ASP.NET provides support for page, partial page, and data caching.
Caching a page that is dynamically generated, called **page output caching**,
improves performance by generating the page dynamically only the first
time it is accessed. Any subsequent access to the same page will be returned
from the cache, saving the time it would have taken to dynamically generate the page. The expiration of a cached page must be explicitly set, after

which time the page will be regenerated and recached the next time it is accessed. ASP.NET also supports the ability to cache portions of a page if those portions are encapsulated into a user control.

The other opportunity for performance improvement is to reduce the number of round-trips made to a back-end data server (or even to a local database). Instead of always requesting live data from a data source, you can cache that data in memory and access it locally. Data caching can cause cache coherency problems, but when used correctly, it can dramatically improve application responsiveness. ASP.NET provides a full-featured data cache engine, complete with support for scavenging, expiration, and file and key dependencies. Figure 9-1 shows the two locations where caching can be used to improve performance in ASP.NET applications.

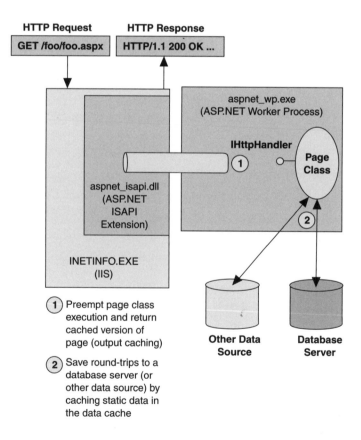

FIGURE 9-1: Caching Opportunities in ASP.NET

9.2 **Output Caching**

For pages whose content is relatively static, it is inefficient to regenerate the page for every client request. Instead, pages can be generated once and then cached for subsequent fetches. The OutputCache directive can be added to any ASP.NET page, specifying the duration (in seconds) that the page should be cached. The code shown in Listing 9-1 is an example of using the OutputCache directive to specify that this particular page should be cached for one hour after its first access. In this example, the page prints the date on which it was generated, so if you try accessing this page, you will notice that after the first hit, all subsequent accesses will have the same timestamp until the duration is reached.

LISTING 9-1: OutputCache Directive Example

```
<%@ Page Language="C#" %>
<%@ OutputCache Duration='3600' VaryByParam='none' %>
<html>

  <script runat="server">
    protected void Page_Load(Object sender, EventArgs e) {
        _msg.Text = DateTime.Now.ToString();
    }
  </script>

  <body>
    <h3>Output Cache example</h3>
    <p>Last generated on:
        <asp:label id="_msg" runat="server"/></p>
  </body>

</html>
```

When using the OutputCache directive, you must specify at least the Duration and VaryByParam attributes. Leaving the VaryByParam attribute set to 'none', as shown in Listing 9-1, means that one copy of the page will be cached for each request type (GET, HEAD, or POST). Subsequent requests of the same type will be served a cached response for that type of request. Table 9-1 shows the complete set of attributes available with the OutputCache directive.

TABLE 9-1: OutputCache Directive Attributes

OutputCache Attribute	Values	Description
Duration	Number	Time, in seconds, that the page or user control is cached
Location	'Any' 'Client' 'Downstream' 'Server' 'None'	Controls the header and metatags sent to clients indicating where this page can be cached. Choosing 'Any' means that the page can be cached on the browser client, a downstream server, or the server. 'Client' means that the page will be cached on the client browser only. 'Downstream' means that the page will be cached on a downstream server and the client. 'Server' means that the page will be cached on the server only. 'None' disables output caching for this page.
VaryByCustom	'Browser' Custom string	Vary the output cache either by browser name and version or by a custom string, which must be handled in an overridden version of GetVaryByCustomString().
VaryByHeader	'*' Header names	A semicolon-separated list of strings representing headers submitted by a client.
VaryByParam	'none' '*' Parameter name	A semicolon-separated list of strings representing query string values in a GET request or variables in a POST request. This is a required attribute.
VaryByControl	Control name	A semicolon-separated list of strings representing properties of a user control used to vary the output cache (applicable to user controls only).

The attributes that you specify in an `OutputCache` directive are used to populate an instance of the `System.Web.HttpCachePolicy` class by calling the `System.Web.UI.Page.InitOutputCache()` method. This class is accessible programmatically through the `Response` property of the `Page` (or `Context`) class, as shown in Listing 9-2.

LISTING 9-2: HttpCachePolicy Class

```
public sealed class HttpCachePolicy
{
  public HttpCacheVaryByHeaders VaryByHeaders {get;}
  public HttpCacheVaryByParams VaryByParams {get;}
  public void AppendCacheExtension(string extension);
  public void SetCacheability(
                    HttpCacheability cacheability);
  public void SetExpires(DateTime date);
  public void SetLastModified(DateTime date);
  public void SetMaxAge(TimeSpan delta);
  public void SetNoServerCaching();
  public void SetSlidingExpiration(bool slide);
  //...
}

public sealed class HttpResponse
{
  public HttpCachePolicy Cache {get;}
  //...
}

public class Page : ...
{
  public HttpResponse Response {get;}
  //...
}
```

The `OutputCache` directive gives you access to a subset of the functionality available in the `HttpCachePolicy` class. One useful feature that is only accessible programmatically is the ability to set a sliding expiration on a page. That is, whenever a page is hit, the timeout is reset. This is a useful way to ensure that only items that are being used are kept in your cache. Pages that are cached once and then never accessed again are a waste of resources. The code in Listing 9-3 shows an example of a page whose expiration is set programmatically and uses the sliding expiration scheme.

LISTING 9-3: Programmatically Setting Page Caching

```
<%@ Page Language="C#" %>
<html>
  <script runat="server">
    void Page_Load(Object sender, EventArgs e) {
      Response.Cache.SetExpires(DateTime.Now.AddSeconds(360));
      Response.Cache.SetCacheability(
                    HttpCacheability.Public);
      Response.Cache.SetSlidingExpiration(true);
      _msg.Text = DateTime.Now.ToString();
    }
  </script>

  <body>
    <h3>Output Cache example</font></h3>
    <p>Last generated on:
            <asp:label id="_msg" runat="server"/>
  </body>
</html>
```

9.2.1 Output Caching Location

So far, we have discussed the advantage of output caching on the server, where it saves server processing time by loading the page from a cached rendering stored in the ASP.NET worker process instead of dynamically generating it. In addition to server caching, there are two other opportunities for page caching. First, many browsers can cache pages on the client machine. This is the most efficient method of all because it avoids any network traffic and renders the page directly from the client machine's cache. Web pages indicate that they should be cached in client browsers through the Expires header of their HTTP response, indicating the date and time after which the page should be retrieved from the server again. Second, the HTTP 1.1 protocol supports the caching of responses on transparent proxy servers, sitting between the client and the server. Pages can indicate whether they should be cached on a proxy by using the Cache-Control header.

If your page is already output cacheable, it usually makes sense to make that page client and proxy cacheable too. It turns out that the `OutputCache` directive on a page enables all three types of caching—server, client, and proxy—by default. This means that when you mark a page with an `Ouput-Cache` directive, you are effectively saying that this page will not change for a specific period of time, and if it is possible to cache it anywhere in the pipeline between your ASP.NET application and the client browser, please do so. This is useful because with one statement, you can advertise the cache friendliness of your page, specifying the expiration time only once, and let ASP.NET render your page appropriately to whatever client asks for it.

On the other hand, sometimes you might need more precise control over exactly where your page is cached. The `Location` attribute of the `Output-Cache` directive lets you specify where you want your page to be cached. Table 9-2 shows the values of the `Location` attribute and how they affect the `Cache-Control` header, the `Expires` header, and the server caching of your page.

TABLE 9-2: Effect of the Location Attribute in Output Caching

Value of Location	Cache-Control Header	Expires Header	Page Cached on Server
`'Any'`	`public`	Yes	Yes
`'Client'`	`private`	Yes	No
`'Downstream'`	`public`	Yes	No
`'Server'`	`no-cache`	No	Yes
`'None'`	`no-cache`	No	No

For example, if you specified a value of `'Client'` for the `Location` attribute of an `OutputCache` directive on a page, the page would not be saved in the server cache, but the response would include a `Cache-Control` header value of `private` and an `Expires` header with a timestamp set to the time indicated by the `Duration` attribute, as shown in Listing 9-4.

LISTING 9-4: Designating Private Caching

```
<%@ OutputCache Duration='120' Location='Client'
                VaryByParam='none' %>
...
————- generates the following response ———
HTTP/1.1 200 OK
Server: Microsoft-IIS/5.1
Date: Tue, 01 Jan 2002 12:00:00 GMT
Cache-Control: private
Expires: Tue, 01 Jan 2002 12:02:00 GMT
...
```

9.2.2 Caching Multiple Versions of a Page

Users can request pages in a Web application in several ways. They can issue a plain GET request, a plain HEAD request, a GET request with an accompanying query string with name/value pairs appended, or a POST request with an accompanying body containing name/value pairs. Caching pages that are retrieved using only a GET request with no query string is straightforward, because the page never changes its contents based on the request (except possibly based on client headers, which we will come back to). Caching pages that are accessed with changing query strings or POST variable values becomes more complex, because a distinct version of the page must be cached for each unique query string or variable combination that is submitted.

Before you decide to enable output caching on an ASP.NET page, you must decide how many versions of that page should be cached. The options are to cache only one copy of the page for each request type (GET, HEAD, or POST); to cache all GET, HEAD, and POST requests (implying separate cached versions of the page for each request); or to cache multiple versions of a page only if a particular variable in a GET or POST changes. This option is controlled through the VaryByParam attribute of the OutputCache directive, whose values are shown in Table 9-3.

If you set the VaryByParam attribute to 'none', only one version of the page is stored in the output cache for each request type. If a user issues a GET request to a page with an accompanying query string, the output cache ignores the query string and returns the single cached instance of the page

TABLE 9-3: VaryByParam Values

VaryByParam **Value**	**Description**
'none'	One version of page cached (only raw GET or HEAD)
'*'	N versions of page cached based on query string and/or POST body
V1	N versions of page cached based on value of v1 variable in query string or POST body
V1, V2	N versions of page cached based on value of v1 and v2 variables in query string or POST body

for GET requests. If, on the other hand, you set the VaryByParam attribute to '*', a new version of that page is cached for each unique query string and each unique collection of POST variables across all client requests. This setting is potentially very inefficient and must be used carefully. For example, suppose a page that accepted a person's name in a query string were marked with the OutputCache directive and specified a VaryByParam value of '*'. For each client request with a different name, a new copy of the page would be stored in the output cache. Unless many people with the same name hit that page, there would likely be very few cache hits, and the cached pages would just be wasting server memory. This scenario is depicted in Figure 9-2.

The VaryByParam attribute can also be set to the name, or list of names, of query string or POST variables. The decision of whether to create a unique entry in the output cache for a page is then based on whether the particular variable (or variables) listed change from one request to another. It is unlikely this capability would be used very often, because query string and POST variables are typically used when you are deciding how to render a page, or at the very least, to store in some back-end data source when the page is posted.

In addition to caching different versions of a page based on the parameters passed by a client request, you can cache different versions of a page for a variety of other reasons. The VaryByHeader attribute of the Output-Cache directive caches a different version of a page whenever a header

Client Requests

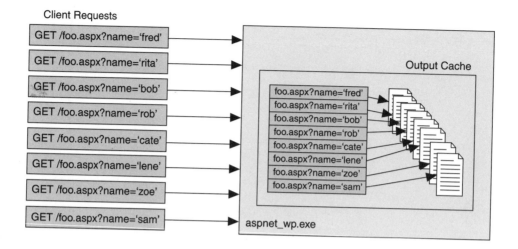

FIGURE 9-2: Caching Multiple Copies of a Page

string (or set of header strings, which you can specify) differs from one client to the next. This is important if you render your page differently based on the headers supplied by the client (which happens implicitly with many ASP.NET controls). For example, if you conditionally render portions of your page based on the `Accept-Language` header passed in by clients, you need to make sure that a separate cache entry is made for each language that clients request. The page in Listing 9-5 prints a message in the client's preferred language (as long as it is French, German, or English). If we applied the `OutputCache` directive to this page without a `VaryBy-Header` constraint, the first client to request it would see his preferred language, but subsequent clients would see the first client's preferred language until the duration expired. Using the `VaryByHeader` constraint with `Accept-Language` as a value causes a distinct rendering of this page to be stored in the output cache for each client request with a unique language preference.

LISTING 9-5: Using VaryByHeader

```
<!-- File: LanguagePage.aspx -->

<%@ Page language='C#' %>
<%@ OutputCache Location='any'
```

```
                VaryByParam='none'
                 Duration='120'
                VaryByHeader='Accept-Language' %>
<html>
  <head>
  <script runat="server">
    protected void Page_Load(Object src, EventArgs e)
    {
       if (!IsPostBack)
       {
          switch (Request.UserLanguages[0])
          {
            case "fr":
              _msg.Text = "Bonjour!  Comment allez-vous?";
              break;
            case "de":
              _msg.Text = "Guten Tag!  Wie geht's?";
              break;
            default:
              _msg.Text = "Hello!  How are you?";
              break;
          }
       }
       Response.Write(DateTime.Now.ToString());
    }

  </script>
  </head>
  <body>
  <form runat=server>
    <asp:Label id='_msg' runat=server />
  </form>
  </body>
</html>
```

Finally, you can cache separate page renderings based on the browser
type and version, or any other criteria you need, through the VaryByCustom attribute. If you know that a page may render differently for different
browsers, it is important that you store a separate cache instance for each
browser type that accesses the page. Setting the VaryByCustom attribute of
the OutputCache directive to Browser causes a unique instance of the page
to be cached for each browser type and major version number that accesses
your page. Note that this is different from using the VaryByHeader option
with a value of User-Agent because that would store a unique instance in
the cache for each user agent string, which would generate many more

entries. It is important to realize that many server-side controls render themselves differently based on the browser type and version, including the `Calendar`, `TreeView`, `Toolbar`, `TabStrip`, and `MultiPage` controls, to name a few. If you use any of these controls in a page on which you have enabled output caching, you should be sure to include a `VaryByCustom` attribute set to `'Browser'`, as shown in Listing 9-6.

LISTING 9-6: Using VaryByCustom Set to 'Browser'

```
<%@ Page Language='C#' %>
<%@ OutputCache Location='Any'
                VaryByParam='none'
                Duration='120'
                VaryByCustom='Browser' %>
<html>
<body>
  <form runat=server>
    <asp:Calendar id='_cal' runat='server' />
  </form>
</body>
</html>
```

If you render your page conditionally based on any other factor, you can use the `VaryByCustom` attribute in conjunction with an overridden implementation of `HttpApplication.GetVaryByCustomString` in your application class. The purpose of this function is to take the string value of the `VaryByCustom` attribute as a parameter and return a string that is unique with respect to some aspect of the page, request, or application. In most cases, the implementation of `GetVaryByCustomString` checks some value in the current `HttpBrowserCapabilities` class and returns a unique string based on that value.

For example, suppose that you have built a page that renders differently based on the client browser's level of `table` support. You might provide an overridden version of `GetVaryByCustomString`, as shown in Listing 9-7.

LISTING 9-7: GetVaryByCustomString Implementation

```
<!-- File: global.asax -->
<%@Application language='C#' %>

<script runat=server>
```

```
public override string
  GetVaryByCustomString(HttpContext ctx, string arg)
{
  switch (arg)
  {
    case "Tables":
      return "Tables=" + ctx.Request.Browser.Tables;
    default:
        return "";
  }
}
</script>
```

This implementation would return a string value of "Tables=true" for client browsers that supported tables and "Tables=false" for client browsers that did not. This string would then be appended onto the other `OutputCache` distinguishing strings and used to index the output cache to store and retrieve renderings of this page. An example of a page that used this `VaryByCustom` attribute is shown in Listing 9-8.

LISTING 9-8: Using VaryByCustom in a Page

```
<%@ Page language='C#' %>
<%@ OutputCache Location='any'
                VaryByParam='none'
                Duration='120'
                VaryByCustom='Tables' %>
<html>
  <head>
  <script runat="server">
    protected void Page_Load(Object src, EventArgs e)
    {
        if (Request.Browser.Tables)
          // render with tables
        else
          // render without tables
    }
  </script>
  </head>
  . . .
```

In general, when you add output caching to a page, it is important to ask yourself if this page will render itself differently in different conditions (different client properties, different times of day, and so on) and make sure you compensate for that by indexing the output cache uniquely for all those different rendering possibilities.

9.2.3 Page Fragment Caching

Even more common than entire pages that change infrequently are portions of pages that change infrequently. For example, there are often navigation bars, menus, or headers that are common to many pages in an application and that change infrequently (especially not between different client requests), which makes them ideal for caching. Fortunately, ASP.NET provides a mechanism for caching portions of pages, called **page fragment caching**. To cache a portion of a page, you must first encapsulate the portion of the page you want to cache into a user control. In the user control source file, add an OutputCache directive specifying the Duration and VaryByParam attributes. When that user control is loaded into a page at runtime, it is cached, and all subsequent pages that reference that same user control will retrieve it from the cache, thus improving throughput. The user control shown in Listing 9-9 specifies output caching for 60 seconds.

LISTING 9-9: Specifying Page Fragment Caching in a User Control

```
<!– File: MyUserControl.ascx –>

<%@ OutputCache Duration='60'
                VaryByParam='none' %>
<%@ Control Language='C#' %>

<script runat=server>
  protected void Page_Load(Object src, EventArgs e)
  {
     _date.Text = "User control generated at " +
                   DateTime.Now.ToString();
  }
</script>
<asp:Label id='_date' runat='server' />
```

In the sample client page shown in Listing 9-10, the page itself is not output-cached, but the user control embedded in it is. In this example, because both the page and the control it embeds print the time at which they were generated, you will see a discrepancy between the printed times as the page is refreshed and the control is drawn from the cache.

LISTING 9-10: Cached User Control Client

```
<!- File: UserControlClient.aspx ->

<%@ Page Language='C#' %>
<%@ Register TagPrefix='DM' TagName='UserCtrl'
             Src='MyUserControl.ascx' %>
<html>
<head>
<script runat='server'>
  protected void Page_Load(Object src, EventArgs e)
  {
      _pageDate.Text = "Page generated at " +
                        DateTime.Now.ToString();

  }
</script>
</head>
<body>
<form runat='server'>
  <DM:UserCtrl runat='server'/>
  <br/>
  <asp:Label id='_pageDate' runat='server' />
</form>
</body>
</html>
```

User controls also can change their rendering based on the type of request the control is responding to or perhaps based on properties exposed by a control. It is important to determine the circumstances under which the contents of a user control will change before you apply the Output-Cache directive to it. There are three ways of indicating that a distinct cache entry is required for a user control caching.

1. You can include a VaryByParam attribute to include different cache entries based on the parameters of the current POST.
2. You can include a VaryByControl attribute to cache different entries based on programmatic values of controls embedded in the user control (such as a combo box selecting some appearance aspect of the control).
3. User controls will automatically be cached in different entries if the user control is instantiated in a page with properties specified in the tag.

The first of these three options is probably the least likely to be useful, since user controls are typically used from several different pages, whose POST variables will be different. It can be complicated to correctly identify the variables to vary by because of the way the parameters are parsed and sent to user controls (they are scoped by the control name).

The second of the three options was added to simplify the process of identifying which parameters should determine unique cache entries for your user control. Instead of referring to POST or GET variables directly, your user control can specify which of its child controls should affect its cache entry. For example, if you built a user control that changed its rendering based on the value of a drop-down list, you would want to be sure that there was a unique entry for every value of that drop-down list. By specifying the drop-down list in the VaryByControl attribute, you ensure that a unique cache entry will be stored for each value selected in the list. The user control shown in Listing 9-11 demonstrates this.

LISTING 9-11: Specifying VaryByControl in a User Control

```
<!- File MyUserControl.ascx ->
<%@ OutputCache Duration='120'
                 VaryByControl='_favoriteColor' %>
<%@ Control Language='C#' %>

<p>Select your favorite color</p>
<asp:DropDownList AutoPostBack='true' id='_favoriteColor'
                  runat='server'>
    <asp:ListItem>red</asp:ListItem>
    <asp:ListItem>green</asp:ListItem>
    <asp:ListItem>blue</asp:ListItem>
</asp:DropDownList>
<p>Here it is!</p>
<span
   style='width:50;background-color:
<%=_favoriteColor.SelectedItem%>'>
</span>
```

The third option for uniquely specifying cache entries for user controls is to expose public properties. There is nothing special you have to do to enable this except to expose public properties and set the property values in the user control creation. For example, if we had a user control that exposed a single public property called `FavoriteColor`, adding an output cache directive to the control would cache separate versions of the control based on the value of that property on creation. A sample user control that does this is shown in Listing 9-12, and a sample client is shown in Listing 9-13.

LISTING 9-12: Specifying Unique Cache Entries by Exposing a Public Property

```
<!- File MyUserControl.ascx ->
<%@ OutputCache Duration='120' VaryByParam='none' %>
<%@ Control Language='C#' %>

<script runat='server'>
private string _color;
public string FavoriteColor
{
    get { return _color; }
    set { _color = value; }
}
</script>

<p>Here is your favorite color:</p>
<span style='width:50;background-color:<%=_color%>'>
</span>
```

LISTING 9-13: Client to Cached User Control with Public Property

```
<%@ Page Language='C#' %>
<%@ Register TagPrefix='DM' TagName='UserCtrl'
            Src='MyUserControl.ascx' %>
<html>
<body>
<form runat='server'>
  <DM:UserCtrl FavoriteColor='green' runat='server'/>
</form>
</body>
</html>
```

9.2.4 Output Caching Considerations and Guidelines

As we have seen, you have many options to consider when enabling output caching for a page. It is important to balance the estimated increase in throughput with the additional overhead of saving one or more renderings of a page in memory. While this trade-off is not easy to calculate precisely, here are some guidelines you should consider when deciding whether to enable output caching on a page.

1. *Enable output caching on a page that is frequently accessed and returns the exact same contents for many of those accesses.*

It is useless to cache a page if it is rarely accessed. It wastes memory and incurs more overhead on the few requests that the page gets. Keep this in mind as you begin deciding on which pages in your application to enable output caching. Good candidates for output caching are pages that are accessed frequently and render themselves identically for all or most of those accesses. This is somewhat alleviated by the fact that output-cached pages are stored in the data cache and that pages are evicted from the cache on a "least recently used" basis when memory is constrained.

2. *Cache as few versions of a page as possible.*

This guideline relates to the first one in that it advises you to cache as few versions of a page as possible. If you cache every possible version of a page (assuming it varies with a query string or POST body), you will populate the cache with a large number of page renderings, many of which will probably never be accessed again. Try to anticipate the most common use of your pages (or use site statistics to understand common use), and use the attributes of the OutputCache directive to cache only the most frequently accessed versions of a page.

3. *If a page is accessed frequently, but portions of its contents change with each access, consider separating the static or semistatic portions of the page into output-cached user controls.*

Before deciding that a frequently accessed page is uncacheable because it changes with each request, you should look carefully at the entire contents of the generated page. If any portions remain static from one request to another, especially if those portions are somewhat expensive to render (if they are generated from a database query, for example), you may want to consider using page fragment caching to cache only those portions of the page. By encapsulating portions of the page in one or more user controls, you can then enable output caching on the user controls themselves.

4. *When enabling output caching for a page, be sure not to introduce incorrect behavior and/or rendering for any particular client.*

In addition to controlling which versions of a page are output-cached for efficiency, you want to be very sure that you are not introducing any incorrect behavior when adding an `OutputCache` directive to a page. For example, suppose you have a page that displays a form with two fields, `name` and `age`, and you add an `OutputCache` directive with the `VaryByParam` attribute set to `'name'`. For each request that comes in with a distinct value for `name`, you cache a new version of the page. However, if someone posts the same name to your page with a different age, ASP.NET still retrieves the rendered page from the cache, which was rendered with the first value for `age` that was submitted, resulting in incorrect behavior.

5. *Determine the duration of the cached page carefully to balance speed of access (throughput) with memory consumption and cache coherency correctness.*

When determining the length of the duration for an output-cached page, you have two important considerations. First, the longer the page stays cached, the longer it occupies memory. This is fine if it is being frequently accessed in the cache, but if it is not being accessed, it is simply wasting space. Second, as with any caching mechanism, you need to be careful that the cached version of your page is not out of date with the data used to generate it (often called the cache coherency problem). To avoid this, choose a duration that is short enough to ensure that the underlying data used to generate the page will not change while the page is cached. In some cases, cached pages with stale data may be acceptable, but be sure you are aware that you have made a decision to potentially serve stale pages.

6. *Consider enabling sliding expiration on a page if you end up using* `Vary-ByParam='*'`.

One of the easiest ways to enable correct output caching on pages that change with requests is to set `VaryByParam` to `'*'`. By doing this, however, you will probably cache many more versions of your page than necessary (in all likelihood, the most commonly accessed renderings of the page will be a small subset of the total set of page renderings). It is advisable, therefore, to enable sliding expiration on a page with `VaryByParam` set to `'*'`. This will keep versions of the page that are accessed frequently in the cache, but those that are not accessed frequently will be removed from the cache as soon as their expiration is reached. Keep in mind, however, that enabling sliding expiration on a page can easily lead to cache coherency problems, and thus this scenario may be best avoided altogether.

9.3 Data Caching

Internally, the output cache is built using a sophisticated data caching engine. This data caching engine is available directly to page developers as well through the `Cache` property of the `Page` class and should be used in addition to output caching (or instead of it, in some cases) to improve response times.

Caching of data can dramatically improve the performance of an application by reducing database contention and round-trips. The data cache provided by ASP.NET gives you complete control over how data that you place in the cache is handled. At its simplest level, data caching can be used as a way to store and restore values in your application, which is trivial to do using its dictionary interface. The example shown in Listing 9-14 demonstrates the caching of a `DataView` that has been populated from a database query. The first time this page is accessed, the database is queried, the `DataView` is populated, and it is then placed in the cache. On subsequent accesses, the `DataView` will be retrieved from the cache, saving the time required to query the database again.

LISTING 9-14: Caching a DataView in the Data Cache

```
<!– File: DataViewCache.aspx –>
<%@ Page Language="C#" %>
<%@ Import Namespace="System.Data" %>
<%@ Import Namespace="System.Data.SqlClient" %>
<html>
<script runat="server">
```

```
protected void Page_Load(Object src, EventArgs e)
{
  // Look in the data cache first
  DataView dv = (DataView)Cache["EmployeesDataView"];
  if (dv == null)   // wasn't there
  {
    SqlConnection conn = new SqlConnection(
         "server=localhost;uid=sa;pwd=;database=Test");
    SqlDataAdapter da =
       new SqlDataAdapter("select * from Employees", conn);
    DataSet ds = new DataSet();
    da.Fill(ds, "Employees");
    dv = ds.Tables["Employees"].DefaultView;
    dv.AllowEdit   = false;
    dv.AllowDelete = false;
    dv.AllowNew    = false;
       // Save employees table in cache
    Cache["EmployeesDataView"] = dv;
    conn.Close();
  }
  else
    Response.Write("<h2>Loaded from data cache!</h2>");
  lb1.DataSource = dv;
  lb1.DataTextField = "Name";
  lb1.DataValueField = "Age";
  DataBind();
}
</script>
<body>
<form runat="server">
<asp:ListBox id="lb1" runat=server />
</form>
</body>
</html>
```

The data cache exists at the scope of the application and in many ways is identical in functionality to the application state bag (HttpApplicationState), with two important differences. First, anything placed in the data cache is not guaranteed to be there when you attempt to retrieve it again (by default). This means that you should always be prepared for a cache miss by being able to retrieve the data from its original source if the cache returns an empty value, as demonstrated in the previous example. The second difference is that the data cache is not intended as a place to store shared, updateable data. Because the cache lives at the application scope, the potential for concurrent access is high, and in fact, the Cache class uses a multireader, single-writer synchronization object (System.Threading.ReaderWriterLock) to ensure that no more than one thread modifies the cache at a time. This synchronization object, however, is not exposed externally and thus cannot be used by clients to perform their own locking. This is in contrast to the HttpApplicationState class, which provides a pair of methods, Lock() and an UnLock() to have clients perform explicit locking whenever modifications are made to the application state. It is also important to keep in mind that the cache lives at the application scope in a particular instance of the ASP.NET worker process and is not shared between processes or machines. This means that cached data is not intrinsically synchronized across machines in a Web farm.

As a result, the proper and intended use of the data cache is to store read-only data or objects for the convenience of access. Note that in the previous example, the DataView that was cached was modified to prevent updates, deletes, or insertions, effectively making it read-only. It is good practice to make cache entries read-only to ensure that cached data is not accidentally modified. The example in Listing 9-15 shows how *not* to use the data cache.

LISTING 9-15: Improper Use of the Data Cache

```
<!— File: BadCache.aspx —>
<%@ Import Namespace="System.Collections" %>
<html>
<script language="C#" runat="server">
protected void Page_Load(Object src, EventArgs e)
{
  // Look in the data cache first
  ArrayList al = (ArrayList)Cache["MyList"];
  if (al == null)  // wasn't there
  {
     al = new ArrayList();
      // Save ArrayList in cache
    Cache["MyList"] = al;
  }
  // Manipulate the ArrayList by adding the time this
  // request was made (bad! may be accessed concurrently!)
  al.Add(DateTime.Now.ToString());
  lb1.DataSource = al;
  DataBind();
```

```
}
</script>
<body>
<form runat="server">
<asp:ListBox id="lb1" runat=server />
</form>
</body>
</html>
```

In this example, an instance of the `ArrayList` class is stored in the cache. It is modified every time the page is hit by adding the time of the current request. This is dangerous because multiple client requests may come in concurrently to this application, and the `ArrayList` class is not thread-safe by default.

The data cache is also used internally to manage the HTTP pipeline. It is often instructive to view the contents of this data cache, including all system-cached objects and any you may have added to the cache. You easily can do this by calling the function shown in Listing 9-16 from within any ASP.NET page.

LISTING 9-16: Displaying the Contents of the Data Cache

```
private void PrintDataCache()
{
  string strCacheContents;
  string strName;

  //display all of the items stored in the ASP.NET cache
  Response.Write("<b>Data cache contains:</b><br/>");
  Response.Write("<table>");
  Response.Write("<tr><td><b>Key</b></td>");
  Response.Write("<td><b>Value</b></td></tr>");
  foreach(object objItem in Cache)
  {
    Response.Write("<tr><td>");
    DictionaryEntry de = (DictionaryEntry)objItem;
    Response.Write(de.Key.ToString());
    Response.Write("</td><td>");
    Response.Write(de.Value.ToString());
    Response.Write("</td></tr>");
  }
  Response.Write("</table>");
}
```

9.3.1 **Cache Entry Attributes**

So far we have seen that the data cache is similar to the application state object except for object lifetime and updateability. There are several other differences as well, primarily related to determining the lifetime of an object in the cache. Each time a new item is inserted into the cache, it is added with a collection of attributes. Every cache entry is represented by an instance of the private `CacheEntry` class, which is created on behalf of your item when you perform a cache insertion. While you don't have direct access to this class when using the cache, you can control the attributes of each instance when you add objects to the cache. Table 9-4 shows the various properties of the `CacheEntry` class and their meanings.

TABLE 9-4: CacheEntry Properties

Property	Type	Description
Key	String	A unique key used to identify this entry in the cache
Dependency	CacheDependency	A dependency this cache entry has—either on a file, a directory, or another cache entry—that, when changed, should cause this entry to be flushed
Expires	DateTime	A fixed date and time after which this cache entry should be flushed
Sliding-Expiration	TimeSpan	The time between when the object was last accessed and when the object should be flushed from the cache
Priority	CacheItem-Priority	How important this item is to keep in the cache compared with other cache entries (used when deciding how to remove cache objects during scavenging)
OnRemove-Callback	CacheItem-RemovedCallback	A delegate that can be registered with a cache entry for invocation upon removal

When the default indexer of the data cache is used to insert items, as was shown in the previous examples, the values of the `CacheEntry` class are set to default values. This means that the expiration is set to infinite, the sliding expiration is at 0, the CacheItemPriority is Normal, and the CacheItemRemoveCallback is null. Basically, your object will remain in the cache as long as no scavenging operation occurs (typically because of excessive process memory usage) and you don't explicitly remove it.

If you want more control over the attributes of the CacheEntry created for your cached object, you can use one of several overloaded versions of the Insert() method. The most verbose version of Insert() takes all the CacheEntry properties as parameters (plus the object to be cached) and passes them into the constructor for the CacheEntry class. For example, the code shown in Listing 9-17 inserts a string into the data cache that is set to expire a second before midnight on December 31, 2001.

LISTING 9-17: Setting Expiration Dates in the Data Cache

```
object obj = // retrieve obj to place in cache somehow
DateTime dt = new DateTime(2001, 12, 31, 23, 59, 59);
Cache.Insert("MyVal", // key
             obj,      // object
             null,     // dependencies
             dt,       // absolute expiration
             Cache.NoSlidingExpiration, // sliding exp.
             CacheItemPriority.Default, // priority
             null);    // callback delegate
```

9.3.1.1 *Cache Object Lifetime*

Whenever data is added to the data cache, you must specify its lifetime (or implicitly accept the default lifetime of *infinite*). This is an important decision because it directly affects the correctness of data retrieval in your application, and if not done correctly, can lead to working with stale data, often referred to as cache coherency problems. How you determine the lifetime of the data that you place in the cache depends entirely on the type of data you are caching. The data may become invalid when a file changes on the system or when another cache entry becomes invalid. It may become invalid after a fixed period of time (absolute expiration). Or perhaps the data is not in danger of becoming stale, but you don't want it to occupy memory in the cache unless it is actually being referenced (achieved with sliding expiration times). Finally, you can register a callback delegate for the data cache to invoke whenever a particular item is removed from the cache if you want to take specific action when the item is removed.

All these options can be specified when you insert an item into the cache using the `Cache.Insert()` method. The code in Listing 9-18 shows an example of adding the contents of a file to the data cache on application start (in the `global.asax` file). This cache entry becomes invalid if the contents of the file used to populate the cache entry change, so a `CacheDependency` is added to the file. We also register a callback function to receive notification of when the data is removed from the cache. Finally, this entry is set to have no absolute expiration, no sliding expiration, and the default value for priority.

LISTING 9-18: Using Cache Dependencies

```
<!- File: global.asax ->
<%@ Application Language="C#" %>
<script runat=server>
public void OnRemovePi(string key, object val,
                       CacheItemRemovedReason r)
{
    // Perhaps perform some action in response to
    // cache removal here
}

public void Application_OnStart()
{
  System.IO.StreamReader sr =
    new System.IO.StreamReader(Server.MapPath("pi.txt"));
  string pi = sr.ReadToEnd();

  CacheDependency piDep =
    new CacheDependency(Server.MapPath("pi.txt"));
  Context.Cache.Add("pi", pi, piDep,
                  Cache.NoAbsoluteExpiration,
                  Cache.NoSlidingExpiration,
                  CacheItemPriority.Default,
           new CacheItemRemovedCallback(OnRemovePi));
}
</script>
```

Any page that was part of this application could then reference the "pi" key in the data cache and be guaranteed that it is always up to date with the contents of the `pi.txt` file. Listing 9-19 shows how it might be used—in this case, to populate the contents of a text box with the value of the string in the file.

LISTING 9-19: Sample Page Accessing a Cache Element

```
<!— File: PiPage.aspx —>
<%@ Page language=C# %>
<html>
<head>
<script runat=server>
protected void Page_Load(Object src, EventArgs e)
{
  if (Cache["pi"] == null)
  {
      // Refresh pi in app
      pi.Text =
          ((global_asax)Context.ApplicationInstance).LoadPi();
  }
  else
    pi.Text = (string)Cache["pi"];
}
</script>
</head>

<body>
<form runat="server">
<h1>The pi Page</h1>
<asp:TextBox id="pi" runat=server Rows=50 Wrap=True
            Width=450px TextMode=MultiLine
            Height=300px/>
</form>
</body>
</html>
```

9.3.2 Cache Object Removal

An object in the data cache can be removed in several ways. You can explicitly remove it from the cache using the `Cache.Remove` method, it can be removed because its lifetime has expired, or it can be implicitly removed from the cache to reduce memory consumption (scavenging). You have direct control over the first two cases. You explicitly call `Cache.Remove`, and you explicitly set the expiration date of items in the cache. Removal because of scavenging, however, is not always under your direct control.

You can indicate a preference for how your cache items should be treated during a scavenging operation, however.

When scavenging is performed, the data cache removes items with low priority first. By default, your cache items have normal priority. If you want to directly control the priority of your cache items, you can set the priority value when you perform the insertion into the cache. Table 9-5 shows the various values for `CacheItemPriority` and their meanings. Note that you can request that an item in the cache *not* be removed during scavenging. Most of the time, it is wise to leave these priority values at their defaults and let the cache use its scavenging algorithms to decide which objects to remove.

TABLE 9-5: CacheItemPriority Values

`CacheItemPriority` Value	Description
AboveNormal	Item *less* likely than `Normal` items to be removed from cache during scavenging
BelowNormal	Item *more* likely than `Normal` items to be removed from cache during scavenging
Default	Equivalent to `Normal`
High	Least likely to be deleted from the cache during scavenging
Low	Most likely to be deleted from the cache during scavenging
Normal	Deleted from the cache after all `Low` and `BelowNormal` items have been deleted during scavenging
NotRemovable	Never removed from the cache implicitly

9.3.3 Data Cache Considerations and Guidelines

As with the output cache, using the data cache effectively involves making important decisions about data lifetime and estimating trade-offs in memory consumption and throughput. The following guidelines and considerations are designed to help you use the data cache as efficiently as possible.

1. The data cache is not a container for shared updateable state.

You should always anticipate the possibility that a request for an item in the data cache will return `null`, and you should never modify existing items (although replacing them with new objects is fine). The data cache does protect against concurrent writes to the `Hashtable` that is used internally to store cache entries, but that concurrency protection does not extend to accessing and modifying objects in the cache. In general, it is a bad idea to use any shared updateable state at the application scope anyway, because it often can become a bottleneck in application performance.

2. Cache data that is accessed frequently and is relatively expensive to acquire.

The effectiveness of caching data in a Web application depends on two factors: how often the data is accessed and how often it changes. As with output caching, if the data changes with each client request, caching it is a complete waste of resources. On the other hand, if the data does not change frequently but is almost never accessed, it is also a waste of resources to cache it (especially if it is big). Caching data retrieved from a database, especially if the database is on a remote machine, is almost always beneficial.

3. If data is dependent on a file, directory, or other cache entry, use a `Cache-Dependency` *to be sure it remains current.*

Many cache entries may have dependencies on external resources, or perhaps other cache entries. It is easy to ensure that these entries stay current by adding a `CacheDependency` when inserting them into the cache. Note that you can also signal that a cache entry is out of sync with a database value by adding a trigger to the database that modifies a file whenever the data is changed.

4. Beware cache coherency problems.

With the dramatic performance improvement that data caching brings, it is easy to begin relying on it too much and introducing cache coherency problems into your system. When you add data to the cache, carefully think through the different ways in which it will be accessed, and make sure that the data is not stale or that stale data is acceptable. In most cases, you can still achieve significant performance improvements even with short cache lifetime durations, especially if the data is accessed frequently.

SUMMARY

ASP.NET introduces two significant caching features to improve application performance: output caching and data caching. Output caching provides a mechanism for caching rendered versions of pages so that subsequent access to those pages will not have to go through the entire rendering process. You enable output caching on a page by specifying an `OutputCache` directive, in which you can control the duration the page should be cached, how many different versions of the page should be cached, and whether the page should be cached on downstream proxies and in client browsers. Output caching is also applicable to user controls, where it is called page fragment caching. Applying the `OutputCache` directive to an .ascx file caches the rendering of that control the first time it is used on a page.

An application-level data cache is available through the `Cache` property of the `HttpContext` class. Any object can be inserted into the data cache, and each entry in the cache has its own set of attributes that control its lifetime. Cache entries can specify how long they should stay in the cache either by specifying a fixed time when they should be removed, a duration after the most recent access after which they should be removed, or a dependency on another cache entry or file that should trigger their removal. Entries in the cache are subject to scavenging according to priority, which gives ASP.NET a last recourse for reclaiming memory before bouncing its worker process.

■ 10 ■
State Management

B EFORE WE BEGIN discussing state management in ASP.NET, let's get
one thing straight: Attempting to manage state in Web applications
goes against the fundamental design principles of the Web. One of the primary goals of the Web and its underlying protocol, HTTP, is to provide a
scalable medium for sharing information. Adding user state inherently
reduces scalability because the pages shown to a particular user will be different from those shown to another user and thus cannot be reused or
cached.

In spite of this fact, many applications deployed on the Web require user-
specific state to function properly. Applications ranging from e-commerce
shopping sites to local company intranet sites depend on the ability to track
individual requests from distinct users and store state on behalf of each
client, whether it's items in a shopping cart or which days were selected on
a calendar as requested vacation days. Although maintaining client-specific
state is not officially part of the HTTP protocol, there is a proposal in place
for adding state management to HTTP. RFC 2109[14] defines a proposed standard for state management for HTTP also known as cookies. Although it is
only a proposed standard and not yet an official part of the HTTP specification, cookies are in widespread use today in almost all browsers, and many
Web sites rely on cookies for their functionality.

---

14. See http://www.w3.org/Protocols/rfc2109/rfc2109.

As a consequence, Web programmers must be very conscious about state management. Unlike traditional applications, Web applications must be very explicit about any state that is maintained on behalf of a client, and there is no one standard way to maintain that state.

10.1 **Types of State**

One of the most important decisions you face when designing a Web application is where to store your state. ASP.NET provides four types of state: application state, session state, cookie state, and view state. In this chapter, we explore each type of state, when it is most applicable, and any disadvantages you should be aware of if you decide to make use of it.

ASP.NET, like its predecessor, ASP, provides a pair of objects for managing application-level state and session-level state. Application state is where information that is global to the application may be stored. For efficiency, this state is typically stored once and then read from many times. Session state is maintained on a per-client basis. When a client first accesses any page in an application, an ASP.NET generated session ID is created. That session ID is then transmitted between the server and the client via HTTP either using client-side cookies or encoded in a mangled version of the URL (URL mangling is discussed in detail later in this chapter). On subsequent accesses by the same client, state associated with that session ID may be viewed and modified. Cookies provide the ability to store small amounts of data on a client's machine. Once a cookie is set, all subsequent pages accessed by the same client will transmit the cookie and its value.

Finally, view state is a yet another way of storing state on behalf of a client by saving and restoring values from a hidden field when a form is posted. Although this technique for retaining state has been used by Web developers in the past, ASP.NET provides a simplified mechanism for taking advantage of it. As we have seen in Chapter 8, it is possible to place items into the `ViewState` property bag available in every `Page`-derived class. When that page issues a `POST` request to itself, the values placed in the `ViewState` property bag can then be retrieved, the key restriction being that view state works only when a page posts to itself. Table 10-1 summarizes the advantages and disadvantages of each of the four types of state available in ASP.NET.

TABLE 10-1: State Type Comparison in ASP.NET

Type of State	Scope of State	Advantages	Disadvantages
Application	Global to the application	• Shared across all clients	• Overuse limits scalability • Not shared across multiple machines in a Web farm or processors in a Web garden • Primary purpose subsumed by data cache in ASP.NET
Session	Per client	• Can configure to be shared across machines in a Web farm and processors in a Web garden	• Requires cookies or URL mangling to manage client association • Off-host storage can be inefficient
Cookie	Per client	• Works regardless of server configuration • State stored on client • State can live beyond current session	• Limited memory (~4KB) • Clients may not support cookies or may explicitly disable them • State is sent back and forth with each request
View	Across POST requests to the same page	• Works regardless of server configuration	• State is retained only with POST request made to the same page • State is sent back and forth with each request

10.2 **Application State**

Application state is something that should be used with care, and in most cases, avoided altogether. Although it is a convenient repository for global data in a Web application, its use can severely limit the scalability of an application, especially if it is used to store shared, updateable state. It is also an unreliable place to store data, because it is replicated with each application instance and is not saved if the application is recycled. With this warning in mind, let's explore how it works.

Application state is accessed through the Application property of the HttpApplication class, which returns an instance of class HttpApplicationState. This class is a named object collection, which means that it can hold data of any type as part of a key/value pair. Listing 10-1 shows a typical use of application state. As soon as the application is started, it loads the data from the database. Subsequent data accesses will not need to go to the database but will instead access the application state object's cached version. Data that is prefetched in this way must be static, because it will not be unloaded from the application until the application is recycled or otherwise stopped and restarted.

LISTING 10-1: Sample Use of Application State for Data Prefetching

```
    // Inside of global.asax
  void Application_Start(object src, EventArgs e)
  {
    DataSet ds = new DataSet();
    // population of dataset from ADO.NET query not shown

    // Cache DataSet reference
    Application["FooDataSet"] = ds;
  }


      // In some page within the application
  private void Page_Load(object src, EventArgs e)
  {
    DataSet ds = (DataSet)(Application["FooDataSet"]);
    // ...
    MyDataGrid.DataSource = ds;
    // ...
  }
```

Because it is likely that multiple clients will be serviced by the same application, there is a potential for concurrent access to application state. The `HttpApplicationState` class protects access to its collection of objects with an instance of the `HttpApplicationStateLock` class, a derivative of the `ReadWriteObjectLock` class. This class provides two alternate mechanisms for locking, one for reading and one for writing. Multiple reader locks may be acquired simultaneously, but to acquire a writer lock, all other locks must be released first. This type of locking mechanism is particularly useful for protecting state in the application state bag because it allows multiple readers to pass through concurrently, and restricts access only when a request tries to write to the state bag. The general usage model of application-level state is to update it infrequently and read it frequently, so concurrent readers are a common occurrence.

In traditional ASP, it was always on the shoulders of the developer to call `Lock` and `Unlock` on the application object whenever it was modified or accessed. In ASP.NET, however, these calls are made implicitly for you whenever you insert items into or read items from the state bag in the form of either `AcquireWrite()` or `AcquireRead()`, depending on whether an item is being inserted or accessed. There is typically no need to explicitly call `Lock()` and `UnLock()` when working with the application state bag. These methods do exist, however, and internally calling the `Lock()` method acquires a writer lock on the internal `HttpApplicationStateLock` class. It is important to note that making explicit calls to `Lock()` and `UnLock()` defeats the multiple-reader efficiency of this new locking mechanism and should therefore be avoided in most cases.

The one case in which you still need to explicitly call the `Lock()` and `UnLock()` methods on the application state bag is when you are updating a shared piece of state. For example, Listing 10-2 shows a sample page that uses shared, updateable application state. In this example, each time the page is accessed, the string identifying the client browser type (`Request.Browser.Browser`) is used as an index into the `HttpApplicationState` collection, where a count is maintained to keep track of how many times this page was accessed with each client browser type. The page then renders a collection of paragraph elements displaying the browser names along with how many times each browser was used to access this page. These statistics continue to accumulate for the lifetime of the application. Note that before the value in the application state bag is retrieved and updated, `Application.Lock()` is called, and once the update is complete, `Application.UnLock()` is called. This acquires a writer lock on the application state bag and guarantees that the value will not be read while the update is being performed. If we did not take care to call `Lock`, a potential race condition would exist, and the value keeping track of the number of browser hits for a particular browser type would not necessarily be correct.

LISTING 10-2: Sample Use of Application State

```
<%@ Page Language='C#' %>
<script runat='server'>
private void Page_Load(object sender, System.EventArgs e)
{
  Application.Lock();

  // Modify a value in the HttpApplicationState collection
  if (Application[Request.Browser.Browser] != null)
    Application[Request.Browser.Browser] =
            (int)Application[Request.Browser.Browser] + 1;
  else
    Application[Request.Browser.Browser] = 1;

  Application.UnLock();

  // Print out the values in HttpApplicationState
  // to show client browser access statistics
  for (int i=0; i<Application.Count; i++)
    Response.Output.Write("<p>{0} : {1} hits</p>",
              Application.GetKey(i), Application[i]);
}
</script>
```

In almost every scenario that would have used application state in a traditional ASP application, it makes more sense to use the data cache in ASP.NET, discussed in Chapter 9. The most common need for application state is to provide a share point for accessing global, read-only data in an application. By placing global, read-only data in the data cache instead of in application state, you gain all the benefits of cache behavior, with the same ease of access provided by application state. Probably the most compelling advantage of the data cache over application state is memory utilization. If the memory utilization of the ASP.NET worker process approaches the point at which the process will be bounced automatically (the recycle limit), the memory in the data cache will be scavenged, and items that have not been used for a while will be removed first, potentially preventing the process from recycling. If, on the other hand, data is stored exclusively in application state, ASP.NET can do nothing to prevent the process from recycling, at which point all of the application state will be lost and must be restored on application start-up.

The one feature of application state that cannot be replaced by the data cache is the ability to have shared updateable state, as shown earlier in Listing 10-2. Arguably, however, this type of state should not be used at all in a Web application, because it inherently limits scalability and is unreliable as a mechanism for storing meaningful data. In the previous example, we were using application state to save statistics on browser type access. This information is maintained only as long as the application is running, and it is stored separately in each instance of the application. This means that when the process recycles, the data is lost. It also means that if this application is deployed in a Web farm (or a Web garden), separate browser statistics will be kept for each running instance of the application across different machines (or CPUs). To more reliably collect this type of statistical information, it would make more sense to save the data to a central database and avoid application state altogether.

10.3 Session State

Maintaining state on behalf of each client is often necessary in Web applications, whether it is used to keep track of items in a shopping cart or to note viewing preferences for a particular user. ASP.NET provides three ways of maintaining client-specific state: session state, cookie state, and view state. Each technique has its advantages and disadvantages. Session state is the most flexible and, in general, the most efficient. ASP.NET has enhanced session state to address some of the problems associated with it in previous versions of ASP, including the abilities to host session state out of process (or in a database) and to track session state without using cookies.

Session state is maintained on behalf of each client within an ASP.NET application. When a new client begins to interact with the application, a new session ID (or session key) is generated and associated with all subsequent requests from that same client (either using a cookie or via URL mangling). By default, the session state is maintained in the same process and AppDomain as your application, so you can store any data type necessary in session state. If you elect to house session state in another process or in a database, however, there are restrictions on what can be stored, as we will discuss shortly. Session state is maintained in an instance of the HttpSessionState class and is accessible through the Session property of both the Page and HttpContext classes. When a request comes in to an application, the Session properties of the Page and HttpContext class used to service that request are initialized to the current instance of HttpSessionState that is associated with that particular client. Listing 10-3 shows the primary methods and properties of the HttpSessionState class, along with the property accessors in both the Page and HttpContext classes.

LISTING 10-3: HttpSessionState Class

```
public sealed class HttpSessionState : ICollection,
                                       IEnumerable
{
    // properties
    public int CodePage {get; set;}
    public int Count {get;}
    public bool IsCookieless {get;}
    public bool IsNewSession {get;}
    public bool IsReadOnly {get;}
    public KeysCollection Keys {get;}
    public int LCID {get; set;}
    public SessionStateMode Mode {get;}
    public string SessionID {get;}
    public HttpStaticObjectsCollection StaticObjects {get;}
    public int Timeout {get; set;}
    // indexers
    public object this[string] {get; set;}
    public object this[int] {get; set;}
    // methods
    public void Abandon();
    public void Add(string name, object value);
```

```
      public void Clear();
      public void Remove(string name);
      public void RemoveAll();
      public void RemoveAt(int index);
      //...
  }

  public class Page : TemplateControl, IHttpHandler
  {
      public virtual HttpSessionState Session {get;}
      //...
  }

  public sealed class HttpContext : IServiceProvider
  {
      public HttpSessionState Session {get;}
      //...
  }
```

Because the `HttpSessionState` class supports string and ordinal-based indexers, it can be populated and accessed using the standard array access notation that most developers are familiar with from traditional ASP. There are some new properties, however, including flags for whether the session key is being maintained with cookies or with mangled URLs (`IsCookie-less`) and whether the session state is read-only (`IsReadOnly`). Also note that although the `CodePage` property is accessible through session state, this is for backward compatibility only. The proper way to access the response's encoding is through `Response.ContentEncoding.CodePage`.

For an example of using session state, let's consider an implementation of the classic shopping cart for a Web application. As a user navigates among the pages of an application, she selects items to be retained in a shopping cart for future purchase. When the user is done shopping, she can navigate to a checkout page, review the items she has collected in her cart, and purchase them. This requires the Web application to retain a collection of items the user has chosen across request boundaries, which is exactly what session state provides. Listing 10-4 shows the definition of a class called `Item`. Instances of this class are used to represent the selected items in our shopping cart.

LISTING 10-4: Item Class

```
public class Item
{
  private string _description;
  private int     _cost;

  public Item(string description, int cost)
  {
    _description = description;
    _cost = cost;
  }

  public string Description
  {
    get { return _description; }
    set { _description = value; }
  }
  public int Cost
  {
    get { return _cost; }
    set { _cost = value; }
  }
}
```

To store Item instances on behalf of the client, we initialize a new
ArrayList in session state and populate the ArrayList with items as the
client selects them. If you need to perform one-time initialization of data in
session state, the Session_Start event in the Application class is the
place to do so. Listing 10-5 shows a sample handler for the Session_Start
event in our application object, which in our case is creating a new
ArrayList and adding it to the session state property bag indexed by the
keyword "Cart".

LISTING 10-5: Initializing Session State Objects

```
// in global.asax
public class Global : System.Web.HttpApplication
{
  protected void Session_Start(Object sender, EventArgs e)
  {
    // Initialize shopping cart
    Session["Cart"] = new ArrayList();
  }
}
```

A sample page that uses the shopping cart is shown in Listings 10-6 and 10-7. In this page, two handlers are defined: one for purchasing a pencil and another for purchasing a pen. To keep things simple, the items and their costs have been hard-coded, but in a real application this information would normally come from a database lookup. When the user elects to add an item to her cart, the `AddItem` method is called. This allocates a new instance of the `Item` class and initializes it with the description and cost of the item to be purchased. That new item is then added to the `ArrayList` maintained by the `Session` object, indexed by the string "`Cart`". Listings 10-8 and 10-9 show a sample page that displays all the items in the current client's cart along with a cumulative total cost.

LISTING 10-6: Session State Shopping Page Example

```
<!- File: Purchase.aspx ->
<%@ Page language="c#" Codebehind="Purchase.aspx.cs"
         Inherits="PurchasePage" %>

<HTML>
  <body>
    <form runat="server">
      <p>Items for purchase:</p>
      <asp:LinkButton id=_buyPencil runat="server"
                  onclick="BuyPencil_Click">
          Pencil ($1)</asp:LinkButton>
      <asp:LinkButton id=_buyPen runat="server"
                  onclick="BuyPen_Click">
          Pen ($2)</asp:LinkButton>
      <a href="purchase.aspx">Purchase</a>
    </form>
  </body>
</HTML>
```

LISTING 10-7: Session State Shopping Page Example—Code-Behind

```
// File: Purchase.aspx.cs
public class PurchasePage : Page
{
  private void AddItem(string desc, int cost)
  {
    ArrayList cart = (ArrayList)Session["Cart"];
```

continues

```
      cart.Add(new Item(desc, cost));
    }

    // handler for button to buy a pencil
    private void BuyPencil_Click(object sender, EventArgs e)
    {
      // add pencil ($1) to shopping cart
      AddItem("pencil", 1);
    }

    // handler for button to buy a pen
    private void BuyPen_Cick(object sender, EventArgs e)
    {
      // add pen ($2) to shopping cart
      AddItem("pen", 2);
    }
}
```

LISTING 10-8: Session State Checkout Page Example

```
<!- File: Checkout.aspx ->
<%@ Page language="c#" Codebehind="Checkout.aspx.cs"
        Inherits="CheckoutPage" %>
<HTML>
 <body>
 <form runat="server">
   <asp:Button id=Buy runat="server" Text="Buy"/>
   <a href="purchase.aspx">Continue shopping</a>
 </form>
 </body>
</HTML>
```

LISTING 10-9: Session State Checkout Page Example—Code-Behind

```
// File: Checkout.aspx.cs
public class CheckOutPage : Page
{
  private void Page_Load(object sender, System.EventArgs e)
  {
     // Print out contents of cart with total cost
     // of all items tallied
    int totalCost = 0;

    ArrayList cart = (ArrayList)Session["Cart"];
    foreach (Item item in cart)
    {
      totalCost += item.Cost;
```

```
      Response.Output.Write("<p>Item: {0}, Cost: ${1}</p>",
                           item.Description, item.Cost);
    }

    Response.Write("<hr/>");
    Response.Output.Write("<p>Total cost: ${0}</p>",
                        totalCost);

  }
}
```

The key features to note about session state are that it keeps state on behalf of a particular client across page boundaries in an application, and that the state is retained in memory on the server in the default session state configuration.

10.3.1 Session Key Management

To associate session state with a particular client, it is necessary to identify an incoming request as having been issued by a given client. A mechanism for identifying a client is not built into the essentially connectionless HTTP protocol, so client tracking must be managed explicitly. In traditional ASP, this was always done by setting a client-side cookie with a session key on the first client request. This technique is still supported in ASP.NET (in fact, it is the default technique) and is demonstrated in Figure 10-1.

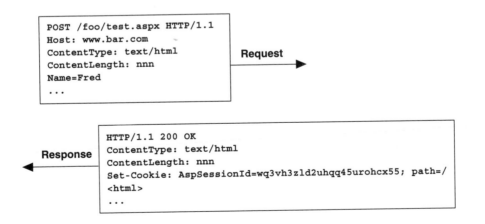

FIGURE 10-1: Session Key Maintained with Cookies

Because session keys are used to track clients and maintain potentially sensitive information on their behalf, they must not only be unique, they must also be next to impossible to guess. This has been a problem in the past when programmers used Globally Unique Identifiers (GUIDs) as session keys. Because the original algorithm for generating GUIDs was deterministic, if you knew one of the GUIDs generated by a server machine, you could guess subsequent GUIDs and thus access the session state associated with another client. Although GUIDs are no longer generated this way, ASP.NET takes the precaution of generating its own session keys by using the cryptographic service provider and its own encoding algorithm. Listing 10-10 shows some pseudocode demonstrating the technique used by ASP.NET for creating session keys.

LISTING 10-10: Session Key Generation in ASP.NET

```
// Generate 15-byte random number using the crypto provider
RNGCryptoServiceProvider rng =
                        new RNGCryptoServiceProvider();
byte[] key = new byte[15];
rng.GetBytes(key);

// Encode the random number into a 24-character string
// (SessionId is a private class - not accessible)
string sessionKey = SessionId.Encode(key);
```

Using cookies to track session state can be problematic. Clients can disable cookie support in their browsers, and some browsers do not support cookies. As an alternative to using cookies, ASP.NET also supports a technique called URL mangling to track session keys without using client-side cookies. This technique works by intercepting the initial request made by a client, inserting the session key into the URL, and redirecting the client to the original page requested. When this page receives the request, it extracts the encoded session key from the request URL and initializes the current session state pointer to the correct block of memory. This technique is demonstrated in Figure 10-2. This technique works even with clients that have disabled cookie support in their browsers. On any subsequent navigation, either via anchor tags or explicit programmatic redirections,

ASP.NET will alter the target URL to embed the session key as well. This implicit URL mangling works only for relative URLs, however, so care must be taken with all links in an application using cookieless session key management to avoid absolute URLs.

Controlling whether cookies or URL mangling is used to manage your session keys (along with several other session state–related features) is performed through the sessionState element in your application's web.config file. Table 10-2 lists the various configuration settings available for the sessionState element of web.config. Listing 10-11 shows a sample web.config file that enables cookieless session key management for an application.

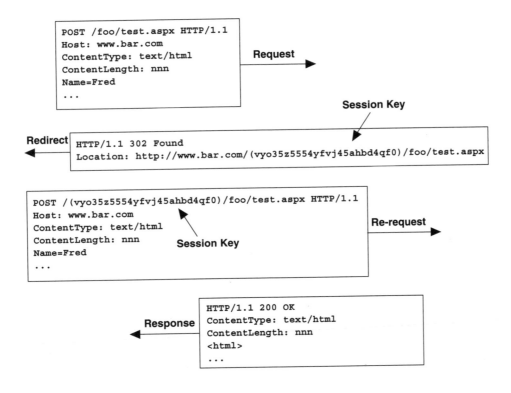

FIGURE 10-2: Session Key Maintained with URL Mangling

TABLE 10-2: sessionState Attributes

Attribute	Possible Values	Meaning
cookieless	True, False	Pass SessionID via cookies or URL mangling
mode	Off, InProc, SQLServer, StateServer	Where to store session state (or whether it is disabled)
stateConnection-String	Example: '192.168.1.100:42424'	Server name and port for StateServer
sqlConnection-String	Example: 'server=192.168.1.100; uid=sa;pwd='	SQLServer connection string excluding database (tempdb is implied)
timeout	Example: 40	Session state timeout value (in minutes)

LISTING 10-11: Sample web.config File Enabling Cookieless Session Key Management

```
<configuration>
  <system.web>
    <sessionState cookieless="true" />
  </system.web>
</configuration>
```

The choice of whether to use cookie-based or mangled URL–based session key management must be made at the application level. It is not possible to specify that the application should use cookie-based management if the client supports cookies, and otherwise default to mangled URL–based management. The trade-offs to consider when making this decision include efficiency, universal client support, and dealing with relative URLs. Cookies are more efficient because they avoid the redirection necessary to perform the URL mangling, although only one redirection per session will occur with URL mangling. Mangled URLs work with clients that don't have cookies enabled (or that don't support them). The mangled URL technique requires that your application avoid absolute URLs so that the mangling can take place properly. Finally, URL mangling also prevents easy bookmarking and thus may be an inconvenience for your users.

10.3.2 **Storing Session State out of Process**

In addition to requiring cookies to track session state, traditional ASP only supported the notion of in-process session state. Confining session state to a single process means that any application that relies on session state must always be serviced by the same process on the same machine. This precludes the possibility of deploying the application in a Web farm environment, where multiple machines are used to service requests independently, potentially from the same client. It also prevents the application from working correctly on a single machine with multiple host processes, sometimes referred to as a Web garden. If session state is tied to the lifetime of the Web server process, it is also susceptible to disappearing if that process goes down for some reason. To build traditional ASP applications that scale to Web farms and/or maintain persistent client-specific state, developers must avoid session state altogether and rely on other techniques for tracking client-specific state. The most common approach is maintaining client-specific state in a database running on a network-accessible server. To distinguish one client's state from another, the table (or tables) used to store state is indexed by the session key, as shown in Figure 10-3.

ASP.NET introduces the ability to store session state out of process, without resorting to a custom database implementation. The session-State element in an ASP.NET application's web.config file controls where session state is stored (see Table 10-2). The default location is in-process, as it was in traditional ASP. If the mode attribute is set to StateServer or SqlServer, however, ASP.NET manages the details of saving and restoring session state to another process (running as a service) or to an SQL Server database installation. This is appealing because it is possible to build ASP.NET applications that access session state in the normal way, and then by switching the sessionState mode in a configuration file, that same application can be deployed safely in a Web farm environment.

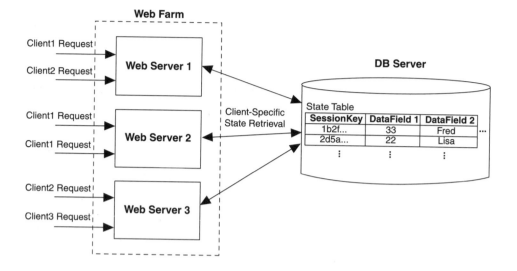

FIGURE 10-3: Maintaining Client-Specific State in a Web Farm Deployment

Whenever out-of-process session state is specified, it is also important to realize that anything placed into session state is serialized and passed out of the ASP.NET worker process. Thus, any type that is stored in session state must be serializable for this to work properly. In our earlier session state example, we stored instances of a locally defined Item class, which, if left in its existing form, would fail any attempts at serialization. The ArrayList class we used to store the instances of the Item class does support serialization, but since our class does not, the serialization will fail. To correct this, we would need to add serialization support to our class. Listing 10-12 shows the Item class correctly annotated to support serialization, which is now compatible with storage in out-of-process session state.

LISTING 10-12: Adding Serialization Support to a Class

```
[Serializable]
public class Item
{
  private string _description;
  private int    _cost;
  // ...
}
```

For session state to be transparently housed out of process, ASP.NET must assume that a page has all of its session state loaded before the page is loaded, and then flushed back to the out-of-process state container when the page completes its processing. This is inefficient when a page may not need this level of state access (although it is somewhat configurable, as we will see), so there is still a valid case to be made for implementing your own custom client-specific state management system, even with ASP.NET.

The first option for maintaining session state out of process is to use the `StateServer` mode for session state. Session state is then housed in a running process that is distinct from the ASP.NET worker process. The `State-Server` mode depends on the ASP.NET State Service to be up and running (this service is installed when you install the .NET runtime). By default the service listens over port 42424, although you can change that on a per-machine basis by changing the value of the `HKLM\System\CurrentControlSet\Services\aspnet_state\Parameters\Port` key in the registry. Figure 10-4 shows the ASP.NET State Service in the local machine services viewer.

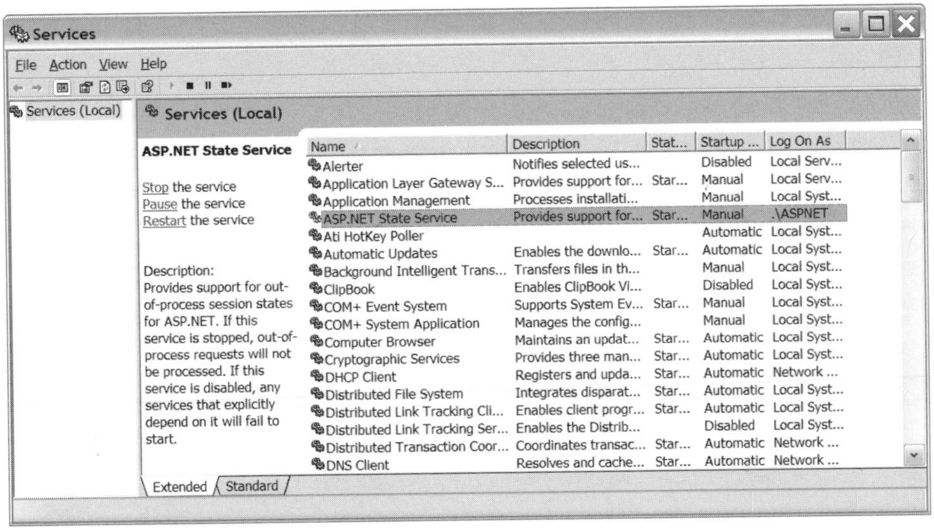

FIGURE 10-4: The ASP.NET State Service

The State Service can run either on the same machine as the Web application or on a dedicated server machine. Using the State Service option is useful when you want out-of-process session state management but do not want to have to install SQL Server on the machine hosting the state. Listing 10-13 shows an example web.config file that changes session state to live on server 192.168.1.103 over port 42424, and Figure 10-5 illustrates the role of the state server in a Web farm deployment scenario.

LISTING 10-13: web.config File Using State Server

```
<configuration>
  <system.web>
    <sessionState mode="StateServer"
      stateConnectionString="192.168.1.103:42424"
    />
  </system.web>
</configuration>
```

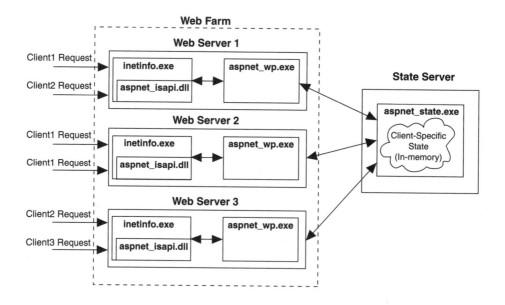

FIGURE 10.5: Using a State Server in a Web Farm Deployment

The last option for storing session state outside the server process is to keep it in an SQL Server database. ASP.NET supports this through the SQLServer mode in the sessionState configuration element. Before using this mode, you must run the InstallSqlState.sql script on the database server where session state will be stored. This script is found in the main Microsoft.NET directory.[15] The primary purpose of this script is to create a table that can store client-specific state indexed by session ID in the tempdb of that SQL Server installation. Listing 10-14 shows the CREATE statement used to create the table for storing this state. The ASP state table is created in the tempdb database, which is not a fully logged database, thus increasing the speed of access to the data. In addition to storing the state indexed by the session ID, this table keeps track of expiration times and provides a locking mechanism for exclusive acquisition of session state. The installation script also adds a job to clean out all expired session state daily.

LISTING 10-14: ASPStateTempSession Table

```
CREATE TABLE tempdb..ASPStateTempSessions (
   SessionId          CHAR(32) NOT NULL PRIMARY KEY,
   Created            DATETIME NOT NULL DEFAULT GETDATE(),
   Expires            DATETIME          NOT NULL,
   LockDate           DATETIME          NOT NULL,
   LockCookie         INT               NOT NULL,
   Timeout            INT               NOT NULL,
   Locked             BIT               NOT NULL,
   SessionItemShort   VARBINARY(7000)   NULL,
   SessionItemLong    IMAGE             NULL,
)
```

Listing 10-15 shows a sample web.config file that has configured session state to live in an SQL Server database on server 192.168.1.103. Notice that the sqlConnectionString attribute specifies a data source, a user ID, and a password but does not explicitly reference a database, because ASP.NET assumes that the database used will be tempdb.

---

15. On most 1.0 installations, this should be C:\WINNT\Microsoft.NET\Framework\v1.0.3705.

LISTING 10-15: web.config File Using SQL Server

```
<configuration>
  <system.web>
    <sessionState mode="SQLServer"
     sqlConnectionString=
        "data source=192.168.1.103;user id=sa;password=" />
  </system.web>
</configuration>
```

Both the state server and the SQL Server session state options store the state as a byte stream—in internal data structures in memory for the state server, and in a VARBINARY field (or an IMAGE field if larger than 7KB) for SQL Server. While this is space-efficient, it also means that it cannot be modified except by bringing it into the request process. This is in contrast to a custom client-specific state implementation, where you could build stored procedures to update session key–indexed data in addition to other data when performing updates. For example, consider our shopping cart implementation shown earlier. If, when the user added an item to his cart, we wanted to update an inventory table for that item as well, we could write a single stored procedure that added the item to his cart in a table indexed by his session key, and then updated the inventory table for that item in one round-trip to the database. Using the ASP.NET SQL Server session state feature would require two additional round-trips to the database to accomplish the same task: one to retrieve the session state as the page was loaded and one to flush the session state when the page was finished rendering.

This leads us to another important consideration when using ASP.NET's out-of-process session state feature: how to describe precisely the way each of the pages in your application will use session state. By default, ASP.NET assumes that every page requires session state to be loaded during page initialization and to be flushed after the page has finished rendering. When you are using out-of-process session state, this means two round-trips to the state server (or database server) for each page rendering. You can potentially eliminate many of these round-trips by more carefully designing how each page in your application uses session state. The session manager then determines when session state must be retrieved and stored by querying the current handler's session state requirements. There are three options for a page (or other handler) with respect to session state. It can express the need to view session state, to view and modify session state, or no session state dependency at all. When writing ASP.NET pages, you express this preference through the `EnableSessionState` attribute of the `Page` directive. This attribute defaults to `true`, which means that session state will be retrieved and saved with each request handled by that page. If you know that a page will only read from session state and not modify it, you can save a round-trip by setting `EnableSessionState` to `readonly`. Furthermore, if you know that a page will never use session state, you can set `Enable-SessionState` to `false`. Internally, this flag determines which of the tagging interfaces your `Page` class will derive from (if any). These tagging interfaces are queried by the session manager to determine how to manage session state on behalf of a given page. Figure 10-6 shows the various values of `EnableSessionState` and their effect on your `Page`-derived class.

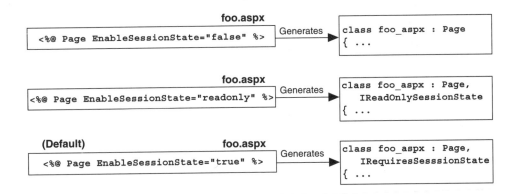

FIGURE 10-6: Indicating Session State Serialization Requirements in Pages

10.4 Cookie State

Although not part of the HTTP specification (yet), cookies are often used to store user preferences, session variables, or identity. The server issues a Set-Cookie header in its response to a client that contains the value it wants to store. The client is then expected to store the information associated with the URL or domain that issued the cookie. In subsequent requests to that URL or domain, the client should include the cookie information using the Cookie header. Some limitations of cookies include the fact that many browsers limit the amount of data sent through cookies (only 4,096 bytes are guaranteed) and that clients can potentially disable all cookie support in their browser.

ASP.NET provides an HttpCookie class for managing cookie data. Listing 10-16 shows the HttpCookie class definition and the cookie collection properties exposed by the request and response objects. Note that the request and response objects both expose the collection of cookies through the HttpCookieCollection type, which is just a type-safe derivative of the NameObjectCollectionBase class, designed for storing HttpCookie class instances. Each cookie can store multiple name/value pairs, as specified by RFC 2109, which are accessible through the Values collection of the HttpCookie class or indirectly through the default indexer provided by the class.

LISTING 10-16: The HttpCookie Class

```
public sealed class HttpCookie
{
  public string                 Domain           {get; set;}
  public DateTime               Expires          {get; set;}
  public bool                   HasKeys          {get;     }
  public string                 this[string key] {get; set;}
  public string                 Name             {get; set;}
  public string                 Path             {get; set;}
  public string                 Secure           {get; set;}
  public string                 Value            {get; set;}
  public NameValueCollection    Values           {get;     }
  //...
}

public sealed class HttpRequest
{
  public HttpCookieCollection Cookies {get;}
```

```
  //...
}

public sealed class HttpResponse
{
  public HttpCookieCollection Cookies {get;}
  //...
}
```

To request that a client set a cookie, add a new `HttpCookie` instance to the response cookie collection before your page rendering. To access the cookies that the client is sending with any given request, access the `Cookies` collection property of the request object. Listing 10-17 shows an example of a page that sets and uses a cookie named "`Age`". If the cookie has not been set, the page adds the cookie to the `Response.Cookies` collection with a value from a field on the form (`ageTextBox`). If the cookie has been set, the current value is pulled from the `Request.Cookies` collection and is used instead.

LISTING 10-17: Using Cookies in ASP.NET

```
protected void Page_Load(Object sender, EventArgs E)
{
  int age = 0;
  if (Request.Cookies["Age"] == null)
  {
    // "Age" cookie not set, set with this response
    HttpCookie ac = new HttpCookie("Age");
    ac.Value = ageTextBox.Text;
    Response.Cookies.Add(ac);
    age = Convert.ToInt32(ageTextBox.Text);
  }
  else
  {
    // use existing cookie value...
    age = Convert.ToInt32(Request.Cookies["Age"].Value);
  }
  // use age to customize page
}
```

Although cookies are typically used to store user-specific configuration information and preferences, they can be used to store any client-specific state needed by an application (as long as that state is converted to string form). It is interesting to contrast our earlier shopping cart implementation using session state with an equivalent implementation using only cookies. The major change in our implementation is the population and retrieval of the shopping cart contents from cookies instead of directly from session state. This can be done by converting the contents of the shopping cart into string form so that it can be sent back as cookies to the client and later restored on subsequent requests. To facilitate this, we have added two new functions to our `Item` class: `HydrateArrayListFromCookies` and `Save-ArrayListToCookies`. The first function is called from within the `Load` event handler of our shopping `Page` class, and the second function is called from within the `PreRender` event handler. The implementation of these two functions is shown in Listing 10-18. The rest of our code remains the same because we have changed only how the `ArrayList` is persisted. Listing 10-19 shows the cookie-based implementation of our shopping cart application.

LISTING 10-18: Item Class with Cookie Serialization Support

```
public class Item
{
  public static ArrayList HydrateArrayListFromCookies()
  {
    int itemCount=0;
    HttpCookie itemCountCookie =
          HttpContext.Current.Request.Cookies["ItemCount"];
    if (itemCountCookie != null)
      itemCount = Convert.ToInt32(itemCountCookie.Value);
    else
    {
      itemCountCookie = new HttpCookie("ItemCount");
      itemCountCookie.Value = "0";
      HttpContext.Current.Response.Cookies.Add(
                                        itemCountCookie);
    }

    ArrayList cart = new ArrayList();
    for (int i=0; i<itemCount; i++)
    {
      HttpCookieCollection cookies =
         HttpContext.Current.Request.Cookies;

      int cost = Convert.ToInt32(
                  cookies[i.ToString()+"cost"].Value);
```

```
      string desc = cookies[i.ToString()+"desc"].Value;
      cart.Add(new Item(desc, cost));
    }

    return cart;
  }

  public static void SaveArrayListToCookies(ArrayList cart)
  {
    // Save array size first
    HttpCookie itemCountCookie =
                      new HttpCookie("ItemCount");
    itemCountCookie.Value = cart.Count.ToString();
    HttpCookieCollection cookies =
          HttpContext.Current.Response.Cookies;

    cookies.Add(itemCountCookie);
    int i=0;
    foreach (Item item in cart)
    {
      HttpCookie descCookie =
              new HttpCookie(i.ToString() + "desc");
      descCookie.Value = item.Description;
      cookies.Add(descCookie);

      HttpCookie costCookie =
              new HttpCookie(i.ToString() + "cost");
      costCookie.Value = item.Cost.ToString();
      cookies.Add(costCookie);
      i++;
    }
  }
  // remainder of class unchanged from Listing 10-4
}
```

LISTING 10-19: Cookie State Shopping Page Example

```
public class PurchasePage : Page
{
    // Maintain private cart array variable
  private ArrayList _cart;

  private void Page_Load(object sender, System.EventArgs e)
  {
    _cart = Item.HydrateArrayListFromCookies();
```

continues

```
      }

      private void Page_PreRender(object src, EventArgs e)
      {
        Item.SaveArrayListToCookies(_cart);
      }

      private void AddItem(string desc, int cost)
      {
        _cart.Add(new Item(desc, cost));
      }

      // remaining code identical to Listing 10-7
    }
```

Although it is technically possible to store any type of client-specific state using cookies, as shown in the previous shopping cart example, there are several drawbacks compared with other models. First, all of the state must be mapped into and out of strings, which in general requires more space to store the same amount of data. Second, as mentioned earlier, clients may disable cookies or may have a browser that does not support cookies, thus rendering the application inoperative. Finally, unlike session state, cookie state is passed between the client and the server with every request.

10.5 View State

In addition to session state and cookie state, ASP.NET introduces the ability to store client-specific state through a mechanism called view state. View state is stored in a hidden field on each ASP.NET page called __VIEWSTATE. Each time a page is posted to itself, the contents of the __VIEWSTATE field are sent as part of the post. The primary use of view state is for controls to retain their state across post-backs, as described in Chapter 2, but it can also be used as a mechanism for storing generic client-specific state between post-backs to the same page.

View state is accessible from any control and is exposed as a StateBag that supports storing any type that is serializable. Because the Page class is derived from the Control base class, you can access the view state directly from within your pages and indirectly through server-side controls. Listing 10-20 shows the `ViewState` property of the `Control` class. The view state for a control is loaded just before the `Load` event firing, and it is flushed just before the `Render` method being invoked. This means that you can safely access the `ViewState` in your `Load` event handler and that you should make sure it has been populated with whatever state you need by the time your `Render` method is called.

LISTING 10-20: ViewState Property Accessor

```
public class Control : //...
{
  protected virtual StateBag ViewState {get;}
  //...
}
```

For an example of using view state, let's reimplement our shopping cart example one more time, this time using view state as the container for client-specific state. Because the `StateBag` class has a default indexer just as the `HttpSessionState` class does, the code needs to change very little from our original session state–based implementation. The `Item` class can be used in its original form with serialization support (not the altered form required for cookie state). The most significant change is that view state does not propagate between pages in an application, so to use it, we must aggregate all of the functionality that relies on client-specific state into a single page. In our example, this means that we must implement the `Check-OutPage` and the `ShoppingPage` together in one page. Listing 10-21 shows this implementation.

LISTING 10-21: ViewState Shopping Page Example

```
public class PurchasePage : Page
{
  private void Page_Load(object sender, EventArgs e)
  {
    ArrayList cart = (ArrayList)ViewState["Cart"];
    if (cart == null)
    {
      cart = new ArrayList();
```

continues

```
        ViewState["Cart"] = cart;
    }
      // Print out contents of cart with total cost
      // of all items tallied
    int totalCost = 0;

    foreach (Item item in cart)
    {
      totalCost += item.Cost;
      Response.Output.Write("<p>Item: {0}, Cost: ${1}</p>",
                            item.Description, item.Cost);
    }
    Response.Write("<hr/>");
    Response.Output.Write("<p>Total cost: ${0}</p>",
                          totalCost);
  }

  private void AddItem(string desc, int cost)
  {
    ArrayList cart = (ArrayList)ViewState["Cart"];
    cart.Add(new Item(desc, cost));
    _itemsInCart.Text = cart.Count.ToString();
  }

  // remaining code identical to Listing 10-7
}
```

Notice that in contrast to the cookie state implementation, we were able to save the ArrayList full of Item instances directly to the ViewState state bag. When the page was rendered, it rendered the ArrayList into a compressed, text-encoded field added as the value of the __VIEWSTATE control on the form. On subsequent post-backs to this page, the view state was then reclaimed from the __VIEWSTATE field, and the ArrayList was once again available in the same form. Like cookie state, view state is sent between the client and the server with each request, so it should not be used for transmitting large amounts of data. For relatively small amounts of data posted back to the same page, however, it provides a convenient mechanism for developers to store client-specific state.

SUMMARY

State management influences almost every aspect of a Web application's design, and it is important to understand all the options available for state management as well as their implications for usability, performance, and scalability. ASP.NET provides four types of state, each of which may be the best choice in different parts of your application. State that is global to an application may be stored in the application state bag, although it is typically preferable to use the new data cache instead of application state in ASP.NET. Client-specific state can be stored either in the session state bag, as client-side cookies, or as view state. Session state is most commonly used for storing data that should not be sent back and forth with each request, either because it is too large or because the information should not be visible on the Internet. Cookie state is useful for small client-specific pieces of information such as preferences, authentication keys, and session keys. View state is a useful alternative to session state for information that needs to be retained across posts back to the same page. Finally, enhancements to the session state model in ASP.NET give developers the flexibility to rely on session state even for applications that are deployed on Web farms or Web gardens through remote session storage.

▪11▪
Security

A SP.NET PROVIDES AUTHENTICATION and authorization services in
conjunction with IIS, supporting Basic, Digest, and Windows authentication. Impersonation using client credentials is also supported on a per-
request basis. Role-based security is provided in much the same way as it is
with COM+, and allows customized content based on role membership.
Finally, forms-based authentication allows applications to provide their
own login UI and perform their own credential verification, greatly sim-
plifying a technique already used by many Web sites.

11.1 **Web Security**

Security is often one of the last issues addressed by developers. It requires
thinking about your applications in a different light from what you are
accustomed to. As you build your applications, your goal is to make them
as useful and easy to use as possible. When you consider security, however,
the goal is often quite the opposite. You find yourself asking questions such
as "How can I be sure that these people cannot access this portion of my
application?" or "How can I validate that the request coming into my application is from who I think it is, and not some person pretending to be someone else?"

With Web applications, the issues of security are magnified because
almost all communication to and from the application is performed across

long connections. For this reason, one of the most important security issues in Web applications is authentication. Clients want to know whether the site they are looking at is indeed produced by the company it purports to be from, and servers often need to know the identity of a particular client, especially if the application is modifying data on behalf of a client (as with a bank account). The level of security required is very application dependent. Web applications that are simply informative may not care about client credentials and are happy to deal with all clients as anonymous users. Web applications that provide customized content may want to identify clients only if they want to be identified (for customization), and are otherwise happy to let anonymous clients browse the application at their leisure. Web applications that provide client services (stock portfolios, bank accounts, and so on) typically need to be much more careful about client identity and often require client authentication before any pages on the site can be displayed.

As a Web application developer, you must be aware of the level of authentication required by your application and add only the security services necessary. Each additional security requirement of your application makes it more complex and may have significant impact on its design.

11.1.1 Server Authentication

Server authentication is often very important to clients. They want to be sure that the Web site they are viewing is in fact being published and run by the authority it claims to be. This is especially true if a client is sending sensitive information, such as credit card or bank account numbers, to the server. If the server has not somehow authenticated itself with the client, the client cannot be sure that someone is not surreptitiously pretending to be that site just to collect information from clients.

Authenticating servers in a well-controlled local network is a solved problem. A particular machine is designated as the domain controller and takes responsibility for validating that each communication is authentic. Protocols such as Kerberos work well in this environment. As soon as we try to scale these techniques to the Web, however, we quickly run into client firewall constraints that make it impossible to exchange secret keys safely.

One solution to this is to use a technology labeled **digital certificates**. Digital certificates rely on public key cryptography that lets servers maintain a private key and publish their public key, which clients can use to authenticate that the server is indeed who it says it is. There is still a problem, however; someone may intercept the sending of the public key and replace it with his own. The person in the middle who swapped in his own public key can then potentially intercept and modify subsequent communication between that client and the server.

The solution to this is to designate a trusted authority that can vouch for the public keys of anyone that registers them with this authority. Companies (such as Verisign) have set up such a system and, for a fee, will store and vouch for your public key. As long as everyone trusts that the third-party company is telling the truth, and clients make the effort to verify server certificates, digital certificate authentication of servers works reasonably well. The one issue remaining is how to verify that the third party is who it claims to be (how do you know that Verisign is in fact the one performing the verification of a public key?). Distributing the public keys of companies like Verisign with browser installations solves this.

11.1.2 Client Authentication

With server authentication, there is little question about the purpose of the authentication. It is always to guarantee the identity of the server to the client. Client authentication, on the other hand, can be used for several different purposes. Some Web sites need to authenticate clients so that they can customize their content based on the preferences of those clients (for example, an e-commerce site may want to display on the front page items it thinks you will purchase when you visit it). Other sites control access to all or portions of the site based on client identity. Finally, some sites require that clients have credentials on the server (Windows logins) so that operations performed through the Web site can be done with the credentials of the client (very common with intranet applications). Each of these types of client authentication requires different levels of assurance and can be implemented in several ways.

Through IIS, you can specify the level of client authentication to use for a given Web application (or a page within an application). By default, IIS prefers not to perform client authentication because it will incur more server involvement with each request, slowing down the system. If no client authentication is selected (Anonymous), every request is treated as anonymous, and a designated account (IUSR_*MACHINE*, where *MACHINE* is the name of your machine) is used for credentials. To force client authentication with IIS, you can disable anonymous access and then choose one of the available client authentication methods. Figure 11-1 shows the IIS configuration form controlling client authentication for a virtual directory.

The options for client authentication in IIS are Basic authentication, Integrated Windows authentication, and Digest authentication. Basic authentication requires that the client pass his password as clear text, which makes sense only if it is being encrypted, thus the use of Basic authentication is typically restricted to sites using SSL as their protocol. Even with the password being encrypted, however, it is still available to scripts within the Web application through the AUTH_PASSWORD intrinsic variable, which may not be something you want.

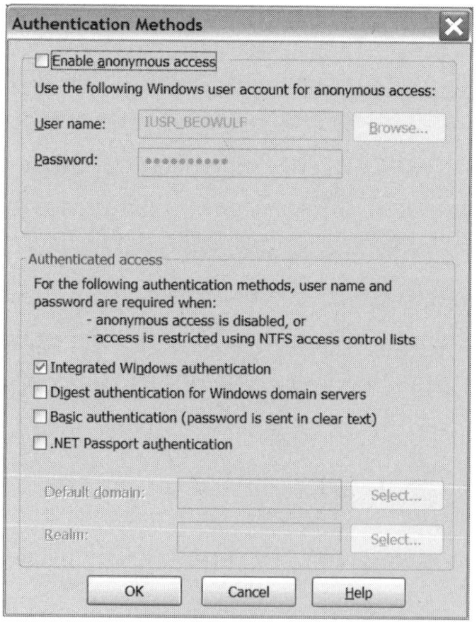

FIGURE 11-1: IIS Client Authentication Settings

Integrated authentication attempts to use native Windows authentication. This works by negotiating Kerberos or NTLM with proprietary extensions to HTTP, and works only for clients running IE who have a valid account on the server and who are not separated from the server by a firewall or proxy, because Kerberos is typically inhibited by a firewall, and NTLM becomes nonoperational through a proxy. This option may be useful for local intranets, but is typically much less useful for Internet servers.

Digest authentication uses a challenge/response technique to verify a client password. This means that the password must be available on the server, and thus the server must be a domain controller on the server network, which is usually not advisable, because having someone hack into your domain controller could be disastrous. It is also possible to configure IIS to accept client certificates for authentication. Certificate authentication is similar to the certificate authentication used to authenticate servers, but the server requests a certificate of the client instead of the other way around. For this to work, all clients must have valid certificates to present to the server to gain access to the site, as well as the server requiring a valid certificate.

In general, a large percentage of Windows-based Web applications do not rely on IIS to perform client authentication because it requires that clients do something special (obtain a server account or a certificate, for example), and most sites want to allow as many users access as possible. Instead, these sites typically authenticate clients at the application level and manage the details of keeping passwords and accounts themselves. This gives them much more flexibility and control in designing their client authentication system.

11.2 Security in ASP.NET

As we will see, you can also require client authentication in ASP.NET applications by adding the appropriate elements to your application's web.config file. Once the client has been authenticated, whether it was specified by IIS or by ASP.NET, information about that client is available through the

User property of the Page class. This property is a pass-through property pointing to the User property of the current HttpContext class on any given request. Listings 11-1 and 11-2 show the definition of this property in each class.

LISTING 11-1: User Property in the Page Class

```
public class Page : TemplateControl, IHttpHandler
{
    public IPrincipal User {get;}
    ...
}
```

LISTING 11-2: User Property in the HttpContext Class

```
public class HttpContext :
        IObjectServiceProvider
{
    public IPrincipal User {get;set;}
    ...
}
```

The User property points to an implementation of the IPrincipal interface. If the client was authenticated using Windows authentication, it points to an instance of the WindowsPrincipal class. Otherwise, it may point to a custom IPrincipal implementation or, more likely, an instance of the GenericPrincipal class. (We will show an example of using the GenericPrincipal class later to implement custom roles.) The IPrincipal interface is shown in Listing 11-3 and consists of a property and a method. The property (Identity) is an interface pointer to the identity of the current client, and the method (IsInRole) can be called to query whether the client is in a particular role. If the client was authenticated using Windows authentication, IsInRole simply checks group membership in the user's access token. If the client was authenticated in some other way (forms authentication, for example), this method should be able to tell you whether the client belongs to a particular named role, which is defined by the application.

LISTING 11-3: The IPrincipal Interface

```
public interface IPrincipal
{
     IIdentity Identity {get;}
     bool IsInRole(string role);
}
```

Listing 11-4 shows the `IIdentity` interface, consisting of three read-only properties: `IsAuthenticated`, `Name`, and `AuthenticationType`. You can use `IsAuthenticated` to distinguish between authenticated and anonymous clients, and you can use `Name` to query the identity of the client. If the client was authenticated, you can then use the `AuthenticationType` property of this interface to query the type of authentication that was used. Listing 11-5 shows an example of accessing an authenticated client's information. In this case, when the page loads, we extract the current client's name and type of authentication, and display them in labels on our page.

LISTING 11-4: The IIdentity Interface

```
public interface IIdentity
{
     string AuthenticationType {get;}
     bool IsAuthenticated {get;}
     string Name {get;}
}
```

LISTING 11-5: Accessing Authenticated Client Information

```
<!- File: AccessClientInfo.aspx ->
<%@ Page language=C# %>
<html>
<script runat=server>
  void Page_Load(Object src, EventArgs e)
  {
    AuthUser.Text = User.Identity.Name;
    AuthType.Text = User.Identity.AuthenticationType;
  }
</script>
<body>
<form runat="server">
```

continues

```
<h1>My test security page</h1>
<h2>Can you read this?</h2>
  <h3>user:</h3><asp:label id=AuthUser runat=server />
  <h3>authType: </h3><asp:label id=AuthType runat=server />
</form> </body> </html>
```

11.2.1 Client Authentication and Authorization

As we have seen, you can configure client authentication through IIS, and once that is in place, it applies to ASP.NET files as well. You can also specify authentication and authorization in ASP.NET via the web.config file of your application. You specify the client authentication type by using the authentication element, as shown in Listing 11-6. There are four possible values for the mode attribute of the authentication element: Windows (default), Forms, Passport, or None. If you use Windows authentication, you are shifting responsibility for authentication to the Web server, so you must pick an authentication mode in IIS, such as Integrated, Basic, Digest, or SSL client authentication.

LISTING 11-6: Setting the Authentication Mode with web.config

```
<!- File: web.config ->
<configuration>
  <system.web>
    <!- mode can also be Forms, Passport, or None ->
    <!- the default is Windows ->
    <authentication mode="Windows"/>
  </system.web>
</configuration>
```

Once you have configured the type of authentication you would like ASP.NET to use, you need to give it a reason to authenticate clients. You do this by restricting access to all or portions of your application via the authorization element. To control access to your site, you add deny and allow subelements to the authorization element, specifically denying or allowing access to users or roles. The wildcard "*" is used to represent all users, and the wildcard "?" is used to represent anonymous users. For example, to deny anonymous users access to your site, you would specify an authorization element with a single deny subelement set to"?", as shown in Listing 11-7.

LISTING 11-7: Denying Anonymous Users

```
<!— File: web.config —>
<configuration>
  <system.web>
    <authorization>
        <deny users="?" />
    </authorization>
  </system.web>
</configuration>
```

Both the `deny` and `allow` elements provide three attributes—`users`, `roles`, and `verbs`—and the values of these attributes support comma-delimited lists of users, roles, or verbs. In Listing 11-7, we used the `users` attribute to deny anonymous users access to our application. We could also construct more complex authorization requirements by adding multiple `deny` and `allow` elements. For example, in Listing 11-8, we explicitly grant authenticated users `MyDomain\bob` and `MyDomain\alice` complete access to our application. The second `allow` element grants all users the right to issue `GET` requests to pages in our application, and the final element, `deny`, restricts access to unauthenticated users. When ASP.NET checks the `authorization` element, it traverses the list of `allow` and `deny` elements in declaration sequence, and the first element that matches the credentials of the client request determines whether access is granted or denied. In our example, if the incoming client has been authenticated as Bob or Alice, he (or she) will be granted complete access. If an anonymous user attempts to access our site with a `GET` request, the request will be serviced because of our second `allow` statement. However, if an anonymous client attempts to access a page in our application with a `POST` request, she will be either given a chance to authenticate or simply denied access.

LISTING 11-8: A More Complex Authorization Declaration

```
<configuration>
  <system.web>
    <authorization>
      <allow users="MyDomain\bob, MyDomain\alice"/>
      <allow users="*" verbs="GET" />
      <deny users="?" />
    </authorization>
  </system.web>
</configuration>
```

One last question to ask about the example in Listing 11-8 is, What happens if Bob or Alice issues a GET request to one of our pages? Because GET requests are allowed via anonymous access by our second `allow` element, even the initial requests from Bob and Alice will typically be processed as anonymous requests. Only when the client attempts to do something that is prevented for anonymous users will authentication take place. In general, try to keep your authorization logic simple and obvious, because the more complex the rules become, the more likely you are to make a mistake and grant access where you should have denied it.

Authorization can be specified differently for different files and subdirectories in your application. To change the authorization settings for different directories in your application, you can add a `web.config` file to each subdirectory specifying authorization settings. Authorization is always applied with local `web.config` file settings first, and only if no match is found will it look in additional configuration files in the hierarchy above. Thus, if you grant anonymous users access to your top-level site but add a `web.config` file that denies anonymous users access to a particular subdirectory, clients must authenticate before they can access pages in that subdirectory. Alternatively, you can specify different authorization settings for different files (and subdirectories) from the top-level `web.config` file of your application using the `location` element. Listing 11-9 shows an example of restricting access to a top-level file called `secret.aspx` and a subdirectory called `secret`, while granting anonymous access to the remainder of the pages in the application.

LISTING 11-9: Using the location Element for Fine-Grained Authorization

```
<!- File: web.config ->
<configuration>
  <system.web>
    <authorization>
      <!- allow all users by default ->
      <allow users="*" />
    </authorization>
  </system.web>

  <!- use location element to restrict access to a
      particular file ->
  <location path="secret.aspx">
  <system.web>
```

```
    <authorization>
      <deny users="?" />
    </authorization>
  </system.web>
  </location>

    <!- use location element to restrict access to a
        subdirectory ->
  <location path="secret">
  <system.web>
    <authorization>
      <deny users="?" />
    </authorization>
  </system.web>
  </location>
  </configuration>
```

One final note on ASP.NET authentication to keep in mind is that ASP.NET can enforce authorization and authentication only when requests are dispatched to the ASP.NET worker process. This means that if you create an authorization scheme for your application using ASP.NET's configuration files, and a user requests a plain .htm file or .gif file, the ASP.NET authentication is not consulted, and whatever settings IIS has for your virtual directory are applied (typically granting anonymous access). The only work-around for this now is to route all file requests to the ASP.NET worker process by configuring the IIS metabase to use the `aspnet_isapi.dll` ISAPI extension as the handler for all Web file types (.htm, .gif, .jpg, and so on). Keep in mind, however, that this also slows down access to these file types for your application.

11.2.2 Forms Authentication

As mentioned earlier, relying on Windows authentication is rarely what you want for an Internet application with a broad user base because it would require that each client have a valid Windows account on your server. Instead, in your `web.config` file, you can specify one of two cookie-based authentication models (`Passport` or `Forms`), which provide many of the details of managing application-level authentication. `Passport` mode uses a cookie-based authentication technique that relies on Microsoft's Passport authentication technology, which lets sites and clients register with Microsoft to have a central point for client authentication. `Forms` authentication also uses cookies but leaves the details of authentication in your hands. You do not have to build your own cookie-based authentication scheme, as developers have had to do in the past, because ASP.NET takes care of the details of enforcing authorization and managing an authentication cookie.

The idea behind forms-based authentication is shown in Figure 11-2. When a user first requests a resource that requires authentication, the server redirects him to a designated login page. This login page collects the user's name and password, PIN, or some other bit of proof, and the application then authenticates him (through some database of users and passwords, presumably). Once the user successfully logs in, the server grants him an authentication cookie (which should be a cryptographically secure value that is infeasible to guess). The user is then redirected to the original page that he requested, but this time he presents an authentication cookie with the request and is granted access to the page. This authentication cookie lasts throughout the session, and thus the client can access all pages allowed by the authorization policy by presenting this cookie with each access. If this cookie is made persistent on the client's machine, it can be used for subsequent sessions from that same machine as well (this is manifested in the commonly seen "remember my password" check box many sites provide). Be aware, however, that persistent authentication cookies can easily be hijacked by anyone with access to the client machine. Forms-based security works well for servers that intend to service a large number of clients and want to manage client registration and authentication at the application level rather than relying on system-provided authentication requiring much more setup.

ASP.NET provides much of the infrastructure necessary to put together a cookie-based authentication Web application. First, if you specify `Forms` authentication in your `web.config` file, you can specify a `loginUrl` attribute, which should point to the page you want users to be redirected to if they attempt unauthenticated access to your application. If you then explicitly deny anonymous users by using the `authorization` element, ASP.NET takes care of routing unauthenticated clients to your designated login page for authentication. An example of a `web.config` file configured for forms-based authentication is shown in Listing 11-10.

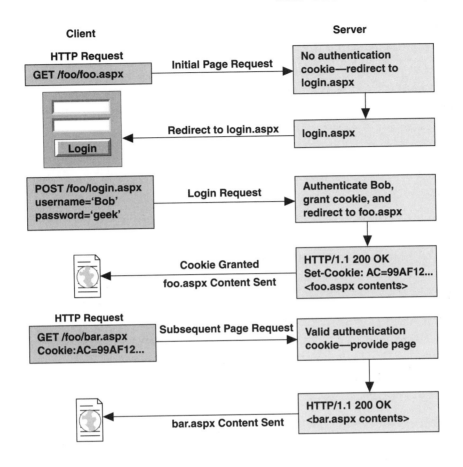

FIGURE 11-2: Forms Authentication

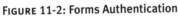

LISTING 11-10: Specifying Forms Authentication

```
<!-- File: web.config -->
<configuration>
  <system.web>
    <authorization>
      <deny users="?"/>
    </authorization>

    <authentication mode="Forms">
      <forms loginUrl="login.aspx" />
    </authentication>
  </system.web>
</configuration>
```

Your only other major task to get cookie-based authentication working is to implement the login page to grant or deny the authentication cookie. ASP.NET provides the class `FormsAuthentication`, shown in Listing 11-11, so that you can do this. This class consists primarily of a number of static methods that control the authentication cookie. For example, to grant an authentication cookie to a client, you call the `SetAuthCookie` method, and ASP.NET makes sure that a new cookie is generated and set for the client. ASP.NET also checks incoming requests to verify that they are in fact presenting a valid authentication cookie, and if not, routes them to your designated login page. This class also gives a useful method called `HashPasswordForStoringInConfigFile`, which takes a string and perform a one-way hash on it (using either SHA1 or MD5 algorithms). The next time a user presents her password to you, you can verify it by running the hash algorithm on it again and comparing the resultant string with the hash you stored earlier. This lets you avoid storing passwords in clear text in your database. We discuss password security in more detail later in this chapter.

LISTING 11-11: FormsAuthentication Class

```
public class FormsAuthentication
{
  public static string FormsCookieName {get;}
  public static string FormsCookiePath {get;}

  public static bool Authenticate(string name,
                                  string password);
  public static FormsAuthenticationTicket
                  Decrypt(string s);
  public static string Encrypt(
                  FormsAuthenticationTicket tk);
  public static HttpCookie GetAuthCookie(string userNm,
                                  bool bPersist);
  public static string GetRedirectUrl(string userNm,
                                  bool bPersist);
  public static string
              HashPasswordForStoringInConfigFile(
                          string psswd, string format);
  public static void RedirectFromLoginPage(string userNm,
                          bool bPersist);
  public static void SetAuthCookie(string userNm,
                                  bool bPersist);
```

```
      public static void SignOut();
      //...
   }
```

Listing 11-12 shows a sample login page implementation. Note that in this example, we are calling the `FormsAuthentication.RedirectFrom-LoginPage` method, which takes care of granting the authentication cookie to the client and then redirecting the client to the page she originally requested. In this example, we have hard-coded the user checks, but in a real application, this information would most likely live in a database.

LISTING 11-12: Forms-Based Authentication Example—login.aspx

```
<!- File: Login.aspx ->
<%@ Page language=C# %>
<html>
  <script runat=server>
  public void OnClick_Login(Object src, EventArgs e)  {
     if (((_username.Text == "Bob") &&
         (_password.Text == "geek")) ||
          ((_username.Text == "Alice") &&
          (_password.Text == "geek")))
         FormsAuthentication.RedirectFromLoginPage(
               _username.Text, _persistCookie.Checked);
     else
        _message.Text = "Invalid login: Please try again";
  }
  </script>
  <body>
    <form runat=server> <h2>Login Page</h2>
       User name:
       <asp:TextBox id="_username" runat=server/><br/>
       Password:
       <asp:TextBox id="_password"
                      TextMode="password" runat=server/>
       <br/>
       Remember password?:
       <asp:CheckBox id=_persistCookie runat="server"/>
       <br/>
       <asp:Button text="Login" OnClick="OnClick_Login"
                 runat=server/><br/>
       <asp:Label id="_message" ForeColor="red"
                 runat=server />
    </form></body>
  </html>
```

If you want further control over the authentication cookie used by the forms authentication module, there are several additional attributes that you can apply to the `forms` element, as listed in Table 11-1. First of all, by default the cookie will timeout after 30 minutes, so if you expect users of your application to submit requests more than 30 minutes apart, and you don't want to force them to reauthenticate, you can increase this value. On the other hand, it may often be wise to decrease this value to something closer to 5 or 10 minutes, because if someone were accessing private information from an Internet café, for example, they wouldn't want someone else to come in within 30 minutes after they leave and be able to view that private data. The `protection` attribute lets you specify how much care is taken to protect the cookie. By default, the cookie is both encrypted and Message Authentication Code (MAC) verified so that it cannot be easily tampered with or read. If for some reason you want to decrease the amount of protection on the cookie, you can do so with this attribute. Unless you have a really good reason to change this setting, however, you should leave it alone. Finally, the `path` attribute lets you specify the path that will be prepended to the cookie. This defaults to "/", which is the preferred setting, since some browsers treat cookie paths with case sensitivity and others without it; so leaving it as "/" works with the largest number of browsers.

TABLE 11-1: Attributes of the forms Authentication Element

Attribute	Values	Default	Description
name	String	.ASPXAUTH	Name of the cookie
loginUrl	URL	login.aspx	URL to redirect client to for authentication
protection	All, None, Encryption, Validation	All	Protection mode for data in cookie
timeout	Minutes	30	Duration for nonpersistent cookie to be valid (reset on each request)
path	Path	"/"	Path to use for cookie

11.2.3 **Authentication Cookies in Web Farms**

By default, authentication cookies used by the forms-based authentication module are both encrypted and MAC verified. The decryption and validation keys used to perform these tasks are automatically generated machine by machine. This means that if you are using forms-based authentication in a Web farm environment, where each request potentially can be served by a different machine in the farm, the key validation will quickly fail. To deal with this, you can use the `machineKey` element in your application's `web.config` file (or you can modify the one in the systemwide `machine.config` file) to use a fixed value for both keys. If all machines in a Web farm are configured to use the same pair of keys, the cookie protection in forms authentication will work properly. Listing 11-13 shows a sample `web.config` file that has explicitly set the `machineKey` element to use fixed key values for both the validation key and the decryption key.

LISTING 11-13: Using Explicit Validation and Decryption keys

```
<configuration>
  <system.web>
  <authentication mode="Forms"/>
  <authorization>
    <deny users="?"/>
  </authorization>
<machineKey
validationKey="F18815BDA3E05869EEFA53C531A696B187DA31A0F298E0FAB869AC9
2E292F1008CD5EC1B5C887B39F9559C7ED6BE66242A42E028CC5B8306D0CD1F5784A4F
BC9"
decryptionKey="9F9E881DFCED3092FDE726CA286B0459375E42DFD3000C20"
            validation="SHA1"/>
  </system.web>
</configuration>
```

This example uses a 64-byte validation key and a 24-byte decryption key, the maximum length allowed by the encryption and validation algorithms in ASP.NET. It is wise to create these keys using strong random algorithms, such as those provided by the `RNGCryptoServiceProvider`. Listing 11-14 shows a sample console application that you can use to generate keys of arbitrary length by passing in the desired length on the command line to the program.

LISTING 11-14: Program to Generate Strong Random Keys Using RNGCryptoServiceProvider

```
// File: genkey.cs
using System;
using System.Text;
using System.Security;
using System.Security.Cryptography;

class App
{
  static void Main(string[] argv)
  {
    int len = 48;
    if (argv.Length > 0)
      len = int.Parse(argv[0]);

    byte[] buff = new byte[len];
    RNGCryptoServiceProvider rng =
                         new RNGCryptoServiceProvider();
    rng.GetBytes(buff);
    StringBuilder sb = new StringBuilder(len);
    for (int i=0; i<buff.Length; i++)
      sb.Append(string.Format("{0:X2}", buff[i]));

    Console.WriteLine(sb);
  }
}
```

11.2.4 Optional Authentication

Another scenario that comes up frequently is the need to let clients authenticate themselves if they want to or to let them simply use the site anonymously. Once a client has authenticated himself, you may elect to customize the contents of the site, or perhaps some subset of the pages of the site are available only if the client has been authenticated. In this scenario, we do not want to send every unauthenticated client to a default login form. More often, it makes sense to have a login form integrated into your main page. This way, the user can authenticate if he wishes or can remain anonymous.

ASP.NET supports this type of cookie authentication as well. Figure 11-3 shows an example of a client using an optional login form on a page. Once the client has been authenticated, the page displays additional information

default.aspx   **Anonymous, Unauthenticated Client**

Form-based Security Example	

Login
 	
Username
`Alice`
Password
`••••`
 	
`Logon`
☐Remember login?
	General messages:
	Message 1 - blah, blah, blah

default.aspx   **Customized Form for Alice**

Form-based Security Example	
Login You are logged in as Alice `Logout`	**Here are your messages, Alice** Message 1 - blah, blah, blah Message 2 - blah, blah, blah Message 3 - blah, blah, blah Message 4 - blah, blah, blah

FIGURE 11-3: Forms-Based Authentication

that is relevant to that client. The implementation is similar to the cookie authentication example discussed earlier, except that anonymous clients are not prevented from accessing the site. Instead, an integrated login form is shown on the main page. If a user logs in and authenticates successfully, she is granted an authentication cookie and can then potentially do additional things or view additional material on the site. Programmatically, our login form looks very similar to the one shown earlier, but instead of directly calling RedirectFromLoginPage, we explicitly grant the user an authentication cookie by calling SetAuthCookie and then redirect the user to the current page so that additional content may be displayed. Then, in any of the pages of our application, we can check the credentials of the current user and display elements of the page conditionally based on her login.

11.2.5 Password Storage

One of the dangers of performing your own authentication, as is required by forms authentication, is that if a hacker manages to break into your database where the passwords are stored, she can then use the usernames and passwords freely, possibly at other Web sites if users established the same credentials elsewhere. To prevent this, you should avoid storing passwords in clear text altogether and instead prefer to store MD5 or SHA1 hashes of users' passwords. The FormsAuthentication class provides a method to perform MD5 and SHA1 hashes on arbitrary strings with the static method HashPasswordForStoringInConfigFile, as shown in Listing 11-15.

LISTING 11-15: Hashing Passwords

```
<%@ Page language=C# %>
<html>
  <script runat=server>
  public void OnClick_Login(Object src, EventArgs e)
  {
    // Calculate hash of password to check against
    // database entry
    string passHash = FormsAuthentication.
        HashPasswordForStoringInConfigFile(_password.Text,
                                           "sha1");
    // use passHash in a database query here to look up
    // password hash instead of clear text password
    // then call FormsAuthentication.RedirectFromLoginPage
    // if username and password hash are correct
  }
  </script>
  <body>
    <form runat=server> <h2>Login Page</h2>
      Username:
      <asp:TextBox id="_username" runat=server/><br/>
      Password:
      <asp:TextBox id="_password"
                    TextMode="password" runat=server/>
      <br/>
      Remember password?:
      <asp:CheckBox id=_persistCookie runat="server"/>
      <br/>
      <asp:Button text="Login" OnClick="OnClick_Login"
                  runat=server/><br/>
    </form></body>
</html>
```

You might have noticed that the name of the function used to hash passwords is not just `HashPassword` but `HashPasswordForStoringInConfig-File`. This is not just because the Microsoft developer building this class wanted the title of "longest API function in .NET" but also because you can store user credentials directly in your `web.config` file. It is unlikely that you will want to take advantage of this feature in any reasonably sized application, because managing usernames and passwords is a task much better suited to a database. Listing 11-16 shows a sample `web.config` file that stores user credentials, and Listing 11-17 shows a sample page that uses the `Forms-Authentication.Authenticate` method to query those credentials.

LISTING 11-16: Storing User Credentials in web.config

```
<configuration>
  <system.web>
    <authorization>
      <deny users="?"/>
    </authorization>

    <authentication mode="Forms">
      <forms loginUrl="login.aspx">
        <credentials passwordFormat="SHA1">
          <user name="Alice" password="9402F2262..."/>
          <user name="Bob"   password="EA9003E95..."/>
        </credentials>
      </forms>
    </authentication>
  </system.web>
</configuration>
```

LISTING 11-17: Authenticating Users with web.config-Based Credentials

```
<%@ Page language=C# %>
<html>
  <script runat=server>
  public void OnClick_Login(Object src, EventArgs e)
  {
    if (FormsAuthentication.Authenticate(_username.Text,
                                          _password.Text))
      FormsAuthentication.RedirectFromLoginPage(
              _username.Text, _persistCookie.Checked);
```

continues

```
      else
        _message.Text = "Invalid login: Please try again";
    }
    </script>
    <!- body and form not shown - see earlier examples ->
  </html>
```

11.2.6 Salted Hashes

In the previous examples, we performed one-way hashes on passwords to prevent anyone from viewing them should they somehow fall into the wrong hands. Unfortunately, this may not be enough to protect the passwords, because someone who gains access to the hashed passwords could run a dictionary attack against them. That is, a dictionary of prehashed words could be compared with all the passwords, and if there were any matches, the attacker would know one or more passwords.

To counter this, many password storage facilities use what are called "salted" hashes to store passwords. To perform a salted hash on a string, you prefix the string with a randomly generated string of fixed length (the "salt") before performing the hash. This ensures that comparisons with hashed strings drawn from a password dictionary will never match. To verify a client's password, you must prefix the password he sends you with the salt string used when the original password was hashed. This means that you need to store both the hash and the salt in your password database.

Although there is no direct support for performing salted hashes in ASP.NET, it is relatively straightforward to do. Listing 11-18 shows a function, HashWithSalt, that performs a salted hash. It takes as parameters the hashing algorithm, the password as plain text, and the salt string by reference (for which you pass null if this is the first time you are hashing a password), and the hash is returned as an out parameter. The function then creates a 16-byte salt string if no salt is passed in, prepends it to the password, and passes the resulting string onto the FormsAuthentication class's HashPasswordForStoringInConfigFile.

LISTING 11-18: HashWithSalt Routine

```
public static void HashWithSalt(string algName,
                                string plaintext,
                                ref string salt,
```

```
                                  out string hash)
{
  const int SALT_BYTE_COUNT = 16;
  if (salt == null || salt == "")
  {
      byte[] saltBuf = new byte[SALT_BYTE_COUNT];
      RNGCryptoServiceProvider rng =
                    new RNGCryptoServiceProvider();
      rng.GetBytes(saltBuf);

      StringBuilder sb = new StringBuilder(saltBuf.Length);
      for (int i=0; i<saltBuf.Length; i++)
        sb.Append(string.Format("{0:X2}", saltBuf[i]));
      salt = sb.ToString();
  }

  hash = FormsAuthentication.
      HashPasswordForStoringInConfigFile(salt+plaintext,
                                         algName);
}
```

11.2.7 Role-Based Authentication

It is often useful to build Web applications in terms of roles. ASP.NET supports role-based authentication through the `IsInRole()` method of the `IPrincipal` interface. If Integrated Windows authentication is used, the `IsInRole()` method checks Windows group membership. If you are using cookie-based authentication and would like to use roles in your security checks, you must define those roles and create the mappings of users to roles. Fortunately, there is a convenient helper class called `GenericPrincipal` that implements `IsInRole()` for you when you give it a string of role names.

For an example of when roles might be useful in a Web application, consider the roles and code shown in Figure 11-4. This application defines five roles: Doctors, Nurses, Administrators, Patients, and Janitors. Each user that logs in to the application belongs to one or more roles, and within each page, you can specifically check to see which roles the current user belongs to, and grant access or display additional information based on role membership.

To implement role-based security checks, you must define the roles and the mapping of users to roles. You may have a registration form that assigns roles based on information that users check, or you may assign roles to

Roles	Users Assigned to Role
Doctors	Alice, Bob, George
Nurses	Hannah, Michael, Emily
Administrators	Alice, Sarah, Matthew
Patients	Madison, Nicholas, Brianna
Janitors	Christopher, Michael, Joseph

```
void Page_Load(Object src, EventArgs e)
{
  if (User.IsInRole("Doctors"))
    // show doctor-specific page elements
  else if (User.IsInRole("Nurses"))
    // show nurse-specific page elements
  //...
}
```

FIGURE 11-4: Role-Based Authentication

users through some internal management page or some other technique. It is up to you how best to implement this. Once you have established the roles and user-to-role mapping, you must prepare a special IPrincipal implementation to be aware of these roles so that you can program against them in your pages.

The GenericPrincipal class is useful for this purpose. Its constructor takes an array of strings (role names) and a client Identity, and properly implements IsInRole of IPrincipal based on the array of strings. To use this class throughout the pages of your application, you need to prepare an instance of GenericPrincipal initialized with the appropriate array of role names for each request, and assign it to the User property of the current HttpContext.

The application-level event called AuthenticateRequest is your hook to perform these operations before any page requests information about the roles of the current client. Listing 11-19 shows an example global.asax file that defines a handler for the AuthenticateRequest event, prepares a GenericPrincipal class initialized with an array of role names based on the current user, and assigns the GenericPrincipal to the User property of the current `HttpContext`. After this event handler has set up the role-aware principal, your pages can successfully use the `User.IsInRole()` method to query whether a given user belongs to a particular role.

LISTING 11-19: Role-Based Authentication Implementation (global.asax)

```
<%! File: global.asax %>
<%@ Import Namespace="System.Security" %>
<%@ Import Namespace="System.Security.Principal" %>
<script language=C# runat=server>
  void Application_AuthenticateRequest(Object src,
                                       EventArgs e)
  {
    if (Request.IsAuthenticated)
    {
      ArrayList roles = new ArrayList();
      if (Context.User.Identity.Name.ToLower() == "alice")
      {
        roles.Add("Doctors");
        roles.Add("Administrators");
      }
      else if (Context.User.Identity.Name.ToLower() ==
               "bob")
      {
        roles.Add("Doctors");
        //...
      }

      // Assign a GenericPrincipal class initialized with
      // our custom roles for this user
      String[] rgRoles =
              (String[]) roles.ToArray(typeof(String));
      Context.User =
       new GenericPrincipal(Context.User.Identity, rgRoles);
    }
  }
</script>
```

11.3 System Identity in ASP.NET

Throughout this chapter, we have discussed authenticating clients and how to work with the "identity" of clients. In all cases, the identity we were referring to was the managed identity of the client, recognized only by the .NET runtime. Another equally important identity to consider is the system identity, which affects the way code runs on a particular machine.

By default, the ASP.NET worker process runs under a special account created for ASP.NET called ASPNET. This account by default is granted only `users` rights, which means that it is quite restricted in what it can do on the machine. This is a good thing, because it prevents potential hackers who might gain access to your machine through this account from doing much damage. If you decide that you want to change the identity of the worker process, it is configurable through the `machine.config processModel` element. The options are to specify a username of `machine` (the default) or `System` (run as the `LOCAL_SYSTEM` account), or some hard-coded username. If you specify `machine` or `system`, you can leave the `password` attribute set to `AutoGenerate`, but if you specify a particular user, you must specify the password for that user in clear text. Listing 11-20 shows the `processModel` portion of a `machine.config` file with the default system identity setting of `machine`.

LISTING 11-20: Using processModel to Control the Identity of aspnet_wp.exe

```
<!- File: machine.config ->
<configuration>
  <!- ... ->
  <system.web>
    <processModel enable="true" timeout="Infinite"
        idleTimeout="Infinite" shutdownTimeout="0:00:05"
        requestLimit="Infinite" requestQueueLimit="5000"
        restartQueueLimit="10" memoryLimit="60"
        webGarden="false" cpuMask="0xffffffff"
        userName="machine" password="AutoGenerate"
        logLevel="Errors" clientConnectedCheck="0:00:05"
        comAuthenticationLevel="Connect"
        comImpersonationLevel="Impersonate"
        responseRestartDeadlockInterval="00:09:00"
        responseDeadlockInterval="00:03:00"
        maxWorkerThreads="25" maxIoThreads="25"/>
    <!- ... ->
  </system.web>
</configuration>
```

If you try to do anything that requires system credentials, such as modifying files on the file system, or writing to the registry, you will find that the default privileges of the ASPNET account will stop you. The best approach to deal with this is to add the ASPNET account to the list of users allowed to perform whatever task you are trying to perform, rather than "punting" and changing the identity of the worker process altogether. For example, if you want to write data to an XML file on your system, modify the permissions of that XML file to include write permissions for the ASPNET account.

If you are using Windows authentication, you may want to take advantage of the fact that you can impersonate the client by using his Windows login credentials on the thread servicing the request within the worker process. To enable impersonation, add an identity element to your `web.config` file and set its `impersonate` attribute to `true`, as shown in Listing 11-21. This gives the thread used to service the request all the privileges associated with the client making the request.

LISTING 11-21: Impersonating a Client

```
<!— File: web.config —>
<configuration>
  <system.web>
    <identity impersonate="true" />
  </system.web>
</configuration>
```

SUMMARY

The primary enhancement that ASP.NET makes to Web application security is its forms authentication infrastructure. Instead of relying on hand-rolled authorization and authentication techniques, ASP.NET provides a framework for building client authentication into applications without relying on operating system credentials. It takes care of granting an authentication cookie, redirecting unauthenticated users to a login page, and enforcing any authorization rules specified in your configuration files. What is left for you to do is to perform the actual authentication of clients, which typically is a simple query into a database. ASP.NET also defines a role-based authorization mechanism that is convenient for building applications in terms of roles of users instead of hard-coding checks for identities. Finally, the programmatic interface to the security settings in an application are generic enough that you can easily switch between using different authentication mechanisms, with very few changes to your application code. This means that you can build a system based on Windows authentication, and then if you decide to scale out your user base, you can switch to a forms-based authentication system relatively easily.

Index

www.informit.com

YOUR GUIDE TO IT REFERENCE

Articles

Keep your edge with thousands of free articles, in-depth features, interviews, and IT reference recommendations – all written by experts you know and trust.

Online Books

Answers in an instant from **InformIT Online Book's** 600+ fully searchable on line books. For a limited time, you can get your first 14 days **free**.

Catalog

Review online sample chapters, author biographies and customer rankings and choose exactly the right book from a selection of over 5,000 titles.

Register
Your Book

at www.awprofessional.com/register

You may be eligible to receive:
- Advance notice of forthcoming editions of the book
- Related book recommendations
- Chapter excerpts and supplements of forthcoming titles
- Information about special contests and promotions throughout the year
- Notices and reminders about author appearances, tradeshows, and online chats with special guests

Contact us

If you are interested in writing a book or reviewing manuscripts prior to publication, please write to us at:

Editorial Department
Addison-Wesley Professional
75 Arlington Street, Suite 300
Boston, MA 02116 USA
Email: AWPro@aw.com

Addison-Wesley

Visit us on the Web: http://www.awprofessional.com